The two men, both in grey suits and about the same height, mounted a stage between standards holding a US flag and the Great Seal of the United States. When Mr Nixon began to speak, Mr Trudeau stood with his eyes downcast, moving his arms until finally he folded them across his chest.

Mr Nixon using no notes, spoke for four minutes. The Prime Minister, clasping his hands low in front of him and not changing his position throughout, spoke for less than two.

Responding to the President's words about a commonality of background, Mr Trudeau said this extended to "a common outlook on the world. We have the same values and we tend to face the issues in a common way." Because of that he was looking forward to the discussion ... "to listening to your views on world problems, on the information and the wisdom that you will want to impart upon me in your talks."

Some observers who have travelled extensively with Mr Trudeau said that he had not sounded so humble, or looked so shy, since just before he decided to run for the Liberal Party leadership more than 13 months ago.

Globe and Mail Toronto, March 25, 1969
(as reported by Scott Young)

Close the 49th parallel etc

The Americanization of Canada

Edited by Ian Lumsden
for the University League for Social Reform

University of Toronto Press

© University of Toronto Press 1970
Reprinted 1970 (twice), 1971, 1973
Printed in Canada by
University of Toronto Press
Toronto and Buffalo

ISBN 0-8020-1696-0 (cloth)
ISBN 0-8020-6111-7 (paper)

The title of the book comes from a painting by
Greg Curnoe in the series "The True North Strong and Free."
It is reproduced on the cover through the courtesy of
the Isaacs Gallery, from the collection of
the London Public Library and Art Museum.

Preface

Since I do not claim to have any special knowledge of Canadian history and politics, I am very grateful for the advice of many people who have made my editorial task easier than it might have been. They are too numerous to mention by name, and in any case some of them no doubt may not care to be publicly associated with the final product! Two of my friends – Mel Watkins and Ken Dewar – have, however, been a constant source of encouragement; without their support I would not have attempted to prepare this book. Though I feel obliged to acknowledge their special assistance, I would not wish to associate them with any of the book's shortcomings. For all final editorial decisions have been mine alone. I should also like to thank Gerry Ronan for his assistance, as well as Christine Purden whose help as editorial consultant was invaluable to me. Rik Davidson and Gerry Hallowell were largely responsible for expediting the publication of the book.

IAN LUMSDEN

Contents

Close the 49th parallel etc   The Americanization of Canada

D. Drache

A political scientist. He is an associate editor of *Our Generation*, and has contributed to the *Journal of Canadian Studies* and other periodicals.

The Canadian bourgeoisie and its national consciousness

Dependence, provincialism, colonialism, whatever term is used is not the best kind of life. An inferior status produces an inferior people.

A. R. M. LOWER

Ten years ago the dream of the Canadian bourgeoisie* had an air of reality. Its spokesmen made much of the fact that Canada's survival as a nation was assured, that national unity prevailed, that Canada was a land of prosperity. Now, the claims of the bourgeoisie are contradicted by the hard facts of Canadian life. National disunity, American imperialism, the collapse of federalism, labour unrest, student militancy, and Quebec separatism reveal a different truth about the policies and politics of Canada's ruling class. The disintegration of the country cannot be seen and studied in isolation from the historic mandate of the bourgeoisie to rule Canada. With their unlimited self-assurance they have promoted the view that only one class of people can hold the country together, overcome regional and racial disunity, and build a national state with national policies. But the balkanization of Canada, north-south, east-west, is a fact that the most arrogant of the establishment cannot afford to ignore. Politically the result of this state of affairs is becoming clearer. The bourgeoisie are in the process of dismantling the Canadian state economically,

---

*   The term normally refers to the owners of the means of production who form the governing class. The Canadian bourgeoisie own a fraction of the means of production and retain control of a minority of the country's resources. More correctly, they are part owners and more frequently the national managers and agents of the owners of the means of production. American capitalists have nationalized Canadian resources and industry. There can be no quarrel on this point. (See a special report in the *Toronto Daily Star* headlined, "Foreigners Buy 500 of Our Firms in 20 Months," October 17, 1969.) In speaking of the bourgeoisie I include also their representatives in the fields of education, culture, media, political life, labour, and military and state bureaucracies, who ally with and defend the interests and policies of resident and non-resident bourgeoisie. Marx describes the function of these people "as the active conceptualizing ideologists of the ruling class." A few of the leading spokesmen for the bourgeoisie in the nation include President Bissell of the University of Toronto; Dr Solandt, Chancellor of the University of Toronto, Robert Fulford, literary critic; Patrick Watson, media propagandist; Bruce Hutchison, writer; the late Blair Fraser; a pyramid of civil servants lead by Bob Bryce; Ramsay Cook, historian; George Ignatieff and A.D.P. Heeney, diplomats; etc., etc.

socially, and culturally. By this process, Canadian history has come full circle – from a colony to a colonial dependency.

The Canadian plight between two imperialisms was documented in the 1930s and 1940s by a political economist, Harold Innis,[1] and by the conservative liberal historians, Donald Creighton[2] and A.R.M. Lower.[3] In more recent times its chief exponent has been George Grant. In his *Lament for a Nation*,[4] he has stated the Canadian dilemma in a single sentence: "Canada's disappearance as a nation is a matter of necessity." He argues that American imperialism has destroyed the basis of an independent Canada, and that the Canadian state has become an advanced colonial structure. He claims further that liberal capitalism has become the instrument for destroying the meagre foundations of Canadian independence. To say this is to argue that the policy of continental development adopted by the Liberal government as Canada's national policy is founded on an anti-national logic. That the Canadian economy has thus been placed at the disposal of American capital and in the hands of American capitalists substantiates the general truth of Grant's argument. The Watkins Report presents extensive evidence that the nationalization of Canadian resources by American imperialism has reached an all-time high.

The charge that Canada has become *de facto* a region of the United States is not new, and on one level it does not take Canadian liberals by surprise. For the bourgeoisie who have guided Canada into a deepened colonialism the wide spectrum of dependency is not a disgrace, nor is it regarded unfavourably. Near-prosperity, the illusion of prosperity, the spill-over from imperial prosperity have been reason enough to legitimize their policies in the political and economic spheres. Their success in living off the British and American empires has given the bourgeoisie enough political power to withstand the opposition from a long line of radical and radicalizing movements for social change. In the past, the politics sustained by regional disparity, class struggle, farmer militancy, and Quebec separatism never reached ascendancy. Hence, for good reason, the bourgeoisie were able to pursue policies which guaranteed them their place as managers and middlemen of a colonial economy.

If for the bourgeoisie of the ruling class the imperial presence does not present a crisis of confidence, it has created a crisis of power. They miscalculated the economic and political cost of remaining an advanced colony. While balkanization may suit the government's purposes, its increased economic helplessness in stopping the spread of inflation, regional depression, unemployment, and industrial stagnation does not meet with approval from three critical sections of the Canadian public – Quebec and the provinces, organized and unorganized workers, and students. Their collective reaction to the Americanization of Canada in its many forms represents the beginning of a new era of politics in Canada.

The bourgeoisie are threatened by these political realities, and their paranoia dominates their politics. *Item:* They regard the struggle for a Free Quebec as a national crime. In simpler language, it is a felony to dismember part of the colony and seek national independence. *Item:* The Committee of Ontario Presidents does not lose any time in aping the imperial American universities and issues its liberal stand for law and order. Radical action in Ontario universities will henceforth be prosecuted. An Americanized faculty and Americanized universities will now be protected from Canadian students. *Item:* International construction unions in Toronto support a drive to crush an "upstart" Canadian union. Canada's labour party, the NDP, gives no support to the Concrete Former's Union. *Item:* Inflation and more inflation. The government remedy is to create planned unemployment to cool off the economy. *Item:* Kierans announces reforms of the postal service. His intention is to make it pay its own way. Consequently, raising the postal rates is tantamount to a stamp tax; it is cheaper not to communicate; publish nationally and perish.

That the bourgeoisie view the political environment with hostility has an objective basis. Their once secure world has ceased to exist and their traditional methods of governorship, parliament, federalism, political parties, and compromise no longer function as national institutions. Their legitimacy is dying out; or, more simply, continental imperialism no longer needs the official channels of the bourgeoisie. But the bourgeoisie have no intention of discarding the pillars of their liberal faith. Such deviations from the norm as the class struggle or Quebec separatism are, in their eyes, unresolved difficulties of the present, not permanent features of a new social order – structural dependency. In blocking out the major social and economic forces of the present period of history, the bourgeoisie look upon such realities as class politics, imperialism, the colonialism of Canadian capitalism and nationalism as heresies in the minds of the left and not as the political condition of the real world. In part their refusal to recognize these realities, let alone understand them, reflects their historic role in Canadian history. On this point we shall have more to say presently. In another sense, the estrangement of the bourgeoisie is a self-willed act – the product of their provincialism and their insistence on Canadian exceptionalism. By their logic Canada stands in a unique relationship to history – history is a benign force which somehow has exempted Canada from the political economy of imperialism, class struggle, and racism. When this construct is broken apart by the national revolution in Quebec, by the nationalization of the Canadian economy by American capital, and by the demands of students to Canadianize Canadian universities, the eruption of the underground cannot be easily covered up. The very problems to which the bourgeoisie stringently denied an existence dominate the national politics of Canada.

The case against the bourgeoisie is not made on the grounds of style. Their general dullness, their abject defeatism on the national question, their contempt for democratic politics, their indifference to labour, play an important part in a managerial strategy of depoliticizing Canadian national life. Style is a convenience, the mark of authority. But style, however McLuhanesque and hence attractive in liberal eyes, is not the heart of the matter. The substantive strategic question is why the bourgeoisie support and welcome the American occupation of Canada. What is it that gives the bourgeoisie a vested interest in Canada as a dependency? Why are they powerless to stop the disintegration of the Canadian state? The answers can be found through study of the history of this class as it builds the national consciousness about nationalism and imperialism, and its use of liberalism as its political ideology. It is through an analysis of these questions that one begins to understand the tragedy of Canadian exceptionalism.

THE CONTRADICTION
WITHIN THE NATIONALISM OF SUBORDINATION

Nationalism joins together the linguistic, cultural, and political aspirations of the ruling class in support of the national economic unit,

the nation-state. By virtue of political economy, capitalism is a force
of the national interest and the ideology of national cohesiveness –
that is, nationalism. Liberalism has made much out of appeals to
nationalism, because of the obvious moral and political implications
of this simple theory. But whatever the moral use-value of nationalism, its real power and authority stem from the material interest it
advances. It is the latter part of this statement, "material interest it
advances," which has been relevant to the Canadian experience.

One cannot fault the Canadian bourgeoisie with the charge that
they have not identified with nationalist politics. Their espousal of
national unity, national development, and national survival is evidence in their mind of their national interest. However, their methods
of working towards these rhetorical goals denote a deep-seated
ambivalence and a lack of will to build national economic structures,
and hence a political and cultural nation. In the liberal view, Canada's
problems grow out of the belief that Canada, if it is not a nation now,
can be one in the future and that this idea of nationhood can be
brought about by reasonable men working reasonably for its attainment. For liberal persuaders Canada can be a country, a nation unto
itself, and can survive on the continent as an un-American, yet
sovereign, state by virtue of the fact that the desire is a reasonable
one, non-antagonistic to American interests, and because Canada's
existence as a nation is recognized by law. Their perception of Canadian history resembles, then, a textbook of constitutional and legal
pieties. For them the resilience of liberal optimism is that it acts as
its own surrogate. It wishes away the unreasonable issues of Canada's
situation. The Canadian liberal has never wanted to face the political
economy of his situation. He believes that Canadian nationalism is
essentially a nationalism of, and at one with, empire. This idea of
nationhood was supposed to be a testament to the possibility of how
the contradiction between national sovereignty and imperial control
could be overcome. In the view of the national bourgeoisie, to join
nation to empire was a sign of nationhood, coming of age within the
empire; for the liberal tradition in Canada is founded on the historical
experience that liberalism has grown out of empire and that colonies
have grown into nations. As a colony it had experienced neither the
best nor the worst of the imperial world; and although its place in
the empire was ambivalent in certain respects, the Canadian ruling
class had no serious misgivings about the necessity for empire and

the importance of an imperial domain. But the bargain it attempted to strike first with the British and then with the United States empires failed to prevent Canada's integration economically and politically into the imperial fold.

As burghers of the industrial world in both the nineteenth and twentieth centuries, Canadian businessmen and industrialists have given priority, not to the search for worldwide markets and imperial monopoly after the Anglo-American pattern, but to a national goal of protection and preference, entry and accessibility into imperial markets.[5] This nationalism of empire, although not unlike the national philosophies of the British and American bourgeoisie, differed in a fundamental aspect. Whereas the latter "big" bourgeoisie spoke from a developing if not a well-developed foothold of national capitalism, in Canada the bourgeoisie spoke from a much different position. Canada's economy was that of a colony, characterized by underdevelopment of industry and overdevelopment of staples. The nationalism of Canadian capitalism contained the belief that it sought co-existence with "mature" capitalism, not as an equal, never as a rival, but primarily as a subordinate and lately as a junior partner.* It was this economic outlook which Canadian governments drafted as their chief strategy with Britain before the end of the British Century in 1939. It solved the problem of getting a better deal for Canada in imperial affairs by adopting a rhetoric of Canadian absenteeism from imperial commitments. In reality, government policy amounted to a tactical ploy of hedging its bet in order to bargain for special concessions. It was this same strategy that the long reign of Liberal governments devised to establish Canada's colonial reliability

---

* W. L. Morton, "British North America: A Continent in Dissolution," *History* (June 1962), argues that, for geo-political reasons connected with the American Civil War, the Canadian bourgeoisie would always be dominated and run by the needs of the American empire. The excellent analysis of this question by S. Ryerson in *Unequal Union* (Toronto, 1968), refines Morton's contention. He demonstrates that the petty bourgeois elements in Upper and Lower Canada were developing a national capitalist consciousness which was anti-imperialist. Historically the petty bourgeoisie have lacked political power to beat the imperial policies of Canada's big bourgeoisie. On this last point G. Myers, *History of Canadian Wealth,* is an invaluable source of information.

with Washington. Reversing styles, the Pearson approach called for blanket endorsement of American Cold War politics – a free hand in a Free World for an American-continental market. In both instances the nationalism of subordination fit the material interests of the Canadian bourgeoisie.

If the task of nationalism on the economic level is to ensure the colonial relationship of the governing élite to the imperial establishment, politically nationalism is a dangerous instrument of class rule. This is no less true for the Canadian bourgeoisie than it is for any other colonial élite. By its very definition nationalism in the colony is an anti-imperialist doctrine. Too much talk of independence and economic development arouses the latently antagonistic national consciousness of the people. This is the explosive, socially progressive, politically formidable side of nationalism which the bourgeoisie seek to defuse. They know also that without national unity or a sufficient amount of national identity the economic state of the country suffers. Hence, the bourgeoisie do not relish nationalism. They look upon it as a tightrope which will bridge the distance between local growth and imperial concerns.*

No bourgeoisie, however, can afford to disown the rhetoric, nor the political task, of claiming to be nation-builders and supposedly the saviours of the country. Hence, in the colony or dependency, the bourgeoisie distort nationalism for their own ends. In their actions and in their programmes for national self-determination, they emphasize their support of independence and of continuing the relationship with the imperial metropolis. Their ingenuity in drawing up a nationalist programme deflects the independence movement from its immediate goal of overthrowing colonialism in all facets of life.

The Canadian bourgeoisie are no exception to the general rule – they have taken nationalism in hand and made it safe for domestic

* The most successful colonial politicians, Macdonald and King, put nationalism to work in this manner – home rule rather than national independence. Macdonald's statement, "a British subject I was born and a British subject I will die," was more than idle boasting; it was a statement of Canadian political economy. In this sentence he defined the horizon of Canadian nationalists. Later nationalists of the St Laurent era have been forced to change only one word, "American," putting into practice Pearson's directive to roll with the imperial punch.

consumption. For them it was necessary to turn nationalism on its head by deploying it in support of imperial causes and in defence of their class rights. This concept of nationalism was directed, not to building a country, but to ruling it. On this basis alone, it suited the bourgeoisie to support national endeavours. As long as nationalism dissipated its energies in endless factional strife, they had nothing to fear from it. Thus they turned nationalism against itself; that is, in the past and in the present Canadian nationalism has been self-liquidating and therefore useful as a disabling device politically while losing little of its utility as a tonic economically. By draining nationalism of its progressive content, the bourgeoisie deployed it as a strategy of divide and rule. By turning nationalism into a force of division, they discovered their only basis, short of military dictatorship, for maintaining control of Canada's national affairs.

At all critical times in the nineteenth and twentieth centuries, the method of rule of the bourgeoisie followed the well-established pattern of the colonial era. The politics of a pre-Confederation Canada depended on equal amounts of authority and opportunism. This formula, which had served its purpose of bringing the bourgeoisie together so that a minimum transfer of power could occur, was not abandoned when the imperial authorities withdrew. Instead, it was adopted and used with the same advantage it had provided for pre-Confederation and Confederation politicians. But the birth of national politics so heavily committed to national-colonial or national-imperial principles did not have as its immediate objective a solution to the French-English question, any more than it was interested in developing strong inclusive national institutions. Neither Macdonald nor Cartier, nor later Laurier, practised politics with the crucial objective of establishing a national democratic state. Indeed, within their framework national politics, when stripped of pretentious rhetoric, was a holding action where the centre, be it Ottawa or Bay Street – that is, the English majority, industry, and finance – kept the nation "together" by keeping it apart. For them, as well as for those who followed their example (particularly King), leading the country meant playing off French against English, east against west, labour against business. It is this tradition of opportunism, backed up by the threat of physical and military intervention from the central authority, that has been given the name of Canadian pragmatism.

Conventional politics that have a vested interest in accentuating differences, fear the possibility of the parts combining and amount to a rearguard holding action, describe the purpose of the political nationalism of Canada's bourgeoisie. With this mode of politics they have addressed themselves to three critical problems – Quebec, western regional demands, and class politics.

QUEBEC: BI-NATIONAL NATIONALISM

Quebec has always been threatened by the prospect of national politics. At a bare minimum a nationalist programme had to guarantee French Canada, not merely its inherent language and religious rights, but something more substantive: a political structure and a cultural-economic future of survival in a two-nation state. The eastern bourgeoisie never subscribed to the idea of an equal Quebec. In their eyes the very proposal negated the *raison d'être* of an English-controlled federal state. There was one Ottawa, not two as Quebec required as the only adequate guarantee of its political rights. Without unqualified recognition of its equal status, national politics would play up Quebec's minority status in a majoritarian political system. A nationalism which told Quebec that it was simply one of many strengthened the French-Canadian belief that Confederation was to be equated with the term, "the Second Conquest." Its experience with the realities of federal politics taught the lesson that constitutional guarantees were no protection against the influence wielded by flagwaving Orange legions and Tory men of empire. The confrontation over the public schools question, the scandalous Riel affair, and the two instances of national conscription left no doubt in the mind of French Canada that the national interest of Quebec would always be subordinate to the one-nation interest of English Canada. These events supplied the evidence that, if two peoples had created Canada, only one of those peoples was being served by its political direction.

It is no surprise in these circumstances that even the most reactionary excesses of survival practised by the church and by Duplessis had the support of many in Quebec. Their man of the iron cross stood between them and engulfment. French Canadians were somewhat justified in claiming that Duplessis' policies were no worse than the Anglo-Saxon racism which called French Canada "the cockroach in the kitchen of Canada"[6] and which federal politicians used to win votes in Ontario and the West.

The nationalist offering vis-à-vis Quebec was tantamount to treating
French Canada as a hostage. This attitude on the part of the bourgeoisie has always been grounded in the political fear that the need
for French-English co-existence (as they understood it) might one
day end. It was the eventuality of an ascendant Quebec, more popularly known as "Québec libre," which gave purpose to the efforts of
French-Canadian federalists, Ottawa nationalists, religious interests,
and English industrialists to secure Quebec by opposing and isolating
its national consciousness as a nation in and for itself. By isolating
Quebec with threats and promises, the bourgeoisie created – so it
seemed to them – an unassailable situation. In part, that is why
Liberals in the time of Laurier and King, with the assistance of a
vendu class from French Canada, seized upon the opportunity of
selling the lie to Quebec that, by confining itself to a ghetto within
its borders and in the Liberal party, its political future was assured.[7]

The national self-destructiveness of this act gave the Liberal party
power in Parliament, the myth of national unity, and a nationalist
following deriving its support from the mutual religious fears and
racial suspicions of the English- and French-Canadian masses.* The
tactic of separating Quebec politically from the rest of Canada, which
the Liberal party achieved, ended the possibility of an authentic
French-English state.

* It is standard fare for every Liberal and Conservative government
to condemn strenuously rightist nationalist appeals and to dissociate
their nationalism from them. Indeed, the professional historians who
record the innumerable crises of national leaders give us example upon example of every Liberal prime minister who in the nick of time
has averted national calamity by turning back the evils of a scarring
nationalism. Those Conservative leaders – Meighen, Borden, Diefenbaker – who missed their cue, supposedly failed to wave the magic
wand of mature national reason in time and brought the country to
the edge. Exeunt the villains. Enter stage centre, the hero – Canadian
liberalism. The melodrama picks up as each national figure gives his
five-minute confessional on – right, you guessed it – the evils of
nationalism. Laurier, King, Pearson, Trudeau win the day. It has
never struck Canadian historians such as Ramsay Cook that the most
proficient in this five-and-dime display of political soul-bearing are
also the most apt in their deployment of nationalism as a force of disunity. This contradiction is ignored. Lacking an analysis, the Canadian

THE WEST: NATIONAL REGIONALISM

The West has had reasons to fear eastern nationalism. It paid for the
cost of industrialization in Ontario out of the huge surpluses it sent
east.[8] Little time elapsed before it discovered that it was not regarded
as an equal profit-sharing partner in the plans of eastern capitalism.
As the branch plant of a distant metropolis, it was charged more for
all basic necessities and received proportionately the minimum for
its agricultural efforts. The national economic policies of the Liberal
and Conservative parties relieved neither its indebtedness to eastern
capital nor its enforced dependency on federal whim. In an attempt
to break away from its precast role as the hinterland of the Canadian
economy, it revolted against the monetary grip of the banks, the
corrupt practices of the railways, and the restrictions of the tariff.
The combination of populism, agricultural collectivism, and anti-
capitalism created third-party politics.

In the 1920s the revolt of the West was a great event in Canadian
history. Having its roots in three decades of resentment, it challenged
the monopoly practices of an unrepresentative, corrupt, two-party
system. The national regionalism of the CCF radicals created an
alternative to the colonial policies of Ottawa. Its strength lay initially
in its political character. It was a mass movement committed to
democratizing radically the class structure of a capitalist society. By
itself populism could and did threaten the finance-nationalism of the
centre, but it could not and did not seize power nationally. The West,
in choosing the parliamentary road, redefined its politics and adopted
a strategy which the east understood better and was more skilful at
– coalition politics.

The bourgeoisie traditionally played the middle against the peripheral parts; and the West quickly learned that this strategy was
reversible, with the parts theoretically combining against the centre,

---

historian expects us to believe, as he does, that the nationalism which
played a critical role in precipitating one crisis after another is somehow a pragmatic moderate nationalism of liberal realists. This act
performed by the liberal leaders of disowning their frequent use of
national force and authority as exceptionalism gives them greater
leverage in employing their power against anyone who steps out of
line. It is not too crude conceptually to reduce this strategy to blatant
political opportunism.

Ottawa. What had made King and Laurier apt at manipulating the "middle game" could not, however, work so easily for western farm-labour interests. They had to gamble (*a*) that they could combine with other regional and provincial groups against the eastern-based bourgeoisie, or (*b*) that they could disrupt the coalition that King and his company had built. But as the price of entry into coalition, the Progressives had to abandon their most valuable instrument – a mass democratic political movement. In leaving by the wayside the force which had propelled regional nationalism into a national strata-gem for the parliamentary world of social democratic politics, the West stripped itself of its power. The essential point that King knew better than the West was that national regionalism had appeal as a mass movement, but had much less attraction as just another regionalism. If, in fact, regionalism could be played up to the point where either he or it could bury its anti-capitalist message, the national regionalism of the West would exhaust itself fighting the rival provincialisms which King himself had encouraged. As the man in the centre, ultimately he had more leverage in derailing the regional nationalism of the West by sidetracking it on non-radical issues – the issue of bourgeois nationalism. The farm-labour alliance came to be-lieve that it owed its first loyalty, not to its class, but to the colonial institutions and the national-imperial economy which kept the West powerless.

If expediency and necessity bring together national factions, his-torically coalition has not lead to national consolidation and the more important objective of redistributing the economic and political power of the bourgeoisie. In the case of the West, coalition proved politically acceptable because it perpetuated the illusion that a well-timed squawk on national matters somehow lessened the costs of being a branch plant of eastern interests. On the other hand, the failure of coalition confirmed the worst suspicions of the West that nationalist appeals and national centrist politics were not to be trusted. The experience it learned first hand from the King, St Lau-rent, and Pearson governments was that the national ruling coalition of Liberals did not offer a national spectrum of economic and politi-cal advantage equal to or greater than what the West on its own could win for itself by supporting the spoils system of national politics. Hence, bourgeois nationalism both as a cause and as a pro-gramme aroused all the innate political and economic suspicions that existed nationally.

CLASS AND NATIONALISM

The defeat of the West and the retreat of Quebec played a decisive
role in the nationalist ambitions of the bourgeoisie. As long as both
these "nationalisms" were contained, the only other force which
could and did oppose the internal and external policies of the bourgeoisie was the Canadian working class.

The nationalism of the bourgeoisie grew out of their needs as
industrial employers and as governors of the political state of Canada.
To the extent that the bourgeoisie proclaimed their nationalist intentions, they used nationalism to win the support of the masses for
their economic programme of industrialization and for their parliamentary programmes. Macdonald, Laurier, and King consciously
understood the power of this strategy. Unless the bourgeoisie had
the loyalty of the working man, even the most tentative plan for a
national economy would fail. If, for economic reasons, they saw the
benefits of using nationalist appeals to mobilize the masses, they saw
also the danger of giving the Canadian people a feeling for working
class politics and, more important, a mechanism for class consciousness. The danger of a national economic policy and a programme for
industrial development lay in the fact that, while the bourgeoisie
sought to bring the working class into national politics in directly
appealing to it, they made the working class conscious of its class
interest and its place in a capitalist order.

For the bourgeoisie to sell their nationalist ideas to the working
class was problematic. On the one hand, they were not interested
in allying with Canadian workers on an anti-imperial basis. The
bourgeoisie did not see the contradiction between their nationalism
and the political economy of their capitalism. The two coalesced,
because in the nineteenth and twentieth centuries the unity between
the one and the other was premised on the belief that Canada could
come of age inside the British and American empires, retaining the
imperial capital ties in a colonial-national structure. On the other
hand, the nationalist plans of the bourgeoisie were rooted in capitalist
anti-labour policies. In the national drive for canals and railways in
the 1850s, the bourgeoisie used the state repeatedly against striking
workers. The pattern of sending in the militia to control workers and
to ensure a passive low-paid work force became established governmental policy at the same time as industrial capitalism came to
Canada. Workers quickly learned that "in this setting, notions about

the atomistic market as the governor of labor matters were pushed aside in favor of a system of state intervention. 'Labor relations' ... meant troops and mounted police to 'overawe' the laborers, government spies to learn their intentions, and priests paid by the government and stationed among the laborers to teach them meekness. Here was a full program of intervention, immediately on behalf of the contractors, basically to promote economy for the state ..."[9]

If, for economic reasons, the bourgeoisie required a disciplined, cohesive work force, politically they took measures to destroy the potential power of this class as a leading national force.* It was Mackenzie King in his capacity as deputy minister of labour who devised the first national labour policy at the turn of the century. "He consistently advocated legislation directed to strengthening the state's power to investigate labor disputes, to compel arbitration and conciliation and by this device to blunt the ultimate weapon possessed by the wage-earners, i.e. *their power to withhold labor*.... his policies, as he himself subsequently admitted, had the effect of preventing workers from cooperating together to employ their social power."[10] But neither Laurier nor King was successful in the larger aim of preventing the rise of a Canadian trade union movement.

The emergence of an organized labour movement created a dual threat to the Canadian bourgeoisie. Canadian labour was both a force for national unity and a class enemy. But labour's fight against federal nationalism did not make labour anti-nationalist after the fashion of bourgeoisie nationalism, which defended the colonialism of Canadian dependency. Labour's target was the Canadian state in the hands of the national bourgeoisie. Hence, for labour the national struggle was a class struggle, and working class politics an anti-capitalist pro-Canadian position.[11] For both communist and non-communist unions in the 1930s to link the national and class question together was a logical step politically. Significantly, however, militant labour fought the policies of the bourgeoisie only from an anti-capitalist position.

* "Parties are not, as their philosophers claim, servants of the state cooperating in its service; their real desire is the mastery of the state and the brooking of no opposition or rivalship." Dafoe, *Laurier,* p. 43-4. Ostensibly his subject matter is the career of Laurier. However, this book is one of the few examples of class analysis of Canadian politics by a member of Canada's bourgeoisie.

Their class analysis of Canadian capitalism singled out what they regarded as the central feature of the political economy of Canada. The fact of imperialism was either regarded as a secondary question or ignored altogether. Labour did not see the need for a national-democratic independence movement, based on the needs of the working class. In concentrating their efforts on only one-half of Canada's historical situation, the Canadian left failed to understand the colonial character of Canadian capitalism. This error blinded the left to the reality of continental capitalism – that the American capital interests were more imperialistic than the British in Canada.[12]

The left concluded erroneously that Canadian capitalism and the class struggle in Canada were different in degree but not in kind from the anti-capitalist struggle of labour in the United States and Britain. Therefore, at the bidding of the communists and other radical pro-gressives, the Canadian trade union movement was handed over to the CIO and the Canadian Workers Unity League was disbanded.

The subsequent events are well known. Canadian and American liberal democrats combined to expel the left-wing socialists from positions of leadership in Canadian industrial unions. Canadian trade unions turned their attention to reformist unionism, ultimately settling for a "very junior partnership" in the corporate economy – continental co-existence with capitalism. The effective isolation of Canadian communist trade union officials from the majority of Canadian workers destroyed any possibility of a viable anti-capitalist Canadian working-class party. Had both the communists and social democrats understood the exceptionalism of the political economy of Canadian capitalism, they would never have turned over Canadian workers to an imperialist trade union movement.

Politically this move meant that effective control of Canadian trade unions lay with the internationals and their local "Canadian" branch-plant representatives. Since 1945 the leadership of the Canadian trade unions has indicated the totality of its commitment to liberal ideas by promoting an American political consciousness for Canadian workers: opposition to Canadian unions for Canadian workers. The continentalization of the Canadian trade union movement gave the bourgeoisie a clear field politically. Labour did not contest the direc-tion of bourgeois nationalism, and after the 1950s, represented by the Canadian Labour Congress, it was neither nationalist nor anti-capitalist. It openly supported the economic policy of the bourgeoisie in defending the capital interests of American business. This policy

was an integral part of the metropolitan programme of the "internationals" – acceptance of American capitalism at home and protection of America's imperial presence abroad.*

Nationalism is both an instrument of class rule and an integral part
of the class consciousness of the Canadian working people. Even
bourgeois nationalism opens the door to class consciousness. The
Canadian bourgeoisie could not control nationalism as a political
force, because nationalism is by definition a political programme
which creates a mass movement. An economic nationalism which
mobilizes workers, farmers, students, and intellectuals is taken over
by these groups to advance class demands against the ruling class and
against the foreign exploitation of the country's economy. This
"class" nationalism opposes the national philosophy of the bourgeoisie. Significantly, Canadian labour failed to link its class demands
to the national question. Its analysis passed over the most salient
feature of Canadian capitalism, that without imperial investments
and the support of the British and American bourgeoisie, national
capitalism in Canada would not survive. In terms of strategy labour
did not understand capitalism and imperialism as inseparable realities
any more than they recognized that an anti-imperialist movement is
a precondition to building a socialist Canada.

AN ANTI-IMPERIALIST NATIONALISM

The bourgeoisie are well versed as to their situation. The strategy of
keeping Canada together by keeping it apart is rooted in the liberal
reality of power that accepts imperialism as the bread-and-butter of
its politics. Nationalism and the national consciousness are extensions
of the liberal order of things, recording the mirror images of how the
bourgeoisie have been able to govern Canada. For them there is no
contradiction between imperial demands and national survival. Their
national programmes reflect a simple design – making Canadian resources cheap and accessible to British and American capitalists. This
eagerness to please and profit has an historical explanation.

The survival and prosperity of this class depends on using the

---

* The breaking of the Canadian Seamen's Union strike, 1947-48, by
   an alliance of the federal government, social democratic trade union
   leadership, and Washington illustrates how far to the right the Canadian trade union movement had travelled.

nation for its own advancement in the capitalist world. But the Canadian bourgeoisie have never sat at the high table as an industrial bourgeoisie in their own right. A colonial bourgeoisie gains admittance to the club for its weakness, not its strength. It reveals itself, according to Fanon, "as incapable of giving birth to an authentic bourgeois society with all the economic and industrial consequences which this entails. From the beginning the national bourgeoisie directs its efforts towards activities of the intermediary type. The basis of its strength is found in its aptitude for trade and small business enterprises, and in securing commissions. It is not its money that works, but its business acumen. It does not go in for investments and it cannot achieve that accumulation of capital necessary to the birth and blossoming of an authentic bourgeoisie."[13] The bourgeoisie does not ask for protection; it is protected by the metropolitan authority. Arm and arm with the real power, it plays the part which has been assigned to it. Fanon writes, "They guess that the present situation will not last indefinitely but they intend to make the most of it. Such exploitation and such contempt for the state, however, inevitably gives rise to discontent among the mass of the people."[14]

The bourgeoisie accept the responsibility for legitimizing the political and economic costs of imperialization as their part of the arrangement. They pacify the people and defuse the internal situation, so that each year the economic surplus produced by the people will be shipped to the imperial centre without interruption. The reliability and ultimate status of the bourgeoisie hinges on their performing this critical function.

For the past one hundred years Canada has acted as the safety-deposit box for British and American investments. One can only describe Canada as the hidden colony of two empires, quietly absorbing huge amounts of capital – investments which paid enormous dividends to both imperialist powers. In 1914 Canada accounted for 23 per cent of all US direct investment; in 1964 it totalled 31 per cent. By 1969 the American "trust" in Canada (both direct and portfolio) had jumped to over $20 billion. "Foreigners hold more than half the total assets of our 400 largest corporations. Non-residents, at last report, control 97 per cent of our automobile industry, 97 per cent of rubber, 78 per cent of chemicals, and 77 per cent of electrical apparatus. The mining and smelting industry is 59 per cent foreign-controlled; the petroleum and natural gas industry 74 per cent. Outside interests control at least 60 per cent of manufacturing."[15]

In protecting the massive inflows of American funds, the Canadian bourgeoisie realized their historic mission as an intermediary. As a consequence the governing bourgeoisie are content with a national consciousness of a people without their own history and who have refused to use the available historical forces to create a national economy and a national culture. Owing their primary commitment to foreign benefactors, they put the needs of capital before the needs of the Canadian people. Their anti-national behaviour is a "desirable and necessary" condition of their well-being as a class. The Canadian semi-sovereign state originated with the class policies of a bourgeoisie incapable of independent thought and independent action. The national bourgeoisie "follows the Western bourgeoisie along its path of negation and decadence without ever having emulated it in its first stages of exploration and invention ... We need not think that it is jumping ahead; it is in fact beginning at the end. It is already senile before it has come to know the petulance, the fearlessness or the will to succeed of youth."[16]

There is no mystery about the behaviour of the bourgeoisie in Canada. They are opposed to a political economy of independence. For them, the nation-state is an obstacle to the complete absorption of Canada into the North American empire. For Canadian liberals national sovereignty is an irrelevant and obsolete concept.* In order to promote and protect imperialism it has been necessary to dismantle the cultural and political institutions of Canada. With dependency comes disintegration.

Bourgeois nationalism is a spent force in Canada. The Canadian

---

* St Laurent, Pearson, and Trudeau speak only about the evils of nationalism. All three are obsessed with internationalism, believing that if all states turned internationalist, the majority of the world's problems would disappear. When these men speak of internationalism, their remarks are prefaced with the unspoken adjectival phrase, "American Cold War internationalism." If Canada's example is to be followed, one would expect the Canadian government to call upon such "narrowly nationalist" countries such as North Vietnam and the Provisional Revolutionary Government of South Vietnam to abandon their struggle for independence and accept the "good neighbour" policy of the United States in Asia! To the extent that Canada has a foreign policy, it is to hand out the pathetic advice, "Be like us, follow the imperial leader."

people are indifferent to it and the bourgeoisie themselves have no faith in it. What remains powerful and alive in the national consciousness is the force of sentimental nationalism. It expresses the discontent and the general anxiety of the Canadian people with their future of living in an advanced capitalist and advanced colonial state.

The English-Canadian people are just beginning to recognize that Canada is a semi-autonomous region of the continent. They realize too that a dependent capitalist region is economically depressed. This is reflected concretely in the inability of Canadian capitalism to solve a range of problems: housing, inflation, lack of new jobs, loss of foreign markets, regional poverty, national planning, student unrest, and US control of the economy. Canadian capitalism is passing through a period of extreme vulnerability.

The strength of Canadian capitalism is its power to suppress its own contradictions. However, the more Americanized Canada becomes, the more disruptive are the effects of the contradictions. Soon enough, Ottawa's role will be to defend openly the advanced colonialism it has imposed on the Canadian people – with no intention of doing anything about it.

Sentimental nationalism is not a revolutionary force, because it does not isolate and crystallize the economic contradictions of capitalism. But it does create the conditions out of which will evolve a revolutionary nationalism – namely, anti-imperialism, which provides the only alternative to the policies of the Canadian bourgeoisie. An anti-imperialist struggle is the only way to break through the tight circle of Canadian history. Anti-imperialism, anti-capitalism and Canadian independence are an inseparable unity.

Analysis leads to strategy. Ideas require testing in practice. The central political issues facing the people of Canada are the historic role of the bourgeoisie in selling the country out and the Americanization of all aspects of Canadian life. These problems must be investigated and discussed throughout Canadian society: by trade union members in their locals, by students in universities, by public employees in government, by individuals in cultural institutions, and by sympathetic businessmen. There should be people's committees to investigate, document, then fight American imperialism in Canada.

NOTES

1 *The Fur Trade in Canada* (rev. ed., Toronto, 1956); *Essays in Canadian Economic History,* collected and published posthumously, M. Q. Innis, ed. (Toronto, 1956). I have analysed this key aspect of Innis' thought in "Harold Innis: Canadian Nationalist," *Journal of Canadian Studies,* May 1969.
2 *The Empire of the St. Lawrence* (Toronto, 1956).
3 *The North American Assault on the Canadian Forest* (Toronto, 1938).
4 (Toronto, 1965).
5 See Donald Creighton, *John A. Macdonald: The Old Chieftain* (Toronto, 1955), chap, III, "Fish and Diplomacy." J. W. Dafoe in *Laurier: A Study in Canadian Politics* (paperback ed., Toronto, 1963), chap. III demonstrates Laurier's commitment to an imperial market. The Abbott plan of 1947 is basically an imperial scheme and a continuation of the national-imperial policy of Macdonald.
6 H. S. Ferns and B. Ostry, *The Age of Mackenzie King* (London, 1955) p. 239.
7 See Pierre Elliott Trudeau, "Some Obstacles to Democracy in Quebec," *Canadian Journal of Economics and Political Science,* August 1958; Roger Graham, *Arthur Meighen,* I (Toronto, 1960); and J. W. Pickersgill, *The Mackenzie King Record,* I, 1939-44 (Toronto, 1960). The latter two books record incidents in which the Liberal party used racist appeals to win votes in Quebec and then turned its racism to double advantage outside Quebec by campaigning against Quebec on the same issue.
8 This point is frequently overlooked because political historians do not avail themselves of all sources of evidence, particularly the writing of Canadian political economists. See H. A. Innis, *A History of the Canadian Pacific Railway* (London, 1923), and G. Myers, *History of Canadian Wealth* (Chicago, 1914), as examples of classics that have been overlooked. Another more recent example is H. C. Pentland's study of the Canadian political economy as it relates to labour, "Labor and the Development of Industrial Capitalism," an unpublished Toronto PHD thesis. It is a brilliant examination of the creation of the Canadian proletariat.
9 Pentland, "Labor and the Development of Industrial Capitalism," p. 409.

10 Ferns and Ostry, *The Age of Mackenzie King,* p. 65. Italics added.
11 See Tim Buck, *Our Fight for Canada: Selected Writings, 1923-1959*
     (Toronto, 1959), esp. chaps. 1 and 2, "The Idea of Labour and
     Democratic Unity" and "The People against the Monopolies." See
     also Gad Horowitz, *Canadian Labour in Politics* (Toronto, 1968).
12 It is perplexing in reading Harold Innis' writings in the 1930s and
     1940s on the political economy of Canada and on the theme of
     American imperialism in this country to realize that his work went
     apparently unnoticed by the Canadian left. See his *Essays in Cana-
     dian Economic History,* particularly, "Economic Trends in Canadian-
     American Relations" (1938), "Recent Developments in the Canadian
     Economy" (1941), and "The Canadian Mining Industry" (1941).
13 F. Fanon, "Pitfalls of National Consciousness," in *The Wretched of
     the Earth* (New York, 1965), p. 144.
14 *Ibid.,* p. 140.
15 *Toronto Daily Star,* Oct. 17, 1969. A historical perspective on US
     foreign investment is given in the tables below:

Non-resident Ownership as a Percentage
of Selected Canadian Industries

INDUSTRY	1926	1957
PERCENTAGE OWNED BY ALL NON-RESIDENTS		
Manufacturing	38	50
Petroleum and natural gas	–	64
Mining and smelting	37	56
Railroads	55	30
Other utilities	32	15
Total of above industries and merchandizing	37	35
PERCENTAGE OWNED BY US RESIDENTS		
Manufacturing	30	39
Petroleum and natural gas	–	58
Mining and smelting	28	46
Railroads	15	11
Other utilities	23	12
Total of above industries and merchandizing	19	27

Foreign Long-Term Capital Invested in Canada, Direct and Portfolio

Type	1926 $ billions	1926 Per cent	1957 $ billions	1957 Per cent
ALL COUNTRIES				
Direct	1.8	30	10.1	68
Portfolio	4.0	66	6.5	37
Miscellaneous	.3	4	.9	5
Total	6.0	100	17.5	100
UNITED STATES				
Direct	1.4	44	8.5	64
Portfolio	1.7	53	4.3	33
Miscellaneous	.1	3	.5	3
Total	3.2	100	13.3	100

Geographic Distribution of US Direct Investment, 1897-1964

	1924 $ billions	1924 Per cent	1958 $ billions	1958 Per cent	1964 $ billions	1964 Per cent
Europe	.9	17	4.4	16	12.1	27
Canada	1.1	20	8.9	32	13.8	31
Latin America	2.8	52	12.7	43	10.3	23
Other	.6	11	1.1	9	8.1	19
Total	5.4	100	27.1	100	44.3	100

Sources: Kari Levitt, "Canada: Economic Dependence and Political Disintegration," *New World Quarterly*, vol. IV, no. 2, and Hugh G. J. Aitken, *American Capital and Canadian Resources* (Cambridge, Mass., 1961), pp. 68-9.

16 Fanon, *The Wretched of the Earth*, pp. 124-5.

I love my two boys, my only sons, and they are living in a big city of the United States. My heart is aching to have them home again in some Canadian city. I am afraid they will marry American girls and settle down there, almost forgetting their mother ... Isn't it dreadful? Divorces are so common over there. You will say, "What has all this to do with the tariff?" I will tell you just what. I got a letter two weeks ago from one of my boys. They both work in the same factory. The letter said, "What do you think, mother? We may be back in Canada before long. I heard our manager say yesterday ... that if the Dominion Government should raise the Canadian tariff as high as the

Michael Bliss

Has contributed articles to the *Canadian Historical Review,* the *Queen's Quarterly,* and other journals. He teaches history at the University of Toronto.

Canadianizing American business: the roots of the branch plant

American tariff it would be necessary for our company to start a big branch factory in Canada ... I guess there would be quite a lot of branch factories started in Canada if the tariff should be raised and there would be lots of work for Canadians at home." Now, Mr. Editor, do you see why I am interested in the tariff question? I want my boys to come home, because I think Canada is a purer and better country. They will be better men here. I don't mean that they are not good now. They are both good boys, but I am afraid of the future (From a letter to the *Montreal Family Herald and Weekly Star,* 1903).

Was there a Golden Age of Canadian economic nationalism? Did
Canadians implement a national economic policy in the era of Sir
John A. Macdonald that protected Canada and its resources from the
United States? Can those salad days of energetic nation-building
before the long Liberal sell-out be held up by modern nationalists,
or nationalist-socialists, as an example of what anti-American (or
pro-Canadian) economic nationalism should be trying to achieve
now?

No.

In the light of present issues, the Canadian National Policy of tariff
protection was a very limited form of economic nationalism. Its
effect was to resist only certain kinds of potential foreign domination
of Canadian economic life, while encouraging exactly those other
forms of outside penetration that are now, according to economic
nationalists, our most serious economic problem. There was nothing
accidental about this apparent contradiction. The old economic
nationalism was based on premises about the needs of the Canadian
people that transcended the simple black and white attitudes towards
Americans familiar to readers of this book. These premises have
continued to operate, virtually without regard to the political labels
of governments in power, as the underlying consensus shaping much
of Canadian economic strategy.

The 1911 election seems to have been the apogee of classic Canadian economic nationalism. Laurier's relatively innocuous reciprocity
agreement with the United States roused Canadian protectionists to
one last spirited defence of the old National Policy. Once again, as in
the 1891 campaign, the issue of Canada's commercial relations with
the United States was transfigured into a plebiscite on the future of
the Canadian nationality. Reciprocity, it was argued, would subvert
the economic foundations of Canada (an industrialized central Canada
servicing a dynamic agrarian West through a developed east-west
communications network), leading inevitably first to economic integration and then to political integration with the United States. More
important, the Canadian attempt to preserve a distinctive identity in
the northern half of the continent would be abandoned. Imperialists
and nationalists – who were never very distinguishable – agreed that
continued tariff protection for Canadian industries equalled Canadian
patriotism and *vice versa.* This compelling equation split the Liberal
party as its protectionist wing rallied round the flag, drove pro-

tectionist business organizations like the Canadian Manufacturers'
Association into active politics in the comfortable role of national
guardians, and doomed Laurier's desperate gamble for one final mandate for his crumbling regime. The election campaign was characterized by anti-Americanism ranging from the rational to the paranoid.
John Diefenbaker tried but failed to resurrect its spirit in 1963; one
wing of the NDP keeps trying.

But one of the minor themes of the Conservative-protectionist
argument in 1911 illustrates the paradox of the "nationalism" of the
National Policy. By 1911 there were already enough American branch
plants in Canada to arouse concern when Canadians considered tariff
policy. That concern, though, was not to limit what had already been
called an American "invasion" of Canada,[1] but rather to sustain
and encourage the branch-plant phenomenon. Branch plants were
obviously a creation of the tariff, and it was equally obvious that
tariff reductions under reciprocity might lead to an American withdrawal back across the border. According to the *Financial Post*, the
possibility of such an *undesirable* situation developing was already
worrying the Laurier government in 1910:

Now our ministers at Ottawa have not the slightest desire to do anything, or to agree to anything, that will have any tendency whatever
to check the movement of United States manufacturers to establish
large plants in this country. These American establishments operate
importantly to build our population and trade, and to build up a
good market for the produce of our farms. And it seems that the
existence of our moderate tariff against United States manufactured
goods has been instrumental in many cases in bringing us these industries. Hence a strong argument exists for not meddling overmuch
with the duties.[2]

When the government none the less pushed on with an agreement
that raised the prospect of lower duties on manufactures, Canadian
nationalist-protectionists made the branch-plant issue a minor but
significant part of their campaign. In his landmark speech to the
House of Commons, when he finally broke with the Liberal party,
Clifford Sifton specifically pointed to the good effects the Quaker
Oats Company was having on the economy of Peterborough, cited
an interview in which its president had announced the company's
intention to return to the United States under reciprocity, and

worried that reciprocity would put an end generally to the beneficial development of American branch plants in Canada.[3] Lloyd Harris, another renegade Liberal, read to the House of Commons letters from American manufacturers threatening to withdraw from Canada and/or refusing to expand. Harris spelled out the branch-plant creating effect of the tariff, and concluded: "That is exactly what I want the Canadian policy to do. I want the American manufacturers to be forced to establish plants on this side of the line and provide work for our Canadian workmen if they want to have the advantage of supplying our home markets."[4]

Still another defecting Liberal MP, William German of Welland, was moved by exactly the same consideration. He pointed out that the tariff had caused seven or eight million dollars of American capital to be invested in branch plants in his constituency, had given employment to thousands of workers, and had created a home market for agricultural products. Reciprocity likely would destroy all of this and ruin the economy of the Welland area.[5] German supported the National Policy because it fostered American economic expansion into his constituency.

Canada's leading protectionist publications similarly were worried about the inhibiting effects of reciprocity on the branch-plant movement. The *Montreal Star* compiled lists of the American branch plants in Canada, and the Toronto *News* asked, "Why ratify a reciprocity agreement that will largely remove this necessity for American industries to establish branch factories in this country? Why do anything that may stop the influx of United States capital for industrial enterprises in Canada?"[6] The *Monetary Times* headlined an anti-reciprocity article, "Americans Will Not Establish Branches."[7] *Industrial Canada*, the organ of the Canadian Manufacturers' Association, worried about branch plants in every issue during the campaign; once its cartoonist depicted an American manufacturer standing on the Canadian side of the tariff barrier meditating, "I'd build a factory here if I was sure they wouldn't destroy the dam."[8]

All the while, of course, protectionists were branding Americans as monopolistic marauders lusting to exploit Canada's resources and ravish her political nationality. But it was only American Americans to whom these phrases applied. Let an American move across the border and locate his business in Canada and he immediately became a useful economic citizen whose presence should be appreciated and encouraged. Geography, it seemed, had marvellous pacifying qualities.

The branch-plant-creating effect of the protective tariff was not new in 1911, only a bit more obvious. The 1858 tariff on agricultural implements had caused at least one implement firm to pole-vault into Canada. This was noticed and used in 1875 as an argument for further protection.[9] Although Macdonald did not rely on the investment-creating argument in his speeches defending the National Policy, his supporters were quite conscious of it (one Conservative in 1879 claimed the protective tariff "would bring capital into the country, that that was one of its chief attributes."[10]) As early as 1880, in fact, MPs were read a communication from the manager of a branch-plant-child of the tariff: "Tell the members of the House of Commons that the St. Catharines Cotton Batting Company would not be in Canada today had it not been for the National Policy, and if the duty is taken off they will take the machinery back to the other side, as we can get cotton cheaper and save freight, which is quite a consideration. ... we sell more cotton batting in this part of Canada than all the factories combined. We would ask for a further increase in duty."[11]

Throughout the 1880s and 1890s the establishment of branch plants was noticed in the Canadian press and hailed as one of the finest achievements of the National Policy. From 1882 to 1896, for example, various issues of the *Canadian Manufacturer* (the first organ of the Canadian Manufacturers' Association) contain sixty-nine references to branch plants being considered by Americans, negotiations being carried on towards the establishment of branch plants, branch plants being established, and the benefits of branch plants. Invariably the phenomenon is explained as a result of the protective tariff; the notices often end with comments like "Score another for the N.P.," "the N.P. does it," "more fruit from the N.P. tree," and "another monument to the glory and success of our National Policy." The need to protect American branch plants was used as an argument against unrestricted reciprocity in the 1880s; and the fear that Americans would withdraw from Canada was used as an argument in favour of the Conservative National Policy in both the 1891 and 1896 elections.[12] By the early 1900s it was common knowledge that Canada's protective tariff had encouraged such major American companies as Singer Sewing Machine, Edison Electric, American Tobacco, Westinghouse, Gillette, and International Harvester to establish Canadian subsidiaries. By 1913 it was estimated that 450 off-shoots of American companies were operating in Canada with a total investment of $135,000,000; the triumph of the National Policy in 1911 had greatly encouraged the branch-plant movement.[13] But as early as 1887 a federal royal commission had been told by the secretary of the CMA that there was scarcely a town of importance in Ontario that did not contain at least one branch of some American business.[14]

As economists have long recognized and historians long ignored, the roots of the branch-plant economic structure in North America must clearly be traced to the operations of the National Policy of tariff protection. The situation could hardly have been otherwise; for in an integrated continentalist economy, a branch-plant structure designed for anything but regional economies would have been inefficient and superfluous. The economic nationalism of the late nineteenth century, then, operated and was known to operate to induce Americans to enter Canada and participate directly in the Canadian economy. Accordingly, the National Policy sowed many of the seeds of our present problem with foreign ownership. Possibly it caused more American manufacturing penetration than completely continentalist or free trade policies would have encouraged. From the perspective of the late 1960s it now appears to have been a peculiarly self-defeating kind of economic nationalism. The funny thing about our tariff walls was that we always wanted the enemy to jump over them. Some walls!

The paradox dissolves once the real nature of traditional Canadian economic nationalism is clarified. The impulse behind the National Policy and the whole complex of policies comprising our strategy for national development was not simply or even basically anti-American. It was rather a kind of neo-mercantilism designed above all to secure the maximum utilization in Canada of a maximum of Canadian resources. The nationality of foreigners competing to manufacture Canadian resources in their own countries or to supply Canadians with foreign resources was quite irrelevant. In the early years our tariffs shut out foreign products without regard to their national origin. They probably had a much more negative impact on trade with England than on trade with the United States, and the economic nationalism of Canadian producing classes supplied much of the resistance to any serious system of imperial preferences in the twentieth century.

Similarly, massive inputs of foreign capital were seen to be absolutely central for this concept of national economic development.

Outside money was wooed without regard for either nationality or modern distinctions between direct and portfolio investment. Few people in the half-century after Confederation questioned Canada's absolute reliance on foreign capital. Aside from worrying now and then about our ever being able to pay off our debts, no one was seriously upset about the ultimate consequences of a high percentage of foreign ownership – either British or American – of our resources. Least of all were they worried about the flow of interest and profits to foreign countries. As *Industrial Canada* commented in 1908, "That a portion of the profits made on the development of our latent resources has to be paid out in interest is no hardship, since without the capital there would have been no profits at all."[15]

If the Canadian tariff policy was consciously designed to attract foreign capital to Canada in whatever form it chose to come, there were other more precise policies to encourage the same migration. The applications of export duties on saw-logs in the 1890s and then again on pulpwood in the early 1900s were deliberate and successful attempts to force American lumber and pulp manufacturers across the border to set up their mills in Canada.[16] Intermittently throughout the 1890s and early 1900s both the Dominion and the Ontario governments blustered, cajoled, and legislated in an unsuccessful attempt to force the International Nickel Company to move its main refinery to Canada.[17] And the most important of all of these efforts to induce direct foreign investment has been the least noticed: every Canadian province, every Canadian city, every Canadian hamlet pursued its own "national policy" of offering all possible incentives to capitalists and developers to come into its territory and establish manufacturing enterprises. The practice of granting bonuses to industries in the form of free sites, free utilities, tax concessions, loans, and outright cash grants was universal and persistent, despite the vehement objections of established capitalists. It was responsible for the attraction of countless American branch plants to specific cities as well as for the occasional municipal bankruptcy.[18] The federal government led the way in "bonusing" with its subsidies to the CPR and the general subsidy to manufacturing industries inherent in the tariff. On an even grander scale it conducted an astonishing alienation of public resources by "bonusing" every farmer who came to the Canadian West, regardless of his nationality, with 160 acres of free land. Many American farmers came; and there was more concern about their effect on Canadian national life in the early twentieth century than about all the branch plants combined (in a way every American-owned homestead that had family connections to the United States was a little branch plant).*

The basic assumption underlying all of this activity was the conviction that foreign capital and business enterprise should be Canadianized, that is, that they should be put to work inside Canada on Canadian resources and thereby produce the maximum benefit for the Canadian people and the Canadian nation. This explains precisely why Americans in the United States were competitors and economic enemies, but were invaluable allies once they had crossed the border with their money and skills. The bare fact of their crossing the border Canadianized them. In this sense the Canadianization of foreign business was one of the basic themes of economic nationalism, at least until the First World War.

Vague dreams of a "Big Canada," of population growth, wealth, status, and power undoubtedly all motivated Canadian National Policy-makers.[19] But there was one significant specific variation of these themes that deserves more attention. After defence and public order the most important function of government in nineteenth century Canada was the provision of more and better jobs. Hamlets, towns, cities, provinces, and the nation all assumed that they had a duty to promote jobs for their citizens and for incoming future citizens. They rightly knew that jobless citizens left depressed communities and that such emigration was a sign of communal failure in the most basic way. Particularly in bad times this explains the desire on the part of every political unit to promote industrial development (in good times the "bigness" theme became predominant). The argument of development to create employment was especially important on the national level in the depression of the 1870s. Macdonald's

---

*   In a paper read at the 1969 meeting of the Canadian Historical Association, "The Decline and Fall of the Empire of the St. Lawrence," Donald Creighton argues that the chief subversion of the National Policy came only after the rise to prominence of provincially controlled resources in the 1920s. He implies that the federal government shepherded resources under its control more responsibly, or at least more nationalistically, than the provinces did. My argument may suggest a reconsideration of Creighton's thesis.

concern for the emigrating unemployed echoes (with only a touch of hyperbole) through his great 1878 speech demanding a National Policy:

We have no manufactures here. We have no work-people; our work-people have gone off to the United States. They are to be found employed in the Western States, in Pittsburg, and, in fact, in every place where manufactures are going on. These Canadian artizans are adding to the strength, to the power, and to the wealth of a foreign nation instead of adding to ours. Our work-people in this country, on the other hand, are suffering for want of employment. Have not their cries risen to Heaven? Has not the Hon. the Premier been surrounded and besieged, even in his own Department, and on his way to his daily duties, by suffering artizans who keep crying out: "We are not beggars, we only want an opportunity of helping to support ourselves and our families"? Is not such the case also in Montreal and in Quebec? In fact, is not that the state of things which exists in every part of Canada ...?

... if these men cannot find an opportunity in their own country to develop the skill and genius with which God has gifted them, they will go to a country where their abilities can be employed, as they have gone from Canada to the United States. ... The hon. gentleman opposite sneered at the statement that thousands of our people had left this country to seek for employment in the United States. Why, the fact is notorious that the Government of the Province of Quebec have been taking steps to bring back their people.

... if Canada had had a judicious system of taxation [a protective tariff] they would be toiling and doing well in their own country.[20]

By fostering home industries, protection would give these artisans the jobs they were going to the States to find. It was only a small step to the realization that protection would also draw American manufacturers across the border to provide even more jobs for Canadian artisans. And once this was realized, good nationalists - nationalists concerned with protecting the Canadian community from emigration through unemployment - could only encourage the process. Whether or not this whole argument made or makes sense theoretically is irrelevant; it was the economic theory that Canadians acted upon.

French Canadians faced the same problem even more dramatically.

The greatest threat to the French-Canadian nationality in the late nineteenth century was emigration to the textile mills of New England. Quebec governments had to create jobs to preserve the national identity of their overpopulated community. The colonization programmes that were begun in the 1840s were serious attempts to create employment in agriculture – far more serious and sophisticated than historians have credited them with being. But there were also significant French-Canadian attempts to encourage industrial development of all kinds in the province of Quebec from at least the 1880s. Thanks to William F. Ryan's *The Clergy and Economic Growth in Quebec (1896-1914)*, we now know that French Canadians at many levels of society understood the potential benefits of industrialism to their community and deliberately encouraged manufacturing and resource-development as job-creating alternatives to emigration. Anglophones, usually Americans, were entirely welcome in Quebec because of the ultimate value they had for preserving the French-Canadian nationality. Ryan's discussion of the role of Laurentide Pulp in the community of Grand-Mère summarizes volumes of French-Canadian social and economic history: "Jamais de memoire d'homme on n'avait vu tant d'argent dans la région et dans la paroisse," comments a native about the early years of the pulp mill; "Owing to the new prosperity the curé of Sainte-Flore was able to complete his new church in 1897," remarks Ryan; and a succeeding curé tells the American manager of Laurentide, "Mr. Chahood, you and I are partners – I look after the spiritual welfare of my people while you are responsible for their bodily well-being."[21]

Extreme dependence on capitalists – often foreigners – for initiating crucial economic development with its accompanying employment explains much of the respect for "captains of industry" before the great depression. Capitalists created jobs; they spent money; they enabled curés to build churches. Even when they behaved badly, as the capitalists of the International Nickel Company did before the First World War, the jobs they provided were so critical that neither Ontario nor Canada wanted to stand up to them.[22] The leaders of the province of Quebec often had to genuflect to capitalists by urging deference and docility upon the working class for fear that a militant labour movement would discourage investment in Quebec and thereby create even more desperate poverty leading to emigration and denationalization.

The nineteenth century economy created the role of the capitalist as hero, as nation-builder.* When the foreign capitalist's work led to the development of Canadian resources he too qualified as a builder of the Canadian nation, whether or not he repatriated his profits. Van Horne of the CPR is the most famous Canadianized American (C. D. Howe seems to have won more notoriety than fame, although his contributions to Canada vastly exceeded Van Horne's); but perhaps the most exciting in his day was Frank Clergue, a semi-respectable American promoter who in the late 1890s created the multi-million dollar industrial complex at Sault Ste Marie. Clergue's remarkable ability to turn the wasteland of northern Ontario into a seeming El Dorado amazed, delighted, and shamed Canadians who marvelled at a man with more faith in their country than they had themselves. For a time, in fact, Clergue became a stronger Canadian nationalist than the Canadians, urging them to have confidence in their own country and its resources and campaigning at all levels of government for extensions of Canadian mercantilism (which would, of course, benefit his industries). Clergue's activities aroused concern about the participation of Americans in Canadian development, but only in the form of exhortations to native Canadians to be as enter-prising and dynamic as this American and his Philadelphia backers.[23] Here was a fully Canadianized American businessman, right down to the refurbished Hudson's Bay Company blockhouse he lived in, communing with the spirits of the builders of the empire of the St Lawrence. Despite the spectacular bankruptcy in 1903 that effec-tively ended his Canadian career, Clergue has been the only "Cana-dian" businessman to live on in our fiction, the subject of our most prolonged hymn to capitalist enterprise.[24]

In a 1901 speech to the citizens of Sault Ste Marie, Clergue spelled out the ultimate arguments for the American economic penetration of Canada:

Let me summarize the conditions which the captious critic would discover here. He would find in the different lines of industry we had

---

* This is recognized in our historiography in the popularity of the "Laurentian thesis" and in the interpretation of the construction of the CPR as a national epic. Frank Underhill has been the only major historian to promote a "robber baron" approach to nineteenth century Canadian businessmen.

expended here in the neighbourhood of nine millions of dollars, cash, all of which has been foreign money injected into the circulating medium of Canada, to remain forever to the everlasting blessing of thousands of its inhabitants; that the completion and successful operation of our undertaking will require the expenditure of a sum nearly as large; that several thousands of inhabitants had found new employment in these undertakings at a higher scale of wages than had ever before prevailed in Canada ... that our works sent over $300,000 in cash to Georgian Bay ports last year for purchases; that we sent nearly as much to Hamilton, and nearly as much to Toronto; that the machinery and electrical supplies that we have purchased from Peterborough have amounted to over $100,000; that Brantford, Galt, Dundas and every other Ontario town engaged in mechanical manufactures had received from twenty-five thousand to two hundred thousand dollars of patronage from us; that our requirements had advanced the price of horses and nearly all the farm products in that part of Ontario tributary to Sault Ste. Marie ... Looking over our office staff he would find scientific and classical graduates from every college in Canada, clerks from nearly every bank in Canada and accountants from almost every city in Ontario. Among the artisans, mechanics and laborers he will find nearly every town and city in Ontario represented, and all of these people have assembled here because they found the rewards of labor greater here than elsewhere.[25]

To Canadians of the day these were unanswerable arguments. The citizens of Sault Ste Marie had literally danced at the opening of Clergue's works.

Could things have happened differently in the two or three generations after Confederation? Could a more foresighted and active Canadian government or a more dynamic entrepreneurial class have perceived the ultimate American threat to Canadian society and thwarted it before serious inroads were made? Even if Canadians had recognized an American threat – unlikely inasmuch as Canadianizing American business was integral to Canadian nationalism – there would have been no acceptable alternative to reliance on foreign capital and capitalists for national development. Mel Watkins has suggested that a more thorough-going state capitalism, including a national investment bank, would have obviated dependence on outsiders.[26] In the context of the late nineteenth century this is utopian: Canadian governments were barely competent to run a post office efficiently or anything honestly, let alone be entrusted with hundreds of millions of dollars for national development; the Canadian people fiercely resisted all forms of public appropriation of their incomes; the safety-valve of emigration to the United States put firm limits on the extent to which Canadian development policies could diverge from American, or the Canadian standard of living could fall below that of the United States. Recently Watkins has also argued that a weak and timid entrepreneurial class abdicated from its crucial role as moulder of a natively Canadian economic policy.[27] Such a Schumpeterian or proto-Marxist approach to economic development is probably inadequate in theory. It is at least unproven in fact, for we know virtually nothing about the actual entrepreneurial activities of native Canadians in the formative years of industrialism. My suspicion is that Canadian businessmen did meet ordinary standards of entrepreneurial prowess and that in areas like industrial education they were frustrated by the conservatism and élitism of the cultural establishment, notably professors of the humanities.

This argument has no more implications for present policy than any historical study. It does, I hope, do something to save the past record from the distortions of the present-minded. The economic nationalism of the National Policy was clearly inadequate as a defence against American penetration of the Canadian economy. On the contrary, it encouraged the commencement of American penetration in the form that most worries modern nationalists, and it did this with a fair measure of purposefulness. The great "sell-out" did not begin with Mackenzie King in the 1920s or with C. D. Howe in the 1940s. If anything it was a consistent policy about which there was an extraordinarily broad consensus. If King and Howe are to be criticized for not perceiving that Americans were the "real" threat to Canadian independence, surely Macdonald also must be censured either for not perceiving the future course of North American economic development or for wilfully promulgating a policy that encouraged American economic migration to this country. In all three cases it is much more fruitful to emphasize the force of their desire to create a community of prosperous and happy Canadians (largely happy because prosperous) and their willingness to import outside resources to that end.

Discussions of the role of élites in Canadian history have so far had little to do with historical reality. If élite theory must be used to explain Canadian economic development, some of the points raised in this essay should lead to a reconsideration of the interaction of élites in the late nineteenth century. In so far as industrial employment depended on the existence of capitalists, the industrial worker had a profound common interest with his employer – in the preservation of his job. The benefits of tariff protection in sustaining and encouraging manufacturing, including branch plants, were distributed to the industrial working class in much the same proportion as to the industrial employing class. Instead of a working class being oppressed by a capitalist élite, there was, at least on issues of high commercial policy, a single "industrial élite" which perceived itself as the beneficiary of the National Policy and all its consequences. By the 1890s a few union leaders had developed a working-class consciousness that led them away from paternalism and conventional Canadian economic wisdom. The mass of Canadian industrial workers, though, were still protectionist. The tariff, they thought, protected their jobs and created new jobs in industrial production. After all, the working class supplied the Canadian content of the American branch plants.

Some of the problems and attitudes reviewed here are still directly relevant. The Canadianization of Texas Gulf Sulphur takes another step forward as the Robarts government is egged on by the NDP to force it to transfer its refinery to Canada – creating jobs in Timmins by sacrificing the possibility of native Canadians some day building their own refinery. Joey Smallwood offers to deal with the devil if he has the capital to produce jobs for Newfoundlanders through industrial development (and what are a few Erco-poisoned fish compared to the wages that ex-fishermen can get in factories?); his alternative is the depopulation of the island. Anglophone control of the Quebec economy is despised, but its withdrawal threatens to destroy the economic base of the French-Canadian nationality. In Manitoba Ed Schreyer finds out as the head of an NDP provincial government that he must take capital where he finds it whatever his theoretical doubts about the extent of American investment in Canada. On the whole Canadians continue to believe – wisely, I think – that a limited but prosperous national existence is preferable to a pure, poor nationality.

In 1909 the Canadian Manufacturers' Association launched another crusade for the support of Canadian home industries. One of the first companies proudly advertising its product as "Made in Canada" was Coca-Cola. Things went better ...

NOTES

1 *Financial Post,* June 11, 1910.
2 *Ibid.,* June 4, 1910.
3 *House of Commons Debates,* Feb. 28, 1911, pp. 4394-6.
4 *Ibid.,* March 8, 1911, p. 4905.
5 *Ibid.,* March 2, 1911, pp. 4486-7.
6 Reprinted in *Industrial Canada,* XI, 10 (May 1911), p. 1072.
7 March 4, 1911, p. 918.
8 XI, 7 (Feb. 1911), p. 729. For the issue of branch plants and reciprocity in the United States, see Ronald Radosh, "American Manufacturers,
   Canadian Reciprocity, and the Origins of the Branch Factory System,"
   C.A.A.S. Bulletin, III, 1 (Spring/Summer 1967).
9 William Dewart, "Fallacies of Reciprocity," *Canadian Illustrated News,*
   Feb. 13, 1875.
10 *House of Commons Debates,* March 28, 1879, p. 791. Mr John Weiler
   brought this and the letter cited in the next footnote to my attention.
11 *Ibid.,* March 23, 1880, pp. 836-7.
12 See *Canadian Manufacturer,* May 6, 1887, p. 263; April 17, 1891,
   p. 198; June 5, 1896, p. 468.
13 Fred. W. Field, *Capital Investments in Canada* (Toronto, 1914), p. 25.
   For another account of early American investments see Herbert Marshall *et al., Canadian-American Industry* (Toronto, 1936), chap. 1.
14 Royal Commission on the Relations of Capital and Labor in Canada,
   Evidence – Ontario (Ottawa, 1889), p. 179.
15 VIII, 10 (May 1908), p. 763.
16 H. G. J. Aitken, ed., *The American Economic Impact on Canada* (Durham, NC, 1959), chap. 1; Aitken, "Defensive Expansionism: The State
   and Economic Growth in Canada," in W. T. Easterbrook and M. H.
   Watkins, eds., *Approaches to Canadian Economic History* (Toronto,
   1967). It is significant that the federal government, not the provinces,
   first began the use of export duties on saw-logs as a means of inducing
   manufacture in Canada.
17 O. W. Main, *The Canadian Nickel Industry* (Toronto, 1955), chap. 4.
18 For "bonusing" see any Canadian business periodical for any year
   between Confederation and 1914, but especially the note beginning
   "Belleville ... has organized a little National Policy of its own,"
   Canadian Manufacturer, May 17, 1889, p. 329; also *ibid.,* July 19,
   1895, p. 69, "American firms of every description ... have only to

make public their designs and be inundated by letters from Canadian municipal authorities."

19 R. Craig Brown, "The Nationalism of the National Policy," and John Dales, "Protection, Immigration and Canadian Nationalism," both in Peter Russell, ed., *Nationalism in Canada* (Toronto, 1966).

20 *House of Commons Debates,* March 7, 1878, pp. 857, 859.

21 Ryan, *The Clergy and Economic Growth in Quebec (1896-1914)* (Quebec City, 1966), pp. 62, 64, 67.

22 Main, *The Canadian Nickel Industry,* chap. 4.

23 For Clergue's career, see Margaret Van Every, "Francis Hector Clergue and the Rise of Sault Ste.Marie as an Industrial Centre," *Ontario History,* LVI, 3 (Sept. 1964); for his exhortations to Canadians, see Francis H. Clergue, *An Instance of Industrial Evolution in Northern Ontario, Dominion of Canada; Address Delivered to the Toronto Board of Trade, April 2nd, 1900* (Toronto, 1900); for reaction to Clergue see *Monetary Times,* April 6, 1900, p. 1323; Feb. 1, 1901, p. 987; March 8, 1901, p. 1160.

24 Allan Sullivan, *The Rapids* (Toronto, 1922).

25 *Address by Francis H. Clergue At a Banquet Given in His Honor by the Citizens of Sault Ste. Marie, Ont. Feb. 15, 1901* (n.p.), 29-30.

26 "The 'American System' and Canada's National Policy," *C.A.A.S. Bulletin,* III, 2 (Winter 1967).

27 "A New National Policy," in Trevor Lloyd and Jack McLeod, eds., *Agenda 1970; Proposals for a Creative Politics* (Toronto, 1968).

C. W. Gonick

The editor of *Canadian Dimension,* a member of the Manitoba Legislature, and teaches economics at the University of Manitoba.

Foreign ownership and political decay

Survival has been an historical obsession in Canada – although concern has shifted from sheer physical survival to one of halting the
cultural and economic absorption of Canada into the United States.
Canada has become so deeply penetrated by the American metropolis,
so dependent upon it – economically, militarily, culturally, and psy-
chologically – that we are overcome by our own sense of powerlessness. The possibility of independence appears doubtful, and the cost
of it stupendous.

The question of foreign ownership in Canada has received much
attention in the past decade. Economists, politicians, editors, royal
commissions, and task forces have at various times, and with varying
degrees of sophistication, addressed themselves to the subject. Their
goals and assumptions, usually unstated, often differ, however, and
their discussions have led more to obfuscation than to clarification.
Consequently the issues have become blurred and even incomprehensible. What we need is a new National Policy, a coherent strategy
for independence. We do not have that today. Indeed we have yet to
develop either the analysis or the essential political alliance that can
effectively lead a movement for national independence.

The purpose of this essay[1] is to survey some of the leading positions
in the debate on foreign ownership and compare their underlying
assumptions, to clarify the main terms of the debate, and to provide
a framework for further discussion.

When we talk about Canada and the American empire, we should
keep in mind a fact of central importance: that Canada is a small
regional economy within the metropolitan economy of the United
States of America. We have always been the hinterland of some
imperial system. Our evolution from the British system towards the
American system began with the American Revolution but was not
completed until the early decades of the twentieth century.

The dynamic element in the Canadian economy is not domestic but
export activity. The rate of growth, the pattern of growth, and the
location of growth within the Canadian economy have always been
determined by the export of a small number of staple products. The
shape of the Canadian economy has depended successively upon fish,
fur, timber, wheat, pulp and paper, and metals. Each has its own
peculiarities in terms of the population and the kinds of communities
that it can support, in its technological and capital requirements, in

its regional implications, and in the satellite industries that it can generate. Each, in turn, has been the growth point of the Canadian economy. Economic activity geared to the domestic market has been largely derivative, complementing the staple sectors by processing their raw materials, supplying their buildings, parts, and machinery, and producing the goods and services consumed by their work force. Today, for example, between one-quarter and one-third of the goods produced in Canada are exported to the United States. These are mostly resource-based products – pulp and paper, nickel, iron ore, lead, zinc, and the like. Canadian jobs, profits, and prosperity in general are heavily dependent on the growth of US markets for these products. It is well known that Canada has never prospered in the face of a depression in the US economy, has never been able to stabilize its prices in the face of American inflation, and has never been able to eliminate unemployment in the face of a downturn in the US economy.

The primary economic role of Canada is to supply staple commodities as substitutes for the increasingly depleted resources of the United States. In the 1930s the United States was virtually self-sufficient in iron ore. Currently, about one-quarter of her supplies must be imported from abroad. She was virtually self-sufficient in lead. Now over half of her lead supplies are imported from abroad. The same trend has been evident for many other critical metals.[2]

Canada is a very valuable part of the American empire. Most of the untapped resources in the world are located in backward, non-industrialized, politically unstable, and usually hostile countries. Canada is one of the few countries which has a great frontier of untapped resources and is at the same time highly industrialized, with a stable government friendly to the United States. The financial burden of maintaining access to strategic new materials, in terms of economic and military aid, is very slight. The possibility of these resources being cut off is slim; moreover, Canada offers a northward extension of the US market for manufactured goods which is served largely by the Canadian subsidiaries of the US multinational corporations. In general, American corporate ownership of Canadian resources guarantees, perpetuates, and strengthens a hinterland economy: our resource industry is developed by giant US companies to supply American industry with raw materials; our manufacturing industry is developed by them to supply the limited Canadian domestic market.

The so-called "staples theory," which is commonly used to explain economic growth in Canada, is really a pseudonym for a special kind of imperial relationship.

To get a proper perspective of Canada's relationship to the United States, we should bear in mind that capitalism is an international rather than a national system; that at the centre of this international system is the United States, just as England, France, and Holland were in earlier periods. The entire capitalist world – including the West European countries, their colonies, and their spheres of influence – is profoundly influenced by the movements of the American economy. What distinguishes Canada (and Latin America) within this international system is the extent to which we have become tied to the American metropolis.

Trade ties and us ownership of Canadian industry are the main links which integrate the two nations within one continental economy. They complement and reinforce each other. There is a temptation to debate the primacy of trade ties or foreign ownership in the continentalizing of the Canadian economy. But the distinction is futile, for trade and foreign ownership are ineluctably tied together. Data compiled for 266 of the larger foreign-owned companies in 1964 and 1965 indicate that these firms alone account for about one-third of both Canadian exports and imports. If all subsidiaries and foreign affiliates were included, the proportion would be even greater. A study comparing the import propensities of non-resident-owned firms and resident-owned firms has shown that foreign-owned firms are more import-oriented, less inclined to use local suppliers.[3] Moreover, 70 per cent of all purchases are from parent companies (about 50 per cent of all sales of subsidiaries are to parent companies). A us Department of Commerce Survey (1963) reported that in 1957 close to a quarter of all us export of machinery and parts was sold to subsidiaries and that three-quarters of the machinery and parts imported by all us affiliates were produced in the United States. These statistics demonstrate irrefutably that the setting up of American branch plants and subsidiaries in Canada greatly strengthens trade ties between the two countries. About two-thirds of subsidiary exports go to the United States and about three-quarters of subsidiary imports come from the United States.[4] Much of the trade is intra-company and not subject to market forces. Devaluation of the Canadian dollar in the early 1960s, for example, did not affect these imports. They actually increased by 17 per cent in 1963, whereas total Canadian imports rose by only 7 per cent.

There is, undoubtedly, economic justification for some of this intra-company trade. It would have occurred irrespective of owner-ship ties. Yet, there is some evidence that a portion of this trade, while it no doubt adds to the profitability of the multinational corporation, results in higher production costs for the Canadian sub-sidiary than otherwise might exist. Not long ago, when he was a cabinet minister in the Quebec government, Eric Kierans argued persuasively that Canada, as a major industrial nation, could produce economically thousands of items imported automatically from parent US companies by their subsidiaries.[5] He cited as evidence a major effort by Northern Electric to "buy Canadian." This company succeeded in transferring to Canada the manufacturing of nearly twelve thousand parts and components manufactured principally in the United States. The resulting saving in foreign exchange was $12 million US dollars. The shift generated new jobs for seventeen hundred Canadians, and it evidently produced important savings in costs for the company. If branch plants had the freedom to choose the lowest-cost suppliers, there is little doubt that they would more often opt for Canadian or non-American foreign supplies. This would be more profitable for them and, more to the point, would cut down our heavy dependence on US imports. But, because their primary responsibility is to contribute to the profit maximization of the global corporation rather than their own, they can rationally purchase cost-increasing supplies from the parent.

It may not appear clear why a practice which reduces the profits of subsidiaries can nevertheless contribute more than off-setting increases of profits to the parent company. It might be explained in this way. Most giant manufacturing corporations earn no profits at all over much of their output. Before they earn any profits, they must produce beyond a certain level of output, usually referred to as "the break-even point." This is because of the large overhead capital which yields high per unit costs for low levels of output. For example, a study of US Steel Company shows that the break-even point is 40 per cent of capacity. At 100 per cent of productive capacity the rate of profit is 13 per cent. But it is the last 15 per cent of the corporation's output that accounts for 35 per cent of its profits. Since exports by the typical giant American corporation account for anywhere between 5 and 20 per cent of its total output, these can be of crucial importance for the overall profitability of the corporation. We know, then, that exports to foreign subsidiaries account for a disproportionate share of the profits of parent corporations. Any resulting increased production costs and correspondingly reduced subsidiary profits is a small price to pay for the major contribution subsidiaries make as markets for output which cannot be absorbed by the US domestic market at prevailing prices. In a special report on the multinational corporation *Business Week* magazine has been quite explicit on this relationship: "The goal in the multinational corporation is the greatest good for the whole unit, even if the interests of a single part of the unit must suffer. One large manufacturer, for example, penalizes some of its overseas subsidiaries for the good of the total corporation by forcing them to pay more than necessary for parts they import from the parent and from other subsidiaries."[6]

A manufacturing subsidiary could lose money and still make a net contribution to the parent company's income – by the profit on purchases of raw material, parts, and finished products from the parent, by payment of royalties and fees from management, marketing and research services. Hearings before the US Senate Committee on Ways and Means in 1961 demonstrated that the major purpose of many subsidiaries is not to make a large profit themselves, but to contribute to the profit maximization of the parent firm by providing an automatic export market for equipment, materials, and parts.

The point here, and it is an essential point, is that a significant proportion of Canada's imports from the United States can be explained by the predominance of the American corporations in Canada. This is even more obviously true with regard to exports to the United States. Separation of the trade links which bind the two economies from the corporate links is therefore entirely illegitimate. It is no accident that the new trade relationship between Canada and the Communist countries – especially the Soviet Union and China – all occur in agriculture, one of the few major goods-producing sectors of the Canadian economy which remain under Canadian ownership.

Enough has been said about the structure of Canada's role in the continental economy to allow us to survey the major responses to it. Given the close trade and capital links which now bind together the economies of Canada and the United States and given Canada's regional role within the continental structure, its destiny, national growth, and prosperity are obviously tied to the general movement of the us economy. Grievances inevitably occur when the narrow interests of the hinterland clash with specific policies of the metropolis. And political debate on Canadian-American relations has turned largely on the discovery of the most effective response to these grievances: for example, the Mercantile Bank issue of 1967; the us government guidelines of 1966 (made compulsory some months later), which required American subsidiaries to remit a higher portion of their profits to the United States, to finance their investment more fully out of funds raised on the Canadian money market, and to purchase a larger share of their products and equipment from the United States; the refusal of American-owned drug companies in Canada to sell medical supplies to the Society of Friends for distribution among Vietnamese civilians; the refusal of American-owned flour mill companies to export flour to Cuba (1966); the celebrated Ford of Canada case of the 1950s; and the *Time-Reader's Digest* case of the 1960s. A recurrent grievance is the refusal of parent American companies to permit Canadian investors to acquire shares in their Canadian subsidiaries.

The necessity of continentalism, of Canada's regional role within a continental economic structure, is never doubted, and therefore the question of its desirability is seldom raised. For those who are at all concerned with the problem, the issue is rather how to solve these grievances within the continentalist framework.

Among the Canadian corporate and political élite and their intellectual cohorts appear two schools of thought. One might be termed "passivist," the other "activist." Both schools accept the need for continentalism. Neither envisions Canada as being anything but a regional economy within the continental North American economy. And both agree that the multinational corporation is here to stay, and that it is an agency for economic progress. The activists, among whom the leading figure has been Walter Gordon, complain loud:y about the economic problems which emerge between Canada and the United States. They understand that the grievances are mere symptoms – that they reflect the inevitable conflicts which develop between any region and its centre or metropolis. The activists may have different approaches, but essentially they advocate policies to strengthen Canada's bargaining position within the continental system - to win for Canadians a greater share of the continental pie. The federal government should play a more vigorous role in protecting Canadian interests within the system, and Canadian capital should play a greater role in continental industry. Eric Kierans, another activist, has suggested that Ottawa get from the nine hundred largest US subsidiaries in Canada "detailed analyses" of their imports and prices paid. Once Canadian firms know what companies are importing for their manufacturing processes, and at what prices, they will be in a better position to take advantage of profitable investment opportunities. Kierans has argued also that Canadian economic policy should encourage mergers among Canadian businesses so as to strengthen Canadian capital vis-à-vis US capital. Walter Gordon advocated restricting the sale of Canadian companies to foreigners through a system of financial penalties and the establishment of the Canada Development Corporation that would buy up Canadian firms which would otherwise be sold to Americans, and he put into legislation his programme of providing incentives for American parent companies to permit Canadians to buy shares in their subsidiaries. The *Toronto Star,* the only daily newspaper which supports the activists' position, advocates legislation which would require that all new companies in the resource-field have at least 50 per cent Canadian ownership, and that within ten to fifteen years existing foreign-owned enterprises in the resource-field be required to share ownership with Canadians, to the extent of 50 per cent as a minimum.

The passivists fear these proposals. They downgrade economic difficulties with the United States. For the Pierre Elliot Trudeaus, Jean-Luc Pepins, and E. P. Taylors, they are "misunderstandings" due to "a breakdown of communication." They argue, in effect, that the marginal gains to be made by tinkering with the continentalist mechanism will be more than offset by retaliatory measures by the Americans, or simply by the hostile environment that it will create. They support laissez-faire within the continentalist system – as against the activists who support state intervention to boost Canada's relative position inside it.

The lack of support for the activist position within the ruling circles of Canada is not surprising. Canadian business is thoroughly integrated within the continental economic structure: Canadian-owned corporations often have their own subsidiary companies in the United States; for many, sales and profits depend heavily on continued access to the American market; members of Canada's business élite sit on the boards of directors of US affiliated companies, just as representatives of the American business élite sit on the boards of giant Canadian-owned companies. There is a virtual identity of interests between the Canadian business élite and the American corporate presence in Canada. Their profits and prestige cannot be separated from the economic ties that bind the two countries, and they will not have the Walter Gordons jeopardizing their position. Canadian industry was genuinely worried that Gordon's exploits would scare away American capital, anger the American State Department, and, incidentally, bring more government control into the Canadian economy. His political demise was no doubt a product of its concern.

Before his departure, Walter Gordon, as president of the Privy Council, left behind the report of the task force on *Foreign Ownership and the Structure of Canadian Industry*. This task force, headed by economist Melville Watkins, is an important document in the continuing debate on this subject and deserves separate treatment. Its underlying assumptions are easy to list: foreign investment is essential to Canadian economic development; multinational corporations, the main agency for transmitting foreign investment, are here to stay; these corporations yield both benefits and costs in terms of Canadian economic development and political independence; the policy of government must be to minimize the costs and maximize the benefits.[7] The entire analysis occurs within the confines of the liberal private enterprise economy with a conventional fiscal-monetary role posited for government. The decision not to venture beyond the boundaries of the existing institutional framework explains the decidedly narrow approach to foreign ownership adopted by the task force. The authors of the report, mostly academic economists, bring to their assignment the usual textbook definitions of modern economics: "rational" means those policies designed to maximize the total value of marketable goods and services. They are not interested in what kind of commodities are produced, because this would raise questions about the sovereignty of property and the entire process by which tastes are moulded. Government policies aimed at reclaiming effective Canadian political sovereignty are sanctioned by the task force, but only if they do not interfere with existing property relations. If the recommendations of the task force seem feeble, the underlying explanation lies in its refusal to seek solutions beyond the bounds of the established business framework.

The task force report breaks no new ground. Hurriedly put together, its major purpose seems to have been to bring together current information about the multinational corporation and to place these data within the "conventional wisdom" of modern economics. The policy recommendations follow logically from the assumptions. Facts relevant to the multinational corporation but irrelevant to the frame of reference of the task force are mentioned casually and hurriedly by-passed. These include, among others, the role of the multinational corporation in the American military-industrial complex and the inevitable link it provides in attaching Canada to the global exploits of the American system; also, the entire set of values, tastes, fashions, attitudes, approaches, and organizational patterns which are imported along with the American corporation. Within the static assumptions of the task force, these facts are interesting and therefore worth mentioning, but they are essentially outside the realm of policy considerations. Because they are not central to the analysis they are overlooked, and the analysis is therefore conventional and superficial.

The economist, Thorstein Veblen, once invoked his colleagues to make of economics an evolutionary science – meaning to abandon the mechanical approach of neo-classical economics and to begin to examine the assumptions that lie behind economic institutions, and to trace their historical development. Economists, by and large, have ignored this plea. Certainly the task force report on foreign ownership is devoid of history. It avoids asking the questions which its policies depend upon: what has happened to Canada's capitalist class as American multinational corporations have taken over the commanding heights of the economy? How and why has this development occurred? Is there a business class today with distinctly Canadian interests? The report clearly assumes that there is, and its conclusions rest on this unproven proposition.

The report devotes most of its pages to cataloguing the costs and benefits of foreign ownership. The multinational corporation gives us not only American capital but also American technology, "know-how," and entrepreneurship. On the other hand, easy access to American technology and entrepreneurship discourages the development of indigenous supplies of these critical factors. The multinational corporation gives Canada a ready market in the United States for raw materials and parts. On the other hand, it restricts most subsidiary manufacturing to the small domestic Canadian market.

The economic performance of subsidiaries in terms of exports, costs, research, and innovation is neither much better nor much worse than that of Canadian-owned firms. But it does fall far short of the performance of the parent American company. This is attributed to the generally unhealthy economic environment in Canada. The task force agrees that instead of upgrading the quality of economic performance in Canada, subsidiary firms conform to the general mediocrity of Canadian enterprise. The strategy recommended is one that has become familiar through the writings of Harry Johnson, and through the American-Canadian Committee: enforced rationalization of Canadian industry through a drastic reduction of tariffs. This would eliminate inefficient enterprise, merge Canada and the United States into one market, and dissolve the so-called miniature replica effect of the branch-plant economy. Instead of producing every American model and every American design for the small Canadian market and suffering from the consequent high per unit costs of short runs, the Canadian branch plants would be allotted a few models to be produced for the entire continent.

The task force thus comes out clearly for increased continentalization of the Canadian economy. It is important to emphasize that most of its recommendations are meant for a continentalist economy and seek only to maximize the rewards that can be gained from an integrated North American economic structure. Unlike other free-traders, however, the task force does recognize that in the majority of cases industrial rationalization would benefit the multinational corporations, since they are in the best position to rationalize their operations. Smaller Canadian firms would be less able to make the required adjustment in capital, equipment, and markets, and would in many instances be absorbed by their American counterparts. The task force sees a role for the long-talked-about Canada Development Corporation here. Via loans and equity participation, it could help retain a Canadian presence in the industries affected.

The task force takes up one other Walter Gordon hobby-horse: increased Canadian representation on the board of directors of the multinational corporation, and more widespread participation of Canadian investors in shareholding of US subsidiaries. (It is well known that many of the largest affiliated companies are wholly owned by the parent company and there is, therefore, no way that investors can participate directly in the branch plant.) No economic reasoning is offered by the task force to justify its recommendations. What evidence is produced on the subject indicates that greater Canadian representation on the board of directors and greater Canadian participation in shareholding makes no difference whatever to the performance of the multinational corporation in Canada.*

The one innovation of the task force report is its coining of the term "extraterritoriality," a term which brings together the various instruments of US political intrusion in Canada. The report defines extraterritoriality as "the subjection of residents of one country to the laws and policies of another country," and declares that "the direct investment subsidiary, being resident in one country and owned and controlled by residents of another, becomes a vehicle through which extraterritoriality can be exercised ... and the capacity of [the host country] to effect decisions, i.e. its political independence, is [thereby] directly reduced."[8]

American political intrusion is certainly no new experience for Canada. But it is useful to have its modern version so neatly catalogued. Again, however, the report fails to place this dimension of American-Canadian relations into proper perspective. Canada may not agree with every aspect of the American world view; Canada may not approve of every manifestation of American foreign policy; Canada's economic interest does not always coincide with every new measure emanating from Washington; and Canadian economic groups are understandably unhappy about sacrificing their own short-term gains in order to support some aspect of American foreign policy. Nevertheless, it is important to recognize that political leaders in Canada, and the ruling business circles of this country, do accept the basic premise of the American world view. If anything, they feel grateful to the United States for "protecting us from the *evils* of international communism." They accept, by and large, the assumption of the cold war and the necessity for American hegemony over the western world (and as much of the eastern world as is necessary). They may grumble about losing this market or that market, and they may occasionally feel indignant that Canada's balance of payments is

---

* Canada's businessmen clearly "want in" on the high-growth industries
    represented by the multinational corporations, and the authors of
    the task force report may have felt that indulging them on this score
    would improve the salability of other aspects of the report to the
    business community.

being tinkered with in order to support American military policies in Asia. But they are not prepared to challenge America's right to effectively control the direction of the Canadian economy if this is necessary to "save free enterprise from the onslaught of communist collectivism." For they feel that their own future rests very definitely with America's, and they fully accept what C. Wright Mills once called "the military definition of reality."[9] which has clearly come to dominate American thinking in the post- Second World War world.

It is not surprising, therefore, to find Canada's political and business leaders impatient with proposals to counter American political intrusion in Canada. The most interesting recommendation of the task force report, the establishment of a government export agency to force compliance with Canadian export law, was dismissed out of hand. It would openly challenge American hegemony over Canada, and initiate a clear-cut struggle over the question of Canadian political sovereignty. It would lead to continuous tensions, confrontations, and possible retaliations.

The task force report failed to make an impact in Canada because it addressed itself to the business community and to the political leaders that represent this community and its interests. Effective political sovereignty and independence no longer seem an issue with the Canadian business establishment because it, as an entity, has largely disappeared. The Canadian business class seems to have been submerged within North America, fully accepting the reality of American economic domination, and furthermore feeling no special urge to do anything about it.

Since Keynes and the cold war discovered the cure for unemployment, economic growth has been elevated to a top policy objective. Economists, politicians, and businessmen are all persuaded of its virtues. With economic growth comes wealth ; with wealth come choice and independence. The poor are restricted in their opportunities. Their efforts are monopolized by the need to produce the bare essentials of life. Their freedom is limited by their poverty. Wealth alone frees men from the bondage of necessity.

Put in the abstract, there can be no objection to this line of argument. But put in an institutional context, given historical specificity, its truth can indeed be questioned. And some economists, notably John Kenneth Galbraith and Edward Mishan, have now begun to question the meaning of economic growth in terms of such concepts as choice, freedom, and independence.

The connection between economic growth and independence is made in another context, however, which has yet to be questioned by professional economists. This is the magic *troika* of economic growth, savings, and national independence. Economic growth, spurred on by new investment, generates new wealth and savings which establish the basis for an ever-increasing degree of independence. Anything which contributes to economic growth, in the long run, contributes to national independence. Foreign investment contributes to economic growth. Therefore, *ipso facto,* it eventually contributes to national independence.

The three-stage debtor-creditor theory frequently is advanced in support of this formula. Each capitalist nation undergoes three stages of development. First, as a young debtor nation it imports foreign capital to finance the formative years of industrial growth emerging when commodity imports exceed exports. In the second stage, the trade relationship is reversed, but payment of dividends and interest on past debt keep the current account of the balance of payments, more or less, balanced. Capital investments also balance, new foreign investment just cancelling out new borrowing. In the third stage, the nation moves into a creditor position. Its exports may still exceed its imports, as it supplies the additional purchasing power to importing countries through its own foreign investment. Or it could be financed by gold inflows. But ultimately, in the mature creditor stage, it buys more than it sells, the deficit being made up by dividend and interest received from past foreign investment.

This model seems to fit the historical experience of both the United Kingdom and the United States, and some assume that it fits Canada as well. According to the model, Canada should be advancing to stage three. The truth of the matter is that Canada has yet to advance through stage two. Our present circumstance is that exports normally exceed imports, but there is such an economic outflow of dividends and interest – returns on past investment – that the current account is continuously imbalanced. The deficit has to be offset by still more capital imports from abroad, and the debt keeps rising as the new capital imports add still greater burdens to future balance of payments.

Evidently we are caught in a vicious circle, trapped forever, it seems, between stage one and stage two. Economic independence is as distant as ever. There is neither economic independence, nor a move towards economic independence.

Why has Canada been unable to move through the three stages? Primarily because of the nature of the foreign investment that has been attracted to this country. During the formative years of American industrialization, the United States borrowed large amounts of capital from abroad. Foreign investment took the specific form of loan capital (indirect) rather than equity capital (direct). As the economy grew the loans were paid back and the economy became financially independent. Stage two was complete.

During the formative years of Canadian industrialization, we too received large amounts of capital from abroad. Some of it, that part which was imported from the United Kingdom, was also loan capital. But a growing proportion was equity capital, for during the last quarter of the nineteenth century and with quickened tempo after 1900, American corporations planted subsidiaries in both the resource and the manufacturing sectors of the Canadian economy. Now equity capital has a special quality: as the economy grows, it grows too. When foreign investment takes the form of loan capital, the "foreign sector" of the economy recedes as the economy grows. When foreign investment takes the form of equity capital, the "foreign sector" expands as the economy expands. It may well expand faster than the general economy since it is usually concentrated in the most dynamic, most profitable, branches of economic activity. Unlike loan capital, equity capital is not distant, passive, and self-liquidating. It is, on the contrary, present, active, and self-perpetuating.

Historical statistics on foreign investment can be misleading unless they are broken down and isolated. Through much of the nineteenth century, the United Kingdom was clearly dominant but most of the capital investment in Canada was loan capital. In 1913 the United Kingdom still had over three times as much foreign investment in Canada as had the United States. But total US investment was already beginning to catch up, and, what is more important, in equity (direct) investment she was by 1913 far ahead. In the fourteen years from 1900, American investment increased more than five times in value, and doubled again between 1914 and 1918. American branch plants established before 1900 (including such companies as Imperial Oil, International Nickel, Westinghouse) were expanding with the booming wheat economy, and American companies were opening up new subsidiaries at a record pace so as not to be excluded from this growing market. The large-scale liquidation of British investment during and after the First World War and the continued expansion of American equity investment ended British economic supremacy in Canada. American capital and American capitalism were clearly in control.

No evidence whatever has been produced to show that the Canadian economy has become more independent over the years. Some economists have drawn attention to figures which estimate that in 1926 the value of all foreign long-term assets held in Canada amounted to 117 per cent of Canada's annual output, while the proportion today is 60 per cent. They also point out that the cost of servicing the investment has declined from 3 per cent of GNP in the late twenties to 2 per cent in the early 1960s. However, they neglect to add that these proportions reached their lowest level around 1949 and have been rising ever since. The growth of foreign investment (mostly US) since 1950 has been unprecedented (US equity capital since 1949 has increased over five-fold).

During the Second World War and its aftermath foreign investment in Canada had almost ceased. In fact, Canada was a net exporter of capital. Cut off from foreign capital and from the direction of foreign capitalists, new alliances emerged between the state and Canadian capitalists. An indigenous capitalism seemed to be reviving. The gigantic war effort was internally financed. Foreign control of the economy was dropping off in the case of mining and smelting from 47 per cent in 1930 to 40 per cent in 1948 and rising in manufacturing from 36 per cent in 1930 to 43 per cent in 1948. But the removal of state controls and the readjustment of the world economy once again fully exposed the Canadian economy to the appetite of American capital, and the country easily fell into the old relationship. American control of Canadian manufacturing rose from 39 per cent in 1948 to 46 per cent in 1963; in mining and smelting it rose from 37 to 52 per cent. New American capital flooded into Canada, and together with the reinvestment of subsidiary profits accounted for the remarkable accumulation of foreign-owned capital assets in the post-war period. As late as 1950, half a century after active US investment had begun, total US direct investment amounted to only $4 billion. Over the next fifteen years $11 billion was added to American holdings.*

Defining "economic development" as the development of an indigenous entrepreneurial class and a consequent increasing degree of domestic control over the national economy, Canada thus appears to have stopped developing. As McGill's Kari Levitt has pointed out, the Canadian economy bears many characteristics of underdevelopment.[10] Between 1953 and 1965 Canadian trade as a percentage of that of industrial countries dropped from 9.6 to 7.2 per cent, and her terms of trade have deteriorated parallel to those of countries in the underdeveloped world. These trends can be accounted for by the fact that the composition of Canadian trade closely resembles that of underdeveloped countries. Exports are composed largely of raw materials or semi-processed materials (almost 75 per cent), while imports are mostly finished manufactured goods (almost 80 per cent). Exports remain heavily dependent on a few staples – wheat, metallic ores such as iron, copper, and nickel, petroleum and natural gas – or on partially processed goods such as woodpulp, newsprint, lumber, flour, and aluminum. About two-thirds of the exports of the typical West European country are composed of end-products. For Canada, the proportion is less than one-fifth. Most revealing, the share of consumer goods in total imports has actually risen over the past decade, as has the share of all manufactured goods, reversing a trend that has been operative since the mid-1920s. The importation of machinery and transport equipment – industries particularly indicative of the stage of economic development – has been increasing relative to other commodities since 1910.

The story of the growth of American capital in Canada has yet to be fully told. Contrary to its proponents, its effect has not been to expand Canadian independence but to set in motion the forces of national disintegration. It has choked off Canadian entrepreneurship and technological growth, bought off Canadian capital, and virtually destroyed Canada's once vigorous capitalist class.

* Although US economic control of Canadian industry may have relaxed somewhat during the Second World War, very significant continental co-operation arose from the exigencies of the war itself. There was a proliferation of new US-Canadian governmental committees. Continental bureaucratic integration advanced to hitherto unprecedented lengths. No doubt this had something to do with the ease with which US corporate control resumed its growing dominance of the Canadian economy.

For well over a century the economic foundation of Canada rested on fur. The fur trade nurtured the first indigenous class of capitalists. It ceased to be the centre of economic activity in Canada when the fur country south of the Great Lakes was transferred to the United States (1783) and finally was secured by them in the War of 1812. The fur merchants of Montreal switched their capital into the entrepôt trade. Their goal was to capture the trade between the American midwest and Britain, and the St Lawrence River was their vehicle. But the St Lawrence lost out to an American waterway system; New York was triumphant over Montreal. Nor did the switch from canals to railways change the verdict. The abolition of the Corn laws, and with it the dismemberment of the British mercantile system, ended whatever chance Montreal had of dislodging New York as the entrepôt centre between the new world and the old. The vision of the merchants of Montreal, based in part on continued imperial preference for colonial trade, had utterly collapsed. There was no economic basis for a Canadian future. Tension between French Canadians and English Canadians, aristocratic rule, economic stagnation, and the inability to finance a minimally adequate system of public service brought the country to the point of despair.* Agricultural settlement in Upper Canada had about reached the limit of good land. Civil wars and annexation manifestos were the order of the day in the 1830s and 1840s.

Unable to capture the intercontinental trade, sectionally split, effectively abandoned by England, and without the imagination and resources to open up the Canadian west, Canadian capitalism – and Canada with it – was doomed. The internal market economy was still in its infancy. The possibilities of expansion within it were limited. The economy was cramped. There was only one avenue of escape for Canada – to attach itself to the developing metropolis of the United States. The Reciprocity Treaty of 1854 was the first official step in this direction, and central Canada and the Maritimes were quick to adapt themselves as suppliers of raw material to build industrial America.

---

* This is not to say that there was no new economic activity during these decades. It was simply insufficient to create the kind of widespread prosperity that could provide the markets and opportunities for an industrial take-off.

North American integration was disrupted temporarily by the American Civil War. Internal matters monopolized America's attention. The Reciprocity Treaty lapsed. Once again set adrift, Canadian statesmen and entrepreneurs grasped what then seemed like the only alternative left - a Canadian mercantilism aimed at achieving political and economic unity throughout British North America (the National Policy). They employed the conventional mercantilist instruments: political unity through confederation, economic unity through tariffs, and a national transportation system.

Until the turn of the century, the National Policy seemed an utter failure, however. The economy was in a period of drift. There was some industrialization, but economic development was barely able to maintain the existing population, let alone absorb the new immigrant population. The burden of financing a scarcely used but expensively built railway system was overwhelming. Western leaders, fearful of eastern encroachment and of the disruption of existing settlements, threatened to separate from Canada after the transfer of Ruperts Land from the Hudson's Bay Company to the government of Canada.

Finally the wheat boom did justify the National Policy. Through it, Macdonald's goal was realized. The Canadian West was to be filled by Canadians rather than by Americans. The prairies produced a new staple upon which the economy could depend for its future development. It served as a new link between Canada and Britain and provided a rapidly expanding market for the infant manufacturing industries of central Canada. The new railway system was made economically viable.

Any possibility of the United States gaining formal political sovereignty over Canada was aborted once and for all. But the predominance of an east-west exchange network proved to be only an interlude. The north-south pull that had emerged fifty years before was too powerful to be overcome by half-way measures. Much more state intervention would have been needed to stem the long-term forces of continental integration.

A gross contradiction in the National Policy itself proved to be a major obstacle to containing the north-south pull. The high tariff policy was designed to protect the Canadian market and also to attract foreign capital. It did both. American manufacturers, unable to sell in the Canadian market due to high tariffs, chose to establish branch plants in this country.* As one company located in Canada, other companies felt impelled to follow suit lest the first one gain a monopoly of the Canadian market. In many instances, the American company would look to buy out a Canadian enterprise in a related industry.[11] The result was that the structure of US manufacturing industry was transferred to Canada virtually *in toto*.

The National Policy was incomplete. It developed some of the ingredients for a national economy but it ignored others. And the net result has been the very opposite of the aims and ambitions of those who designed this strategy for development. As Melville Watkins expressed it, "in the absence of complementing programs, the high tariff policy created 'infant industries' but not 'infant firms.'"[12]

A deficient Canadian entrepreneurship guaranteed that high tariffs would protect American subsidiaries rather than new Canadian enterprises. What was needed to complete the National Policy was the kind of programme initiated by the Japanese about the same time and in somewhat the same circumstances – an improved educational system, a network of business and management schools, state construction of new enterprises in partnership with private enterprises or alone, later to be sold to private enterprise. Perhaps it was the conservatism and cliquishness of the existing class of entrepreneurs that blocked programmes designed to broaden and develop new entrepreneurship. Whatever the reason, the National Policy failed to stimulate a Canadian bourgeoisie that could itself grow and prosper behind the wall of protective tariffs and thereby dominate the Canadian economy.

Most of the American-owned companies in Canada were already established by the end of 1920. From the moment of their arrival, they increased their share of industrial output by absorbing Canadian-owned enterprises or by squeezing them out of the market. This is, of course, still happening today. Their easy capture of Canadian enterprise is to be explained in part by a generation gap. By the time major industrial growth had begun in Canada, giant corporations had already formed in America, products of many decades of rapid in-

---

* The founders of the National Policy may have thought of attracting individual American capitalists to Canada rather than getting foreign branch plants. Nevertheless, most foreign capital did not take the form of branch plants.

dustrialization in the United States; Canadian enterprises were still family concerns, not yet part of the corporate world. They were typically small and, by comparison, financially weak or technologically backward. They had neither market power nor government protection. Their absorption was the natural outcome of market forces. Where Canadian ownership persisted, it was usually in industries where "the monopoly leverage of patents, financial power, and exclusive access to markets [was] difficult to establish: examples are found in construction, some forms of merchandising and agriculture."[13] "In the early years of the twentieth century ... employers tended to be vociferous, even strident, in their objection to American influence ... By the 1920's however, Canadian nationalists had either been eliminated from the ranks of Canadian employers or had become clients of American penetration."[14]

Since all US subsidiaries and branch plants operate in oligopolistic market structures with high barriers to entry for new firms, the very considerable growth of Canadian industrial output has been accomplished largely through the internal growth of the American affiliates. Unlike the era of relatively small-scale enterprise, new products and new techniques are usually introduced by existing rather than new firms, and unexploited mineral deposits and timber lands are usually developed by established mining and pulp and paper companies. In short, given the early settlement of US affiliates in the Canadian market and given the nature of the market structures that developed, American enterprise in Canada has grown in size and importance along with the growth of the Canadian economy. There are few signs that this process is abating. As Kari Levitt has remarked, "dependence is addictive and the dynamics of dependence are cumulative."[15]

Canadian business is not highly regarded, even within the business community. It is regularly accused of being unwilling to take risks, lacking in entrepreneurship, and technologically backward. To a degree such criticisms may be valid. But to be fair, the multinational corporation has every advantage over an independent Canadian enterprise. It has much more technological experience and can acquire capital funds more cheaply. It is highly diversified, operating in many countries and producing many products. A new Canadian project is typically a small part of its global operation. The risk is objectively smaller for such a company than it is to an independent, less diversified, Canadian enterprise. Regarding resource industries, the multinational corporation has secured markets and secured prices. But, in general, temporary losses incurred by any subsidiary can be charged back to the parent company and can be offset easily by profit earned elsewhere. Moreover, the parent company is partly or wholly compensated by the automatic export sales that are generated through subsidiaries and by royalties, licence and management fees received by them.

It should be clear by now that it is the very presence of American enterprise in Canada that perpetuates the high degree of dependence on the United States. This is certainly true as regards capital. In the nineteenth century and the early part of the twentieth century, Canada was clearly not wealthy enough to finance great capital-intensive projects such as canals and railways. Heavy capital imports from abroad were needed, and they made a critical contribution to the economic development of this country. Today only a small portion of investment is not financed out of savings generated in Canada. At the same time the volume of foreign investment continues to rise by increasing degrees and Canadian dependence on foreign investment is undiminished. This paradox is to be explained by the fact that a major fraction of savings generated in Canada is owned and controlled by US business. When a portion (about half) of these savings are reinvested in this country, it is termed "foreign investment." The source of this foreign investment and the savings from which it derives are the profits earned in Canada by subsidiaries and branch plants. A very small proportion of foreign (US) investment in Canada actually involves the importation of foreign savings. The biggest proportion is financed from Canadian savings that are controlled by foreign corporations. In 1967, for example, 15 per cent of the increase in gross US investment in Canada was derived from capital imports from the United States. Almost three-quarters was financed from returned earnings and depreciation, and over one-tenth from other Canadian sources.

Canada appears to be entering the third phase of a three-phase evolution within the life of a multinational corporation. Until the mid-1950s, we had been in phase one – receiving more investment from the metropolitan branch of the multinational corporation than we contributed to it. The countries of Western Europe are in this phase today. Over the past decade we have been in an intermediate second phase where the subsidiaries and affiliates of multinational corporations sent to the parent companies about as much as they received from them. In the third phase, the flow of funds from subsidiaries and affiliates in the hinterland economy to the parent companies in the metropolis is greater than the counterflow. (The Latin American countries have long been in the third phase.) Between 1960 and 1967, Canadian subsidiaries and affiliates sent $1 billion more to their parent companies in the form of profits ($2 billion more if royalties, licence and management fees were included) than they received from them in the form of capital imports.

The theme of this essay has been that Canadian capitalism and Canadian capitalists, emergent through much of the nineteenth century, are now deeply submerged in American capitalism. This can be illustrated in still other ways.

Almost every Canadian favours the principle of greater Canadian control of the economy. But whenever measures are hinted at which may harm the narrow interests of particular financial groups, immense pressure is exerted to halt their implementation. Shareholders in Canadian companies have come to regard the prospect of a US takeover as especially rewarding because it makes their holdings a little more valuable; consequently they argue strenuously against any laws that would discourage such a takeover. The government does not favour American ownership in the financial and communication fields but it has done nothing to protect Canadian control over key industries in other highly dynamic sectors of the economy. The $150 million takeover of Canadian Oil Companies, the last of the large, Canadian-owned, well-head-to-consumer companies, was not contested. The recent US bid for Royal Securities, a venerable and large investment house, was not interfered with. In 1968 the Canadian auto industry partially defaulted with production objectives under the auto-pact agreement. The Canadian government gave up $80 million in customs duties to the industry and made no effort to recover any part of the sum for fear that the parent companies would break the pact. In view of the fact that the industry has already become so continentally integrated, it was against the immediate interest of the government to press the issue and assert its rights. In 1968-9 alone there have been a total of five hundred takeovers of Canadian firms by American corporations. The government in Ottawa has done nothing to interfere with these takeovers.

Continental integration has been reinforced and legally sealed by special arrangements granted to Canadian (usually branch-plant) businesses by the United States: the partial free-trade agreement on automobiles alluded to above; exemption from the Interest-Equilization Tax; exemption from import quotas on exports of crude petroleum. As Hugh Aitken has written: "If Canada seriously wishes to retard the process of continental integration, she could refuse to accept such discriminatory treatment when it is offered. It is indeed, by Canada's reaction to such bilateral proposals that outside observers will be inclined to gauge what weight Canadians do in fact attach to their autonomy and what sacrifices of [immediate] economic advantage they are prepared to make to achieve it."[16]

It is not possible to determine whether, in fact, any economic advantage would have to be sacrificed in the long run. This would depend, in large part, on the alternative economic structures that are possible, on what are the objectives of economic growth and in whose material and social interest it is supposed to serve. One could certainly argue, for example, about the inequities, waste, and distortions of American capitalism that are part of the package of American capital, entrepreneurship, and technology that Canada imports. In lieu of an alternative economic structure or strategy of growth, and because of the already existing predominance of American influence and control, Canadian supplies of capital, entrepreneurship, and technology for the most part are absorbed into the American metropolis. We will discuss this process briefly.

It is well known that, on a per capita basis, Canada invests more capital across the border than the US invests in Canada.* The American economy attracts Canadian capital because it *is* the metropolis. Significant branches of the Canadian economy are closed to Canadian investors. Wholly owned subsidiaries do *not* offer their shares to Canadians. Investors, eager to participate in dynamic industries and

---

* Of course, it would be absurd to infer from this that Canada consequently has greater control over the United States. Two other points, however, about Canadian investments abroad should be mentioned. The thirteen largest "Canadian" firms investing equity capital abroad accounted for 70 per cent of the total in 1963; foreign-owned companies contribute a significant portion of Canadian direct investment abroad, amounting to 37 per cent in 1954 and 47 per cent in 1964.

their glamour stocks, must invest in the parent companies (whose shares *are* often listed in Canadian markets) since few, if any, Canadian stocks of these industries are available. IBM is one US corporation with a wholly owned Canadian subsidiary. At the end of 1966 Canadian mutual funds held about $60 million in IBM stock, more than their holdings of any single Canadian stock. Canadians who want to invest in General Motors can do so only by buying shares in the parent US corporation. The point is not to decry the financial policies of US corporations in limiting opportunities for Canadian investors, for a more liberal policy would bring few benefits to the general community. It is rather to demonstrate that the already dominant American position in the Canadian economy limits still further opportunities for Canadian participation and control of the country's economic development, while it induces greater Canadian investment in the economy of the metropolis.

On the matter of entrepreneurship, Kari Levitt reminds us, "... entrepreneurship does not bear any simple relationship to high levels of income, or to high levels of education."[17] Canada, says Levitt, has far higher per capita income than that which prevails in Britain, Germany, and the United States at the peak of their "take-off." Canada has a far higher level of per capita income than contemporary Japan. What this may indicate is that the branch-plant economy is not the product of low incomes and lack of entrepreneurship, but rather the reverse; the lack of entrepreneurship is the product of the branch-plant economy. As we have seen above, local entrepreneurs often become the salaried employees of the multinational corporations. They become citizens of an international corporate empire. And Levitt adds that skilled personnel are attracted and absorbed by "the metropolitan industrial and academic centres by high salaries, superior facilities and the fact that the professionals involved have internationalized the values of the metropolitan society. By means of this 'brain-drain,' the brightest and ablest people from lower-income countries swell the technological resources of the richer countries."

Levitt quotes an account of company policy provided by the Procter and Gamble Company to illustrate the point that this process also includes managerial skill:

When Procter and Gamble moves into a country for the first time, it has to bring in a skilled top-management team, already developed.

The initial cadre goes about building an organization in depth. Just as soon as local talent can be developed, it is. Of the American group in Canada Procter and Gamble had in 1947, only two of us are left. The others have gone to Geneva, to Venezuela, to Cincinnati, and elsewhere ... Today, the General Manager of Procter and Gamble in France is a Canadian, the General Manager in Morocco is a Canadian; the General Manager in Mexico is a Canadian; and the man responsible for all our business in the "outer Seven" including Britain is a Canadian ...[18]

If local entrepreneurship is not necessarily related to national income levels, neither is a nation's ability to develop new technology and to introduce new innovations. And in the same way that the branch-plant economy may itself be the primary agency for choking off local entrepreneurship, so may it be the primary agency for destroying native technological prowess.

As Andre Gunder Frank points out in his insightful book, *Capitalism and Underdevelopment in Latin America,* technological power is the new vehicle of empire and technological dependence has become the clearest indicator of a metropolis-satellite relationship. The Task Force on Foreign Ownership makes abundantly clear that Canada engages in less research than almost any industrial country in the western world. In terms of the welfare of the multinational corporation, it makes no sense for the parent company to assign major research to Canadian subsidiaries. And when research is carried out, it is usually limited to modifying product lines to suit Canadian climatic conditions or other conditions peculiar to this country. Major innovations seem to occur only in those industries that are dominated by Crown corporations. With this exception, new technology appears to trickle into the Canadian economy as American innovations are eventually passed down to the subsidiaries.

Kari Levitt has admirably summarized this process as it involves capital, entrepreneurship, and technology:

For Canada, the result of [the] branch plant economy has been the progressive erosion of Canadian entrepreneurship; an assured and perpetual backwardness in research and technology; a built-in bias toward the importation of supplies from parent companies; a structure of manufacturing industry which is geared to supply the domestic market and creates obstacles to the expansion of Canadian exports (except by special deals and arrangements with metropolitan corporations and their governments), a splintering of the capital market, whereby a large part of savings generated within Canada are not available to potential borrowers in other sectors of the Canadian economy; and a balkanization of the political structure whereby the growing economic powers of the corporations and the provincial governments threaten to destroy the Canadian state.[19]

It is to this latter problem that we must now proceed. The developing continentalization of Canada has led to the deterioration of Canada as a nation-state. The policies which guide the direction of Canada's cultural and economic future emanate more and more from Washington and from the board rooms of the multinational corporation in New York, Chicago, and Detroit. Consequently, it has been the task of Canadian governments to administer this country and its provinces as a region and as sub-regions of the great American metropolis. The inevitable weakening of Ottawa vis-à-vis the United States can only have had the effect of strengthening the position of the provinces relative to Ottawa. Confederation and the old National Policy was predicated on the basis of a strong central government. But the old National Policy could not withstand the power of the north-south pull and a north-south economy dominated by US branch plants; and US resource industry does not need a strong central government.

The former Under-Secretary of State, George Ball, in a speech to the US Chambers of Commerce, put the proposition much more strongly: "The multinational corporation is ahead of, and in conflict with, existing political organizations represented by the nation states." The multinational corporation is seen as a kind of global government, a unifying force throughout the world. It leads not to a world government, however, but to American rule throughout the world. This is not only the view of antagonists of the American empire. It is the view of its advocates. Mr Henry Fowler, as US Secretary of the Treasury, was very explicit when he said:

Let no one forget the crucial importance to the multinational corporation of a United States government that commands world respect for its economic and military progress as well as for its commitment to the highest human ideals – a United States government whose political, diplomatic and military strength is fully commensurate with its role as a leader of the free world ... *for let us understand that the United States Government has consistently sought, and will continue to seek to expand and extend the role of the multinational corporation as an essential instrument of strong and healthy economic progress through the Free World.*[20]

The multinational corporation provides income from abroad without which the United States probably would not be able to meet its world-wide military, political, and economic commitments. On the other hand, Fowler continues, "it is impossible to over-estimate the extent to which the efforts and opportunities for American firms abroad depend upon the vast presence and influence and prestige that America holds in the world."

American foreign policy and the expansion of the multinational corporation are mutually dependent. It is quite impossible to conceive of one without the other. As Mr Ball explained, the multinational corporation cannot prosper within the confines of the nation-state. To the giant corporation the nation-state is economically confining. What is more it has the potential to develop a countervailing force to the authority of the multinational corporation. Fortunately for the multinational corporation, the central government in Canada is gradually disintegrating. It has lost its main purpose to the metropolis and it has given over its main functions to the provinces. This functional fragmentation, in turn, serves to further strengthen the north-south pull; for the provinces are inherently parochial and absorbed entirely in achieving maximum economic growth within their own narrow boundaries. This necessarily involves them in a competitive race for new investment. The scramble for industry easily overrides any concern for the preservation of Canadian economic control and the development of a Canadian identity. And the system of incentives and concessions used to entice industry from one province to another serves only the corporations and the richest provinces who can always offer the biggest incentives.

Put a different way, a national obsession with crude growth has led the way towards American investment in and ownership of Canadian resources and industry – and consequently to the weakening of the nation-state. A national concern for social needs, on the other hand, would have attracted little equity investment from the United States for the American corporation has little to offer in the way of satisfying basic needs of food, clothing, shelter, education, and recreation. Only a strong government can secure these essentials for all.

It must be added that the balkanization of Canada is further promoted by the unwillingness of English Canadians to recognize Quebec for what it is - a province different from all the others, the homeland of a people with a distinct language, history, culture, and institutions. French Canadians fear for their survival as a national entity. They insist that the authority of the Quebec government must be widened if economic control by French Canadians is to be secured. Prime Minister Trudeau is telling them to be patient. "There is no reason to renegotiate the constitution," he says. "Natural forces are bringing about the desired degree of decentralization." The forces are not natural at all. They are located in the multinational corporation, which cannot coexist with a strong central government. Mr Trudeau's advice to Quebec may be sound – for Quebec. It can hardly be said to be sound for English Canada. The Prime Minister approves of the tendency towards greater provincial autonomy. It is his answer to Quebec separatists. But he is unconcerned about national sovereignty. Like other "cosmopolitans," he finds it old-fashioned, irrelevant, and dangerous. During the 1968 federal election he stated that Canada is no more independent of the United States than is Poland of the Soviet Union. We have 10 per cent independence, he remarked, and we can manoeuvre only within that degree of freedom. His price for keeping Quebec in Confederation is to weaken English Canada, which means, in effect, to weaken still further the position of Ottawa vis-à-vis the United States. The insistence of Quebec for greater powers is used as a lever by the wealthier provinces to pry more and more authority and responsibility from the federal government.

It is easy to count up the forces that are leading Canada towards a new colonial status. Unfortunately, it is not so easy to discover the forces that might lead Canada towards a new independence.[21] Perhaps the very failure of the American system, already apparent, will impose conditions upon our imperial relationship which will finally demand a total restructuring of our political economy. No amount of national will, moral pleading, and nationalist sentiment will, by itself, break the pattern of foreign economic control and cultural absorption that has evolved over the past century. But there are signs that, internally and externally, the American system is beginning to disintegrate. No doubt this will be a long process. It is a process that requires immediate study, especially as to its short- and long-term impact on the Canadian economy.

NOTES

1 The author wishes to thank Professors Melville Watkins, Claire Pentland, and Rubin Simkin, and Mr James Laxer, for reading a first draft of this paper and offering suggestions. The first third of the paper is an extended version of a paper read for the DIMENSION Conference on Canada and the American Empire and published in *Canadian Dimension,* vol. 4, no. 4 (May-June 1967), as "The Political Economy of Canadian Independence."

2 Selective Industrial Raw Materials:
Ratio of Net US Imports to US Supply, 1937-9 and 1956 (percentages)

Raw Material	1937-9 Average	1956
Aluminium	0	11.3
Bauxite	53.0	78.1
Petroleum	0.5	13.5
Iron Ore	2.6	20.3
Copper	0.3	22.4
Lead	0.2	56.5
Zinc	6.3	57.8
Fluospar	13.4	59.5
Tungsten	41.8	59.7
Magnesium	–	82.7
Nickel	99.2	95.5

3 *Foreign Ownership and the Structure of Canadian Industry: Report of the Task Force on the Structure of Canadian Industry* (Ottawa, 1968), p. 205.

4 *Ibid.,* p. 202.

5 "Political Economy of Guidelines," in *Canadian Dimension,* vol. 3, no. 3-4.

6 April 20, 1963.

7 "... the important issue today for host countries such as Canada is not whether foreign investment is worthwhile, but rather how to increase benefits and decrease costs." *Foreign Ownership and the Structure of Canadian Industry*, p. 52.

8 *Ibid.*, pp. 310-11.

9 *The Power Elite* (New York, 1956), and *Causes of World War III*, (New York, 1957).

10 "Canada: Economic Dependence and Political Disintegration," *New World Quarterly*, IV, 2 (Crop Time, 1968), p. 128.

11 The early history of foreign investment is set out in Herbert Marshall, Frank A. Southard, Jr, and Kenneth W. Taylor, *Canadian-American Industry: A Study in International Investment* (New Haven and Toronto, 1936).

12 "A New National Policy," in Trevor Lloyd and Jack McLeod, eds., *Agenda 1970: Proposals for a Creative Politics* (Toronto, 1968), pp. 164-5.

13 H. C. Pentland, "A Study of the Changing Social, Economic and Political Background of the Canadian Systems of Industrial Relations." mimeo, 1968, p. 50.

14 *Ibid.*, p. 51.

15 "Canada: Economic Independence and Political Disintegration," p. 114.

16 *American Capital and Canadian Resources* (Cambridge, Mass., 1961), p. 171.

17 "Canada," p. 113.

18 *Ibid.*, pp. 114-15.

19 *Ibid.*, p. 81.

20 Quoted *ibid.*, p. 110 (italics added).

21 I have discussed alternative strategies for Canadian independence in "The Political Economy of Canadian Independence."

I. M. Abella

Teaches history at Glendon College, York University. He has contributed articles to the *Canadian Historical Review* and other journals.

Lament for a union movement

Of the organized workers in this country nearly 75 per cent are in American unions; the percentage in English Canada is naturally higher. But it is not my purpose to discuss the origins and results of this American domination; this task has been undertaken by many others, most successfully by John Crispo in his various books and articles on international unionism. Rather, it is my intention to describe the Americanization process in operation. It seems to me that it is important to analyse not only the causes and the consequences of this American domination, but also how it comes about – how a Canadian labour organization inexorably succumbs before American pressure.

Many students of the Canadian labour movement have argued that the final Americanization of the Canadian labour movement occurred in 1902 when the American Federation of Labor ordered its Canadian affiliate, the Trades and Labor Congress to expel unions whose jurisdictions conflicted with those of the AFL unions in Canada. The reluctant acquiescence of the TLC signalled final capitulation before its American parent organization and marked the end of its bitter struggle to retain its autonomy in Canada. It seems to me, however, that the last lingering hopes for a truly Canadian labour movement were not permanently quenched until the early 1950s when, after a decade of implacable resistance, the Canadian Congress of Labour finally gave way before the persistent pressure of its affiliates in the American Congress of Industrial Organization.

In the 1930s, while the vigorous, aggressive CIO was expanding in the United States, just north of the border hundreds of thousands of unorganized Canadian workers were crying out for organization. At this time there were already two large labour organizations in Canada: the TLC, which was completely dominated by the AFL, and the All-Canadian Congress of Labour, which – as its name suggests – was militantly nationalistic and anti-American. But neither organization was capable of meeting the workers' demands. The ACCL was too small, too poor, and not aggressive enough; and the TLC was simply delinquent. In any case, to create a nation-wide purely Canadian labour organization in a country that was both immense and relatively empty, and which had a comparatively undeveloped industrial base, was an impossible task. Thus, to fill the vacuum, the Congress of Industrial Organization came into Canada.

The CIO came, not entirely because it wanted to, but because it was compelled to. So desperately did Canadian workers desire organization that without official CIO approval scores of unauthorized "CIO" organizers – most of whom were communist – sprang up around the country, organizing workers into "CIO" locals. To legitimize these efforts, and to maintain its image as the champion of the unorganized worker, the CIO had no alternative but to sanction organizing in Canada (though the CIO president, John L. Lewis, grumbled that the CIO had too much to do in the United States to be bothered about Canada).

Canadian workers did not hesitate to join an American union. Having just suffered a ravaging depression, they were understandably more concerned with material benefits than with national identity. They felt they had no choice but to join forces with their fellow workers to the south. After all, their problems were the same, their traditions were similar, and in many cases they worked for the same employers. Above all, the CIO had much more to offer them than any Canadian union. It had the personnel, the large treasury, and, most important, the experience, to provide Canadian workers with the organization they so urgently needed.

To Canadian workers the very name "CIO" had a mystique all its own. It was a magnet that attracted workers in their thousands. What it had done for American workers it could just as easily do for those north of the border. In fact, for the labour movement, the border did not exist. Organizers and union officials crossed the boundary both ways with little difficulty. And in the same way, with even less difficulty, American economic interests were moving with increasing swiftness into Canada. The expansion of the electrical, rubber, automobile, and other mass production industries into Canada in the 1930s provided an industrial base with new jobs for thousands of Canadians, and it was among these workers that the CIO gained its foothold.

Unlike those of the AFL, the leaders of the CIO abdicated most of their responsibilities in Canada to local people. As a rapidly expanding organization in the United States, the CIO could spare neither the time nor the energy for the Canadian operation. Most of the organization's leaders in Canada were native-born. Their experience was almost exclusively Canadian and so were their interests. Thus, when the CIO proposed a merger with the intensely nationalistic ACCL, the threat of American control seemed somewhat mitigated.

From the beginning the ACCL had vehemently opposed the CIO. During the famous Oshawa strike in April 1937 when the CIO first emerged as a viable power in the Canadian labour movement, the ACCL had supported General Motors and Premier Mitchell Hepburn's anti-labour government in their futile attempt to smash the CIO. And it had also called for the forced removal of American unions from Canada, on the grounds that they represented an "obstacle" to Canadian "national unity and culture."[1] But lacking funds and suffering from weak organizing methods, the ACCL was in no position to compete with either the CIO or the TLC; indeed, many ACCL locals were threatening to transfer their allegiance to their more opulent and aggressive American competitors. Consequently, when the CIO leadership, concerned about the overwhelming communist influence in their unions, approached the ACCL to discuss a merger, the Canadian organization was decidedly interested in the proposal.

If the ACCL leaders were eager for the merger to be consummated, its rank-and-file members were not. For this reason Aaron Mosher, the autocratic president of the ACCL, kept his negotiations with the CIO secret – even from his own executive – until the merger arrangements were complete. Most ACCL members were won over only when the CIO unions signed the merger agreement; for the first clause stipulated that "all organizations affiliated with the new Congress shall be autonomous with respect to their economic and legislative policies and shall not be subject to control in these matters outside Canada."[2] This, in turn, caused some anxiety among American CIO leaders who feared that the CIO unions in the newly created Congress would sever their international connections. Paradoxically, while the Canadian CIO leaders were reassuring their American colleagues that the merger would in no way change the relationship between CIO affiliates in Canada and their American parent unions, the ACCL leadership was publicly reassuring its membership that the new Congress would be "strictly Canadian" and would "carry on its own affairs without dictation or interference of any kind from outside Canada."[3]

During negotiations, the one major dispute between the CIO and the ACCL involved those ACCL unions which fell within the jurisdiction of the CIO unions. After a series of tumultuous meetings which threatened to disrupt the merger, the ACCL finally gave in to CIO demands that all locals within the CIO jurisdiction must automatically join the appropriate CIO union. The new Congress constitution – written by the CIO – also called for the same centralized organizing fund and authority which characterized the CIO structure south of the border. In September 1941 the two organizations met in Toronto and created the Canadian Congress of Labour.

With the merger, strongly nationalist unions found themselves in the same fold as unions controlled from the United States. Both were intensely committed to their respective philosophies. The former wished to build a powerful, strictly Canadian labour movement, controlled by its Canadian membership; the latter also wished to build a strong labour movement, but were more concerned with continental problems. The former wished to sever all ties with the American unions; the latter wished to strengthen them. This alliance of antipathetic philosophies bedevilled the Congress for years and, indeed, was never to be resolved. The CCL, therefore, proved to be less of a fusion than a coalition in which each component part attempted to maintain its individual identity.

Part of the problem lay in the inability or the unwillingness of the CIO unions to meet their financial commitments to the Congress. Meetings between the CCL and international union presidents resulted in many promises – but little else. Even some of the international representatives in Canada complained to their parent organizations that the CIO unions were not doing their share for the Congress. As a result, the CCL continued to rely on its chartered unions for the bulk of its revenue; and, as a natural corollary, it rebuffed most efforts of the international unions to take over the chartered locals within their jurisdiction. This only exacerbated the quarrel between the CCL offices in Ottawa and the CIO headquarters in Washington.

ACCL officials also were disturbed that the American unions continued to pay their dues to the CIO. The president of the Congress, Aaron Mosher, complained that it would "be far better to have the Canadian membership pay the per capita tax [directly] than to have it come ... to us from headquarters in the United States."[4] He warned that some "narrow-minded" people might think "that so long as the Congress receives a cheque for per capita tax from ... the United States, it is taking instructions as well from the source of its revenue, and that does not help us in putting it across that the Canadian Congress is an independent Canadian labour body." Mosher also urged that all publications, pamphlets, and other advertising matter used in Canada should be of Canadian origin and that the American unions should "emphasize the CCL affiliation and not that of the CIO."

Both these proposals were turned down by the CIO whose leaders

argued that "there is no reason why people in Canada should not
know what our movement stands for ... It has nothing to apologize
for." Emphatically rejecting Mosher's requests, the CIO added that
"we shall expect that the name CIO will not be held in the background but will be there for everyone to see as the institution which
stands for our democratic way of life."[5] This reply enraged Mosher.
He angrily accused the CIO of ignoring the interests of Canadian
workers, of "returning to the AFL psychology in its treatment of the
Canadian situation," and of refusing to respect Canadian sovereignty
in not permitting its Canadian affiliates "to determine their own
policy and administer their own internal affairs." The CIO curtly
replied that it would do all in its power to maintain its identity in
Canada, though it naturally had no intention of "injuring the standing
or prestige of the Canadian Congress of Labour."[6] The matter was
therefore left in abeyance to be settled at a later date; not surprisingly,
it never was.

Mosher was soon joined in his campaign against the American
unions by the CCL's secretary-treasurer, Pat Conroy, who was himself a member of a CIO union – the United Mineworkers of America.
When Conroy demanded that the CIO pay to the Congress all the
dues it was receiving from its Canadian affiliates, the CIO was aghast.
Instead it offered to hand over this monthly assessment to Charlie
Millard of the United Steel Workers, the leader of the CIO forces in
Canada. It stipulated, however, that these funds were not to be used
for the "general purposes" of the CCL but "that it be deposited in a
separate CIO organizing fund ... to be used specifically for CIO purposes."

This so outraged the volatile Conroy that he threatened to resign.
The CIO proposal, he felt, would undermine the "autonomous" nature
of the CCL, make it the "infant equivalent of the CIO" in Canada, and
"undoubtedly lead to the breaking up of the Congress."[7] He also
chided the CIO for "setting up a Congress within a Congress" and for
not understanding the Canadian situation. Rather than call Conroy's
bluff, the CIO capitulated and agreed to turn over to the Congress its
Canadian assessment.

More victories were soon to follow. Over the violent opposition of
the CIO and its affiliate, the American Newspaper Guild, the CCL
chartered a newspaper local in Vancouver. In this way the Congress
was able to assert its ascendancy over the smaller CIO affiliates in

Canada. But the true litmus test of CCL autonomy was the problem
of jurisdictional disputes. While Mosher and now Conroy maintained
that the Congress was completely independent from the CIO, it
nevertheless remained a fact that jurisdictional conflicts among international unions in Canada invariably were resolved in the United
States. How autonomous and independent could the Congress be if it
could not settle disputes among its own affiliates? If the Congress
could somehow persuade CIO affiliates to have their quarrels settled
directly by the CCL without referral to the CIO, then the "autonomy"
question would finally be resolved.

The issue came to a head in 1942. Jurisdictional conflicts among
the automobile, steel, and electrical unions – all CIO affiliates – were
threatening to tear the Congress apart. When Conroy travelled to the
1942 CIO convention in Boston to discuss this problem with CIO
leaders, he was ignored. Humiliated, on his return to Canada he
announced that he was "fed up" and "damn disgusted with the CIO."
He had made several "fruitless trips" to the United States, he said, to
discuss Canadian problems, but instead found that "no one in the
CIO has, apparently, any time to discuss anything with anybody."[8]

Finally, succumbing to Conroy's relentless threats the three CIO
unions agreed to refer all their jurisdictional conflicts to the CCL,
though the Canadian president of one of these unions, the United
Electrical Workers, warned that the real purpose behind the Congress
request for full jurisdictional rights in Canada "was to give [Mosher]
the power to maintain his balance of power ... against the increasing
strength of the International unions in Canada ... [so that he] ... could
use these powers in order to build up National unions at the expense
of the International unions."[9]

By March 1943, then, the CCL could rightfully proclaim that it was
autonomous. Not only did it receive the entire monthly assessment
ordinarily paid by international unions in Canada to the CIO, but
it had also acquired the power to settle all jurisdictional disputes
involving its affiliates, and to create, if it wished, chartered locals
within the jurisdiction of a CIO union. Yet for the next few years, the
CCL would still be forced to battle to assert its independence.

This struggle took many forms – some serious, some less so. Among
the latter, for example, in July 1943 Conroy suggested to the CIO
director of organization, Allan Haywood, that he stop using the term
"our Congress membership" in his letters to the CCL and substitute

instead "your Congress membership." The former expression, he said, fanned "the prejudices of some Executive members" who thought it undermined the autonomy of the Congress.[10] Another critical issue for the Congress was whether it would be compelled to accept as affiliates all the CIO unions in Canada. When the CCL refused to affiliate several CIO unions on the grounds that they were "communist" organizations, Haywood informed Conroy that since these unions were CIO affiliates "there should be no question in accepting them." Though he informed Conroy that the CIO was "disturbed" with their behaviour, the Congress would not budge.[11] In the end the CIO once again accepted the CCL position.

Whatever prestige had accrued to the Congress in its battle to ward off the pretensions of the CIO was dealt a grievous blow at the World Labour Conference in London in February 1945. The World Federation of Trade Unions, with the support of the CIO representatives, refused to give Canada a seat on its executive body, on the grounds that the CCL and the TLC were made up of locals of United States unions – even though representation was given to smaller powers in Latin America and Europe. But rather than weakening the resolve of the CCL, this humiliation further strengthened its determination to assert its independence from American domination. On behalf of the Congress, Conroy informed the CIO that the CCL would insist on three prerogatives, without which its so-called "autonomy" was meaningless: the right to determine its own foreign and domestic policy, the right to determine what organizations it should accept or reject, and above all the power to compel international unions to follow the policy set down by the CCL conventions.[12]

Haywood, however, was totally indifferent to the sensibilities of the CCL. Because it was comprised of locals of CIO unions, he thought it reasonable that Canada should be refused a seat on the World Federation of Trade Unions executive. Further, in his opinion, the CCL was no different than any CIO state council in that "every local of a CIO union must affiliate" with the CCL in Canada. Finally, he added, the CIO would never allow the CCL the three powers that it demanded.[13]

For the next few years while Haywood made many attempts to "show the flag" in Canada, Conroy consistently repelled them. In 1945, when Haywood urged CCL unions in Canada to "communicate

to their senators their support of Henry Wallace as Secretary of
Commerce," Conroy pointedly responded that Canadians had no
desire to interfere in American affairs "though the contrary could
not be said for some Americans." In 1950, after several more years
of such exchanges and after Haywood had sent a barrage of wires
urging the workers in Conroy's "state" to send telegrams and letters
to their senators voicing their strong opposition to the policies of the
American Congress, Conroy's patience ran out. He informed Haywood that the CCL was not a "state federation and could not be
treated like one," that the 49th parallel was not simply a state line
but an international border, and that after ten years it was "about
time" that the CIO realized that Canada could not be treated like an
American state.[14] This was something the CIO was extremely slow to
accept.

Understandably, finances were the most pressing and persistent of
problems. For years the CIO unions paid the Congress a monthly per
capita tax of five cents. Naturally, when the CIO raised its own per
capita tax to eight cents in 1948, the CCL expected to receive the
extra three cents. To his surprise, Conroy was informed that the extra
three cents was earmarked for an organizing drive in the Southern
States. Conroy immediately sent a series of letters to CIO offices in
Washington stating that the Congress was on the verge of bankruptcy
and needed the extra assessment. Finally, on behalf of the CIO unions
within the CCL, Millard informed the CIO executive that, despite the
fact that the American unions supplied the bulk of the membership,
it was the national and chartered unions which provided most of the
revenues. For this reason CCL officials were encouraging organization
on a national and charter basis. Only if the CIO unions increased their
financial contributions, he added, could this alternative be avoided.
And only then could the American unions within the Congress
achieve the influence commensurate with their numbers to ensure
that "policies of real benefit" to international unionism would be
adopted.[15]

Where Conroy's pleas had gone unheeded, Millard's were quickly
accepted. The CIO agreed to send an annual $50,000 grant to the CCL
to be used only for purposes of political action, education, and
public relations, as Millard had recommended – but, pointedly, not
for organization, as Conroy had demanded. This latter restriction

annoyed Conroy, who correctly regarded it as an "intrusion on the autonomy" of the Congress and an "indirect slap" at its organizational policies.[16] The episode left Conroy deeply disillusioned and humiliated. He felt that his position as secretary-treasurer had been badly undermined and he was rudely apprised of how impotent he was to change CIO policy. The proud and sensitive Conroy was deeply hurt, and this undoubtedly played a large part in the momentous decision he was to make several months later.

In the labour hierarchy, relations between Washington and Ottawa were cool; between Ottawa and Toronto, however, they were absolutely frigid. The chill between CIO headquarters in Washington and the CCL head office in Ottawa was understandable and probably unavoidable, but not overly dangerous for the Congress. The frostiness between the office in Ottawa and the headquarters of its largest affiliate, the Steelworkers, in Toronto was no less comprehensible, but it was infinitely more hazardous. Charlie Millard's position was rather ambivalent. At times he joined with Conroy to beat off the incursions of the CIO. More often, he joined with CIO leaders to deflate the pretensions of the CCL. External pressure from the CIO was an annoyance which Conroy could withstand; the internal pressures from the international unions led by the USW was something else again. Probably the most talented and able man in the Congress, Conroy was also the most moral and intractable; compromise and fallibility were not part of his vocabulary. In all these characteristics, Millard was not far behind. Because of these similar traits, and their antipathetic viewpoints, the two frequently clashed – and when they did the fragile structure of the Congress was shaken. Their last conflict proved disastrous for the CCL.

Conroy was brought into the CCL in the key position of secretary-treasurer because the CIO unions felt that the executive neither understood nor sympathized with the ideals and objectives of international unionism. In Conroy they thought they had found the "perfect man" to represent their point of view. They were sorely disappointed.

As secretary-treasurer Conroy expected to be able to control the Congress – to delineate its economic and social programmes, to decide on its organizational and political policies, and to make its staff appointments. But in all these powers he found himself pitted against the spokesman for the CIO unions – Charlie Millard. In any showdown between the two, Millard usually had the votes. Often the matters in dispute between the two were minor and insignificant, but every defeat, every snub, no matter how inconsequential, added to Conroy's sense of helplessness and frustration.

To help counter the strength of the American unions, Conroy became the champion of those arguing for more and stronger national unions. With the help of the national unions he strove to root out the CIO infrastructure in the CCL. He asked unions to remove the "CIO" from their letterheads and to avoid mentioning, if at all possible, the CIO connection.[17] He appointed as organizers men who were strongly committed to the expansion of national unions. Some of these men were ill-suited for organizing activity, but extremely loyal to Conroy. Unhappily for Conroy, however, his attempts to reduce the power of the CIO unions in the congress failed. He had come expecting to rule, but found that he was powerless to do so. His attempts to get for the Congress the authority over its affiliates he thought so necessary, were doomed. After ten fruitless years of efforts, Conroy sadly lamented that in relation to its large international unions the CCL was "left without any authority ... thereby reducing it to the status of a satellite organization at the mercy of its affiliated unions."[18]

Between the CCL and the CIO there were two major areas of dispute: the CCL organization policies and its appointments, the latter being simply the corollary of the former. In order to build up the strength of the CCL numerically, and especially financially, Conroy and Mosher were dedicated to a policy of organizing as many directly chartered locals as possible. To carry out this policy it was essential to hire men who agreed with it – men who supported national over international unionism. This brought a series of complaints from Millard that no "CIO men" were being given CCL appointments. Though Millard's complaint was exaggerated, it was undoubtedly true that while "CIO partisans" were in charge of the CCL political and educational campaigns, few were given organizational responsibilities.

Relations between the CCL and the CIO were further strained by the innumerable jurisdictional disputes involving CIO unions, but above all, by the refusal of CIO unions to submit to CCL authority. So upset was Conroy by the obstinacy of the CIO unions that he unburdened himself in a long letter to Millard:

My personal opinion is that I should resign from office, and let the
Congress of Industrial Organizations and its International Unions take
over the Congress ... The Congress is supposed to be an autonomous
body ... but ... in matters of jurisdiction ... the Congress is left without any authority, thereby reducing it to the status of a satellite
organization at the mercy of its affiliated unions. These organizations
choose to do whatever they want regardless of Congress desires, and
in accordance with what their individual benefit may dictate they
should do ... My own reaction is that I am completely fed up with
this situation ... In short, the Congress is either going to be the
authority in its field, or it is not. If it is not to exercise authority,
then the more quickly the Executive Council appoints someone to
hold a satellite position, the sooner the Congress will know that it is
a purely subject instrument, with no authority and a servant of the
headquarters of International Unions in the United States ... This
thought has been running through my mind for the last three or four
years, and I have not arrived at it overnight. It is just that as the chief
executive officer of the Congress, I am in an untenable position, and
I am not going to work in that capacity.[19]

If Conroy hoped that such a letter would change the attitudes of
the American unions, he was sorely disappointed. Soon after receiving
this letter, Millard ordered Steelworker organizers to launch a campaign among several of the Congress' chartered locals to bring them
into Steel. And at a meeting with CCL officials Millard warned that
unless the Congress transferred its chartered locals to the appropriate
CIO union, the international unions would begin a concentrated effort
on their own to woo these unions into the CIO.[20]

Whatever their differences in outlook and philosophy, both Conroy
and Millard strove to avoid a public confrontation, realizing how
severely this would damage the CCL. Unfortunately, their differences
were too deep, their temperaments too volatile, their attitudes too
polarized, and their aims too conflicting for a peaceful and satisfactory resolution of their disagreements. In the end they broke over a
seemingly insignificant internal quarrel in 1951 among executive
members of one of the CCL affiliates, the Textile Workers of America.
His authority challenged once too often, Conroy finally went his own
way, much to the astonishment of the labour movement. With Conroy gone, the international unions resolved to weaken the office of

secretary-treasurer, so that Conroy's successor would have less freedom to oppose them. They did not oppose the executive's choice for
the job – Donald MacDonald. As a member of the United Mine
Workers he was acceptable to the international unions; and as a
faithful CCL organizer for more than a decade, he was a favourite of
the national unions. Nevertheless, MacDonald's honeymoon in office
was to be short. It soon became obvious that his sympathies, like
those of Conroy, did not coincide with those of the CIO union
leaders.

MacDonald retained Conroy's policy of drawing CCL staff from
national unions and ordering them to organize and service these same
national groups. He was similarly reluctant to transfer chartered
locals to the appropriate affiliates. Insistent as ever, the international
unions demanded that they be given a voice in making CCL appointments. MacDonald, with equal insistence, refused to surrender this
prerogative.

More serious were the international incursions against CCL locals.
Because of the low dues structures of the chartered locals and the
open opposition of CCL organizers, few of these groups were handed
over to the international affiliates claiming jurisdiction. Though the
CCL Jurisdiction Committee ordered that some Congress gas and
electrical workers' locals in Ontario and Saskatchewan be turned over
to the CIO Oil Workers union, the hostile opposition of CCL organizers
thwarted this move. Efforts by the Steelworkers and Autoworkers to
take over a CCL needleworkers local in Quebec failed when the Congress decided that since there were two claims for the local, it was
better for it to remain in the hands of the CCL. Demands by the
Autoworkers and Steelworkers that their unions be allowed to take
over CCL locals in Orillia were rejected by CCL officials on the grounds
that in that area "psychological factors were against organization by
the International unions."[21]

Dismayed by the attitude of the CCL leaders and convinced that
the only way to change policy was to change its leadership, Millard
resolved to unseat either Mosher or MacDonald – preferably both –
during the next election at the 1952 convention. Instead of risking
defeat by challenging Mosher, Millard decided that it was safer and
also more important to unseat MacDonald. And in this attempt he
was supported by all the CIO leaders. When informed of the campaign
against him MacDonald "blew his top," charged that it was a "stab in

the back ... a doublecross and an insult," and vowed that he would fight "to his last drop of blood" to retain his job.[22]

At first his task seemed hopeless. Of the 934 delegates at the 1952 convention, more than 600 were from international unions, 234 of these from the usw alone. Every leader of every CIO union in the country, with the solitary and insignificant exception of the president of the tiny Retail-Wholesale union, promised to swing his union's support behind the CIO candidate, Bill Mahoney of the usw. There was no doubt in anyone's mind but MacDonald's that he would be defeated. Nevertheless, against all odds, in what was called "the greatest election upset in the history of the Canadian Congress of Labour," MacDonald managed to win. It was the most humiliating setback ever suffered by the international unions in the CCL.

Even with Mahoney's defeat, the CIO unions triumphed. In the elections, aside from Mosher, only one other representative of a national union was elected to the fourteen-seat executive. Even the representative of the Canadian Brotherhood of Railway Employees was defeated in his attempt to retain the seat held by his union since the creation of the CCL. But far more important, over the heated and at times vituperative opposition of Mosher and MacDonald, the CIO unions managed to pass two constitutional amendments which enhanced their control of CCL affairs. The first transferred the power of appointment from the secretary-treasurer to the executive council, which was controlled by the international unions; the council was also given the power to set up and administer a department of organization. The second raised the dues structure of the chartered locals to the level of the international unions, so that there would be less reason for the former not to join with the latter.[23] With these two amendments the CIO unions achieved the full control over CCL affairs that they felt their members and their financial strength merited. Thus, the 1952 convention was not, as most observers believed, a great victory for the national union forces but rather their ultimate decisive defeat. While the national unions celebrated MacDonald's astounding victory, the CIO unions were whittling away the powers of the secretary-treasurer, thus making him the captive rather than the captain of the new team. It was, as a Steel delegate so astutely remarked at the convention, "a brand new" Congress. Though everyone owed "a debt of gratitude forever to the national unions" for their past contributions, it was the international unions with their overwhelming numbers that now controlled the CCL.[24] At the 1952 convention the national union forces had made their last desperate, valiant gesture, had won a final remarkable battle, but in so doing had lost the war. With them the last lingering hopes for a purely Canadian national labour organization disappeared.

This is not to say that the voices urging autonomy for the Canadian labour movement had been stilled. On the contrary, many of the international union leaders – particularly Millard – were in the forefront, urging increased independence for Canadian affiliates from their American parent organization. What it did signify, however, was that CCL policies – organizational, political, and economic – would now be completely in line with those agreed upon by the large American unions. The CCL envisioned by Conroy and Mosher – a congress in which the national affiliates and chartered locals would be numerous, powerful, and wealthy enough to withstand the incursions and override the demands of the American unions – proved chimerical. But Conroy's foremost achievement, the attainment and guarantee of the complete autonomy of the CCL from the CIO, proved unassailable. Decisions made by the executive and approved by the convention were binding on all CIO affiliates in Canada, whether the CIO approved or not. Even controlled by its CIO affiliates, the CCL maintained its autonomy from the CIO to the very end.

It is worth noting, I think, that to most rank-and-file union members, the conflict between national and international unionism was entirely irrelevant. It was among the leadership that this battle was fought. As almost all studies of the labour movement have shown, the average union member plays an unimportant role in the affairs of his union. Only when his own economic well-being is at stake – during strikes and collective bargaining negotiations – does he take more than a passing interest in the activities of his union. And this, of course, was especially true of the unionist in the 1930s and 1940s, when his immediate, and indeed sole, concern was to achieve financial security.

Nevertheless, because of these internal pressures, the CCL did much to benefit the trade union movement in Canada. When the Congress re-merged with the TLC to form the Canadian Labour Congress in 1956, the AFL agreed to loosen its firm grasp over its Canadian affiliates and to follow the pattern forced on the CIO by the CCL. In addition, disregarding the example of the AFL and the TLC, the new

Congress based its autonomy from the AFL-CIO entirely on the precedent set by the CCL in its relationship with the CIO.

Thus, as the first paragraph of its constitution stipulated, the Canadian Labour Congress was from the outset an "autonomous Canadian Labour Centre with full powers over all labour matters in Canada." Most large AFL unions followed the lead of the larger CIO unions and set up Canadian districts and national offices for their affiliates. The struggles of Mosher, Conroy, and their national union forces had not been totally in vain. As a result of their efforts, the international unions within the CLC agree to recognize Canada as a separate entity, to grant their Canadian affiliates limited independence, and to treat their members in Canada differently from members in the United States. This was the CCL's main achievement.

On the other hand, like its predecessor, the Canadian Labour Congress is dominated completely by its American affiliates. No more than in the CCL have the national union leaders in the CLC been able to undermine this ascendancy of the American unions. To Canadian nationalists, especially those in the labour movement, this failure to achieve for the national unions the power to curb the pretensions and designs of their American union colleagues, was the CCL's most conspicuous and crushing defeat. It signified that thenceforward Canadians would be unable to control their own labour movement. The Canadian labour movement was no longer effectively Canadian.

NOTES

1 Public Archives of Ontario, Hepburn Papers, Mosher to Hepburn, April 24, 1937; *Canadian Unionist,* April 1937, p. 273; May 1937, pp. 323-4.
2 Files and correspondence of the Canadian Labour Congress (CLC), Memorandum of Understanding between ACCL and CCIO Nov. 30, 1939.
3 CLC, e.g., Mosher and Dowd to Stevenson, Jan. 18, 1940.
4 CLC, Mosher to Conroy, Dec. 13, 1940.
5 CLC, Haywood to Mosher, Feb. 19, 1941.
6 CLC, Mosher to Haywood, March 1, 1941; Haywood to Mosher, March 10, 1941.

7   CLC, Haywood to Conroy, Dec. 29, 1941; Conroy to Haywood,
    Jan. 2, 1942.
8   CLC, Conroy to Jackson, Nov. 17, 1942.
9   Files and Correspondence of the United Electrical Workers, C. S.
    Jackson to N. Morgan, Dec. 31, 1942.
10 CLC, Haywood to Conroy, June 21, 1943; Conroy to Haywood,
    July 8, 1943.
11 CLC, Haywood to Conroy, Sept. 5, 1944.
12 CLC, Conroy to Haywood, May 26, 1945; June 14, 1945.
13 CLC, Haywood to Conroy, June 20, 1945.
14 CLC, Haywood to Conroy, Jan. 24, 1945; April 10, 1950; Conroy to
    Haywood, Feb. 1, 1945; May 2, 1950.
15 Files and Correspondence of the United Steel Workers (USW),
    Millard to David MacDonald, Nov. 8, 1949.
16 CLC, Conroy to Millard, March 30, 1951.
17 CLC, Conroy to George Burt, March 31, 1944.
18 USW, Conroy to Millard, April 21, 1950.
19 *Ibid.*
20 USW, Bill Sefton to Millard, Dec. 2, 1950; Millard to D. MacDonald,
    Sept. 2, 1951; Interview, Charlie Millard.
21 CLC, Executive Committee Meeting, June 15 and June 3, 1952;
    Jurisdiction Committee to MacDonald, March 27, 1952; Henry
    Rhodes to Burt, Feb. 4, 1952.
22 CLC, Millard to MacDonald, Sept. 13, 1952; Interviews, Millard,
    Fred Dowling.
23 Proceedings, CCL Convention, Sept. 22-6, 1952, pp. 4-16, 68, 81-3,
    84-5.
24 *Ibid.,* Larry Sefton, pp. 82-3.

Philip Resnick

A political scientist. He is an associate editor of *Our Generation* and has contributed articles to *Canadian Dimension* and other periodicals.

Canadian defence policy and the American empire

This paper* sets out to examine Canadian defence policy since the Second World War, with particular reference to the development of a continental defence alliance between Canada and the United States. I am concerned with relating Canadian junior partnership in defence to a larger process – the subordination of Canada to the American empire. For the acceptance by Canada's political and military élites of American direction in the period of the Cold War was linked intimately to the economic development of Canada along liberal capitalist lines, a process which turned Canada into a region in the continental and worldwide American economic system. Moreover, the colonial mentality which characterized Canadian defence and foreign policy vis-à-vis the United States was related in turn to the liberal ideology through which the Canadian capitalist élites viewed, and continue to view, the world. It was only natural that their support of liberal values and free enterprise, combined with their anti-communism, should have led them to define Canadian interests in terms of the American empire.

The colonialism of Canada's élites predates 1945. Ever since 1867 they have tended to look to the outside for direction and capital, and have identified Canadian nationhood with empire. There were no Noah Websters at the time of Confederation to declare in Canadian terms: "America is an independent empire and ought to assume an independent character. Nothing can be more ridiculous, than a servile imitation of the manners, the language, and the vices of foreigners."[1] Instead, Canada during the first fifty years of her existence was a staunch supporter of British imperialism, while national conscious-ness, with the exception of the Alaska boundary settlement of 1903, remained all but dormant. For the Canadian élites, a deferential, hierarchical society at home found its logical counterpart in deference to imperial policy abroad.

The First World War, with its large commitment of Canadian men and resources, brought foreign and defence policy home to Canada with a vengeance and served to tarnish the old imperial connection. Subsequently, Robert Borden was instrumental in pressing for the autonomy of the Dominions at the Imperial War Cabinet meeting of

* The content of this article is in large part extracted from an MA thesis of the same title submitted by the author to the Political Science Department, McGill University, November 1968.

1917, and in securing the admission of Canada to the League of Nations two years later.

It would be wrong, however, to think that the new emphasis on political sovereignty after the First World War meant the disappearance of a colonial attitude on the part of the Canadian political élite. Borden set forth the case for autonomy in the following terms: "I am beginning to feel that in the end and perhaps sooner than later, Canada must assume full sovereignty. She can give better service to Great Britain and the U.S. and the world in that way."[2] The dispatch of a Canadian force to Siberia in 1918-19, in support of the Allied intervention, was an early example of the autonomy Borden had in mind.

If the 1920s and 1930s witnessed growing disengagement of Canada from the British empire, it simultaneously brought an increased Canadian orientation towards the United States. In this period, American investment in Canada soared from under $500 million in 1910 to over $2 billion in 1920, and over $4 billion in 1930.[3] The development of hydro-electric power, pulp and paper, and minerals of the Shield area gave the Canadian economy a new continental direction and allowed American imperialism to dislodge the British. In Harold Innis's words, "Canada moved from colony to nation to colony."[4]

This shift was reflected in Canadian foreign policy. Mackenzie King's vacillation during what Eayrs, paraphrasing Auden, has called "a low dishonest decade" (that is, the thirties), represented more than a strong isolationism in Canadian public opinion. King appeared to be reacting to a rift in the North Atlantic Triangle, to a divergence of interest between the old imperial power and the new. The international crisis in liberal capitalism, but more particularly, the crisis in Anglo-American relations, lay at the root of Canadian indecision.

Although Canada entered the Second World War at Britain's side, Canadian foreign policy was to regain its equanimity only with the forging of a defence alliance with the United States at Ogdensburg in August 1940 and with subsequent American entry into the war. In its rush to commitments after 1945, Canadian policy sought both to compensate for its hesitations in the 1930s, and to align itself forthright with the United States.* The bogey of Soviet imperialism was

---

* Pearson in a speech in 1944, cited in James Eayrs, "Canadian Defence Policy since 1867," *Studies for the Special Committee on Defence* (Ottawa, 1965), declared: "That collective system which was spurned

to provide the excuse, and the post-war defence alliance the instrumentality. Liberalism would reinforce colonialism in making Canada a willing ally of the United States in the Cold War.

Thus it was not by accident that Canadian policy-makers ignored any threat which the overwhelming power of the United States might represent for Canada. In his important Gray Lecture in January 1947, Louis St Laurent declared: "It is not customary in this country for us to think in terms of a policy in regard to the United States. Like farmers whose lands have a common concession line we think of ourselves as settling, from day to day, questions that arise between us, without dignifying the process by the word 'policy.'"[5] And a year later Lester Pearson vouched for the beneficence of American power in these terms: "The power of the United States in the world, a power now decisive, was established against the will of the Americans, who were quite content without it ... It is in the hands of a people who are decent, democratic, and pacific, unambitious for imperial pomp or rule."[6]

When we compare this with the rhetoric which the American political élite used in defence of its empire, a rhetoric laden with liberal terms, the link between Canadian liberalism and junior partnership in the Cold War becomes clearer. Thus in 1967, in defence of US involvement in Vietnam, W. W. Rostow declared:

The United States has no interest in political satellites ... We seek nations which shall stand up straight. And we do so for a reason: because we are deeply confident that nations which stand up straight will protect their independence and move in their own ways and in their own time towards human freedom and political democracy ... We are struggling to maintain an open environment on the world scene which will permit our open society to flourish and survive.[7]

---

in Peace [sic] has proved to be our salvation in war." When we bear in mind the passion which Pearson, Escott Reid, and St Laurent brought to the concept of collective security through an Atlantic Alliance a few years later, the internationalism of post-war liberal foreign policy, directed against communism, appears as the other side of the coin from the isolationism and appeasement that characterized that same foreign policy vis-à-vis fascism in the 1930s.

It was this same "open environment" which the United States sought to maintain through its policy of containment of Russia and later China, and which Canada has supported since 1945. American leadership of the "free world" became the basis of Canadian foreign and defence policy.

Two symbolic dates mark the continental reorientation of Canadian defence policy in the 1940s, and Canada's entry into the American sphere of influence. The first is August 18, 1940, the date of the meeting between Franklin Roosevelt and Mackenzie King at Ogdensburg, at a dark moment of the war, which resulted in the establishment of a Permanent Joint Board of Defence between the two countries. This board was particularly important during the first two years of its operation, serving to mesh Canadian with American defence planning against an anticipated Axis attack. In practice, however, the board confined its activities to the northern half of North America; it involved the United States in the defence of Canada's eastern and western coasts, and in the later stages of the war, of the Canadian northwest Canada, for its part, had only a minor influence on American and Allied policy and, in fact, became increasingly dependent on the United States for both trade and matériel. The Hyde Park Agreement of April 1941, which co-ordinated the mobilization of resources in both countries, was a corollary to the Ogdensburg Declaration and a portent of increasing economic integration between the two nations.

The second symbolic date is less well known than August 1940, but is in some respects more important. On February 12, 1947, Mackenzie King rose in the House of Commons to announce an agreement worked out in the Permanent Joint Board of Defence to extend Canada's wartime defence alliance with the United States into the post-war period:

It is apparent to anyone who has reflected even casually on the technological advances of recent years that new geographical factors have been brought into play. The polar regions assume new importance as the shortest routes between North America and the principal centres of population of the world. In consequence ... when we think of the defence of Canada, we must, in addition to looking east and west as in the past, take the north into consideration as well.[8]

What his listeners did not know was that this agreement was the product of almost a year and a half of discussion in the joint board, and that ever since June 1945, the American military had expressed a strong interest in "the continuing value to continental defence of the facilities developed in northwest Canada during the war."[9] Fewer still were the Canadians who recognized King's sudden interest in the north for what it was – the first step in Canada's defence alliance with the United States in the Cold War.

There is no space here to trace the steps by which Canadian policy-makers yielded to insistent American pressure and in February 1947 accepted the five principles of defence collaboration.[10] Suffice it to say that at the war's end American military planners had already come to see the Soviet Union as a future enemy, and that American diplomacy both in Eastern Europe and over the A-bomb had largely set the stage for the Cold War.[11] Thus if the United States was insistent on defence collaboration with Canada, it was because of the new military strategy which containment of Russia dictated. As General H. H. Arnold declared in 1946, "If there is a Third World War, its strategic centre will be the North Pole."[12]

Canadian policy-makers, while initially wary of sacrificing Canadian sovereignty on the altar of a defence alliance, none the less came to support American military strategy. As early as August 1945, General Foulkes, chief of the general staff, speaking of defence research, had declared: "Canada's future commitments will lie either in fighting with Empire forces or with the forces of the United States of America ... There appears to be no place in Canada's operations in the future for special Canadian equipment of which British or American commanders may not have full knowledge or experience."[13] To be sure, Foulkes still placed Britain and the United States on a par in his strategic planning in the summer of 1945. By July 1946, however, when Pearson in speaking of the Canadian North could claim that "there is no refuge in remoteness" and that "fear and suspicion engendered in Iran can easily spread to Great Bear Lake,"[14] the United States had emerged as the dominant post-war capitalist power. By November 1946 the principles of the February 12 agreement had been accepted, and Canadian defence policy was becoming aligned to that of the United States.

Mackenzie King in his Commons statement downplayed the importance of these new arrangements and stressed Canadian support for the United Nations. But the significance of the agreement had been underscored by A.R.M. Lower some months earlier: "If Canada wishes to become a subordinate state and even a more complete satellite of the United States than she is at present, the surest road for her to take is to accept American assistance in defending her own territories. Should Yugoslavia accept Russian assistance in defending her Adriatic coast line? We all know the meaning of the answer 'Yes' to that. It is the same with us."[15] Canada had become a fortress in the American chain of command in the Cold War.

It was only in the months following the February 12 agreement, after the Truman Doctrine and Kennan's containment policy had been unveiled, that the full scope of Canadian junior partnership in the Cold War became evident. In a speech in Quebec City in October 1947, St Laurent openly revealed his Cold War liberal assumptions: "If theory-crazed totalitarian groups persist in their policies of frustration and futility, we will not, for much longer, allow them to prevent us from using our obvious advantages to improve the conditions of those who wish to cooperate with us."[16] In a major address to the House of Commons on April 29, 1948, he went even further in defining the principle of Canadian foreign policy: "Our foreign policy, therefore, must, I suggest, be based on a recognition of the fact that totalitarian communist aggression endangers the freedom and peace of every democratic country, including Canada."[17]

Nowhere at the time, in either St Laurent's or Pearson's speeches, was there any question of the validity of identifying Canadian with American interests vis-à-vis the Soviet Union. Nor was any consideration given to a policy of neutralism, such as that which Sweden chose to pursue. Instead, the Canadian élite opted for the American camp, disguising behind the catch-word "internationalism" its subordination to American policy.

This rejection of Canadian independence in the Cold War becomes more understandable when one bears in mind the policy of continentalism in economics which Canada's political and corporate élites simultaneously began to pursue. The currency crisis of November 1947, in which Canadian reserves plummeted to a post-war low of $480 million, revealed the fragility of Canada's capitalist structure. The old Atlantic markets had dried up, and it was to the United States that Douglas Abbott, minister of finance, turned in announcing emergency measures.

Specifically, Abbott announced a temporary curb on imports from the United States and provisions for US Marshall Plan purchases in Canada. But more important, as a long-term policy he stated that the Canadian government would seek to develop natural resources, to reduce permanently the lack of balance in Canadian-American trade.[18] Thus the great resource give-away and inflow of American capital of the 1950s was heralded.

Hume Wrong, Canadian ambassador to Washington and one of the architects of the February 12 agreement, brought home the implications of this policy in an address in early 1948: "We certainly do not want to make the two figures of exports between the two countries equal or nearly equal, for that could only be achieved by a most extreme form of economic nationalism, which would gravely lower the Canadian standard of living."[19] Wrong implicitly rejected economic independence in favour of long-term American development of Canada. Canadian trade with the United States would be balanced in the future by closer integration between the two economies.

Integration in defence policy became a logical counterpart to economic continentalism. Following the outbreak of the Korean War and the mobilization of the Canadian economy and Canadian resources in support of American containment of China, the two would in fact go hand in hand. As American strategy became global, so did Canadian. Brooke Claxton, minister of national defence, was quite candid when he stated "that the best place to defend Canada would be as far away from our shores as possible."[20]

The American involvement in Korea dated back to 1945. In November 1947, on US initiative, a UN Temporary Commission was established to supervise free elections in Korea, thus involving the United Nations in a matter involving post-war settlement among the great powers. Interestingly, Mackenzie King opposed participation by Canada on this commission, "conjuring up visions of Canada's being crushed in a conflict between the United States and the Soviet Union," but he was overruled by his "internationalist" advisers – that is, St Laurent and Pearson.[21]

Although there had been indications of a slackening of American interest in Korea in late 1949 and early 1950,* the outbreak of war

---

*   Dean Acheson, in a speech in January 1950, left Korea out in his discussion of those Asian countries covered by the American security umbrella.

brought an instant American response. In particular, the United States turned to the United Nations, and pushed through the Security Council a resolution recommending intervention by UN members.[22] This became the ostensible basis for Canadian intervention, involving the dispatch of three Canadian destroyers and a special brigade to serve in Korea.

The real motivation of Canadian policy was made plain, however, in a statement by St Laurent on July 19, 1950, in which he declared: "The attack of the North Korean aggressors on South Korea is a breach in the outer defences of the free world."[23] It was as a junior partner in the American empire that Canada was reacting to the Korean War and supporting the containment of communism.

In the fall of 1950, when American rearmament began in earnest, the Canadian government secured $450 million in supplementary defence expenditures from Parliament. At the same time, in the spirit of the Hyde Park Agreement of 1941, a Statement on the Principles of Economic Co-operation between the two countries was released in October, tightening Canada's economic ties with the United States.[24]

In January 1951 Brooke Claxton predicted a defence expenditure for 1951-2 in excess of $1,500 million (the final figure exceeded $2 billion) and listed a whole series of developments, ranging from manufacture of radar and electronical devices in Canada, to manufacture of the F-86 and CF-100, to an increase in military personnel to over eighty-five thousand men. "Defence has become today the biggest single industry in Canada," Claxton declared. In a period of only nine months, eighty thousand defence contracts were entered into by the Canadian Commercial Corporation. Canada's role on the production side was to concentrate on such basic materials as steel, nickel, and aluminum, in line with the needs which the 1952 Paley Report on raw materials and American industrial requirements had outlined for the United States.

Canadian junior partnership in defence was now more explicit. As Claxton stated:

We are constantly reviewing our territorial defence with the U.S. services because the defence of the North American continent is a joint operation. Our security does not depend exclusively on what Canada does or what the Americans do, but on the sum of our joint effort. *Every cent spent in Canada helps to defend the United States and vice versa. We have the same interests in our common defence,* and from day to day we are making arrangements to strengthen that defence.[25]

In the first years of the 1950s, the Canadian political élite spent over $2 billion annually in support of these "common defence interests." At the same time, the Korean War and the American rearmament programme sparked a boom in Canadian economic growth between 1950 and 1957 unmatched in Canadian history.

The stimulus for the boom of the 1950's came wholly from the United States, with the result that the east-west structure of the Canadian economy was fundamentally modified by an almost massive north-south integration. Toward the end of the period Canadian trade statistics revealed the emergence of almost entirely new exports to the U.S. of iron ore, uranium, oil, and nonferrous metals which rivaled and in some cases superseded in size the traditional staples which were sold in overseas markets.[26]

Junior partnership in defence thus reinforced continentalism in economies, for it was to US capital that the Canadian élites turned in "opening up Canada's treasure house of base metals, uranium, and rare metals needed for the jet age."[27] While helping to finance the defence of the American empire in both Europe and Asia through its own rearmament programme, the Canadian political élite simultaneously imported large quantities of US matériel and capital, until by 1956-7 approximately two-fifths of net capital formation was being financed directly by non-residents.[28] Even as decisions on Canadian resources and development came to be made most often in the United States, so too decisions on defence increasingly were made outside the country.

Canadian foreign policy over NATO and Korea had already shown the way. Only rarely did Canada seek to dissociate herself from American actions, as in a speech which Pearson made but two days before Truman's firing of MacArthur: "The days of relatively easy and automatic political relations with our neighbour are, I think, over ... Our preoccupation is no longer whether the US will discharge its responsibilities but how she will do it and how the rest of us will be involved." In the same speech, however, Pearson expressed the real substance of Canadian foreign policy, its underlying support for American actions:

We should be careful not to transfer the suspicions and touchiness and hesitations of yesteryear from London to Washington. Nor should we get unduly bothered over all the pronouncements of journalists, and generals, or politicians which we do not like, though there may be some, indeed are some on which we have the right to express our views ... More important, *we must convince the United States by deeds rather than merely by words that we are, in fact, pulling our weight in this international team.*[29]

Why show suspicion towards Washington when one shared the ideological outlook of American policy-makers, welcomed American capital to Canada, and defined Canadian interests in terms of American willingness to lead the free world? With brigades in Germany and Korea, with high defence expenditures, Canada was indeed pulling her weight in the defence of the frontiers of the American empire. Measures for continental defence would not lag far behind.

With the exception of several cold weather manoeuvres in the far north, the agreement of February 12, 1947, was not given immediate priority. The explosion of a Soviet A-bomb in September 1949, however, ended the American nuclear monopoly, and gave the defence of the North American continent, where the US nuclear force was concentrated, a new importance in American military strategy. Soon a new round of militarization of the Cold War began, leading to the installation of three radar networks in Canada between 1951 and 1957, and to total subordination of Canadian defence policy to that of the United States.

Discussions regarding the first of the radar lines, the Pinetree Line, began in the Permanent Joint Board of Defence in 1949. The line, to be built along the Canadian border, was equipped both to detect and to intercept approaching aircraft. The line would almost certainly have remained beyond the realm of military or financial feasibility, had the Korean War not broken out. In August 1951, however, an exchange of notes between the Canadian and American governments formalized the agreement to build the line at an ultimate cost of $450 million, split two-thirds – one-third between the United States and Canada.[30]

The second line, the Mid-Canada Line, was begun even before the Pinetree Line was completed. It was entirely Canadian in equipment and financing, to the tune of $170 million. The third and most important line, the Distant Early Warning Line (DEW), was entirely

American in inspiration, and originated in a study carried out for the US Air Force at the Lincoln Laboratories of MIT in 1951-2. The explosion of a Soviet H-bomb in August 1953 triggered American action, resulting in National Security Council Minute 162 judging the Soviet threat to be total, and recommending much greater efforts to improve continental defence.[31] Eisenhower's first visit to Ottawa resulted in "complete agreement on the vital importance of effective methods for joint defence"; a year later, in November 1954, the decision was announced to proceed with the construction of a distant early warning line.

The costs of financing, about $450 million, were to be borne exclusively by the United States, and US personnel were to be stationed in the North. Elaborate provisions regarding Canadian sovereignty were included in the DEW Line Agreement, but in effect Canada was reduced to providing the real estate while the United States provided the policy.

Ralph Campney, the new minister of national defence, articulated a Canadian defence policy based on protecting the American deterrent:

... it becomes essential that greater efforts be put forward immediately in strengthening the defences of this continent because North America is the base from which operations for the defence of Europe can be supported and also because of the necessity of protecting the thermonuclear retaliatory capacity of the United States, which provides at the present time probably the greatest single deterrent to war.[32]

Canadian spokesmen refused to admit that the American deterrent was part and parcel of a forward strategy which the United States was pursuing around the globe. American concern with continental air defence became *ipso facto* a Canadian concern. The defence of the centre of the American empire was the defence of Canada. Well might Eisenhower declare in 1954: "Our relations with Canada, happily always close, involve more and more the unbreakable ties of strategic interdependence."[33] As the Cold War entered its second decade, interdependence led to integration of the RCAF itself into a USAF command.

The decision to establish NORAD, the North American Air Defence Command, in the summer of 1957, marked a high point in the loss of

Canadian freedom of action in the military-strategic field. For by agreeing to an integrated headquarters in Colorado Springs to plan and oversee continental air defence, Ottawa recognized that control over that air defence "had to all intents and purposes passed to the United States as the major partner in the combined command."[34]

The pressure for NORAD originated with the USAF, which had already set up a Continental Air Defense Command in September 1954 and naturally was eager to extend its scope to embrace the whole of North America. The Canadian military, especially the RCAF, had acquired the habit of working with the Americans ever since the Second World War; and they regarded the arrangements for Arctic defence worked out in 1946-7 as a "weak compromise" which had failed to come to grips with "the realities of a Soviet air attack on this continent."[35]

In 1956 a joint US-Canadian military study group was set up to prepare the groundwork for a joint command, and the recommendation of this body became in turn the basis for NORAD. By a quirk of electoral fortune, it was the ostensibly nationalist Conservative government of John Diefenbaker, newly elected in June 1957, which accepted the agreement on August 1.

General Charles Foulkes later confessed that the Canadian military had "stampeded the incoming government with the NORAD Agreement."[36] But Howard Green has admitted that although the new government might have taken a harder look at the proposed air defence command, in the end it would have been forced to accept it.[37] The Conservatives, no less than the Liberals, were opposed to a policy of neutralism for Canada. Diefenbaker was as insistent as Pearson in maintaining that "Canada by herself cannot provide adequate defence in a modern war ... Our close relationship geographically, with the U.S. makes it natural that we should join together."[38] Ideologically strongly anti-communist, and a firm supporter of a capitalist Canada depending on a massive infusion of American capital,[39] Diefenbaker was ill-prepared to reverse the pattern of junior partnership in Canadian defence policy.

Through NORAD Canada went beyond merely offering her territory for radar installations or communications facilities. The RCAF had in fact become "a colonial military instrument serving the nuclear strategy of the United States."[40] On the pretext of being consulted by the US officer commanding NORAD, previous to the interception of hostile aircraft, Canada ensured well-nigh automatic involvement in any American measures relating to continental defence.

The parliamentary debate of May 1958 failed on the whole to come to grips with the real implications of NORAD. Both Diefenbaker and Sydney Smith chose to emphasize the element of joint consultation which NORAD provided for, overlooking the fact that in an alliance between a great power and a small one, the power relationship, not the forms of sovereign equality, determines its real character. The opposition, for its part, argued strongly for the need to link NORAD to NATO, as though an alliance set up to foster the American military presence in Europe could somehow alter the subordination flowing from continental air defence.

Only Bert Herridge, CCF member from Kootenay West, drew attention to the future consequences of NORAD during the debate. He stressed the increased economic dependence of Canada on the United States that would follow in connection with the design and production of military equipment. He interpreted Sydney Smith's announcement of May 21, 1958, regarding surveys to establish Semi-Automatic Ground Environments (SAGE) in Canada to bolster radar defence, as pointing to the acquisition of Bomarc. And he foresaw the Defence Sharing Agreement of 1959 in his prophetic observation: "The future pattern may well be that Canadian industry, if it is to get any share at all in the production of new and complex equipment needed in the air defence of Canada, may have to be satisfied with participating as sub-contractors in large US production programs."[41]

NORAD, in effect, entailed the complete acceptance of American strategic doctrine, where Canadian defence policy was concerned. At the time of the NORAD negotiations, Tom Kent, future executive assistant to Lester Pearson, wrote: "The first essential interest of Canada in the world today is the security of the United States; that takes overwhelming priority over everything else in Canada's external relations."[42] On the military side, NORAD demanded a fairly high commitment of air defence forces by Canada in succeeding years. Not only would the radar lines have to be modernized, but also Canada would have to embark on costly arms purchases in the United States, necessitating, as Herridge had predicted, economic integration in defence production between Canada and the United States – that is, an end to independent Canadian production. At the same time, the new weaponry would require nuclear armament, forcing Canada in the end to compromise her concern for non-proliferation of nuclear weapons and disarmament, in the name of NORAD's nuclear strategy.

Between 1958 and 1961, Canada's continental defence alignment with the United States took shape. SAGE electronic equipment was installed in the Canadian air defence system to increase the efficiency of the Pinetree Line and to prepare for the introduction of Bomarc. The Bomarc itself was acquired, in line with American estimations of a manned bomber threat to North America, though a substantial body of opinion held that both SAGE and Bomarc would be obsolete by 1962-3, the dates they were scheduled to become operational. The Lockheed F-104F (Starfighter) and the Voodoo F-101 were acquired for the RCAF, both requiring nuclear weapons. While Howard Green was firm in his moral opposition to nuclear weapons, and Diefenbaker insistent that "Canadians wish to make their own decisions in international affairs,"[43] the government, by accepting NORAD and the nuclear weaponry to go with it, surrendered Canadian freedom of action in defence and painted Canadian defence policy into a nuclear corner.

The Cuban missile crisis was an acid test of the automaticity of NORAD. For, despite Diefenbaker's refusal for forty-eight hours to sanction the alert, he was powerless to prevent it. Five years later, an American official, recalling the crisis, admitted: "It wasn't as bad as it looked. This was because the Canadian forces went on full alert despite their government. But this is a hell of a way to operate."[44] The Canadian military, in the crunch, was prepared to accept its orders from Colorado Springs, rather than Ottawa.

The fall of the Diefenbaker government in February 1963 was itself a reflection of the constraint which NORAD had placed on Canadian policy. Once Lester Pearson had made his dramatic reversal of January 1963, and argued that the government "should discharge its commitments ... by accepting nuclear weapons for those defensive tactical weapons which cannot be effectively used without them,"[45] Diefenbaker's procrastination became untenable. Unwilling to come out in support of a policy of neutralism, he fell victim to the logic of the State Department, arguing: "A flexible and balanced defence requires increased conventional forces, but conventional forces are not an alternative to effective NATO and NORAD defence arrangements using nuclear-capable weapons systems."[46] Given a policy of junior partnership, Pearson's position was the only logical one. Nuclear virginity was incompatible with continental integration around a nuclear strategy. NORAD led irrevocably to nuclear weapons.

Although the nuclear weapons question had generated much controversy in the early 1960s, most of the opposition died down once the Liberals returned to power in April 1963, and allowed nuclear weapons onto Canadian soil. Indeed, as the importance of bomber defence began to decline in the middle 1960s, with the advent of the missile era, there was less tendency in Canadian public opinion to see NORAD as a reflection of Canadian colonialism vis-à-vis the United States.

But there was no inclination on the part of the Canadian political élite to scrap NORAD when the agreement came up for renewal in May 1968. Although as early as 1965 US secretary of defense Mac-Namara had told a House of Representatives committee that the radar systems in Canada were either obsolete or of marginal value to overall American defence,[47] Canadian spokesmen continued to hold that the continental defence arrangements "provide security, which is the basis of independence."[48] The Americans for their part were prepared to continue NORAD as a hold-back line, and saw the agreement as providing the United States with a framework to continue overflights into Canada, and the use of Canadian facilities for testing and deployment. They found the Canadian government a pliant partner.

Paul Martin rationalized the renewal of NORAD "as the only option compatible with Canadian sovereignty."[49] Given this mentality, we can understand how Canadian foreign policy-makers could lend support to American policy in the Dominican Republic* and Vietnam,

---

* Pearson, for example, shortly after American intervention in the Dominican Republic, declared: "We have received evidence that there are indeed communists in the directing group who are controlling that particular group seeking governmental recognition (i.e., Caamaño). *House of Commons Debates,* May 11, 1956, p. 1152.

Paul Martin, in response to criticism of the US intervention from some NDP quarters, a few weeks later said: "It is easy enough to criticize countries which bear the brunt of responsibility when dangerous situations develop. Such criticism might best be directed at the imperfections in our international arrangements." *House of Commons*

and continue to style itself independent. In defence, as in foreign policy, the colonial mentality is self-imposed. The Canadian political élite is prepared to give freely what in Czechoslovakia has to be imposed – fealty to imperialist power.

As General Foulkes expressed it: "Canada has now always agreed with U.S. strategic policies, but it is usually frank enough to point out its views, and is staunch enough to support any challenge to our North American way of life."[50] In this support of "our North American way of life" against Russia, against China, in the extension of the American empire in Latin America and in Asia, lies the key to Canadian junior partnership, and to her membership in NORAD.

NORAD represented the culmination of the process whereby Canada accepted American strategic and military direction in her defence policy. In turn, however, continentalism in defence policy reinforced continentalism in defence production and led to the Defence Sharing Agreement of 1959, entailing tight Canadian dependence on the American market in the production of defence commodities. This agreement, even more than NORAD, became in the late 1960s a symbol of Canada's growing involvement in America's imperialist policies through the mechanism of continental defence, and an acid test of the political subordination that follows in the wake of military and economic subordination to a great power.

Continentalism in defence production dated back, of course, to the Hyde Park Agreement of 1941, and was in turn reinforced after the outbreak of the Korean War in 1950. In the early 1950s Canada in fact developed a fairly sophisticated defence industry, so much so that she embarked on the development of the CF-105, a supersonic jet fighter, by herself in the early 1950s. The cost of the Arrow became prohibitive by 1958-9, and in the absence of American sales (reflecting the insistence of the American military-industrial complex on producing its sophisticated weaponry at home), Diefenbaker was forced to cancel production.

The Arrow had been designed to stave off a bomber threat to North America – that is, had been conceived of in terms of a continental, rather than a Canadian, strategy. With the establishment of NORAD, integration of defence policy had been carried a stage

Debates, May 28, 1965, p. 1776. Of such legalism and moralism is the stuff of Canadian junior partnership made.

further, and it was only natural that the Canadian government, faced with the dislocation of its aircraft industry, should have seen integration of Canadian defence production with American as a veritable *deus ex machina*. In his statement cancelling the Arrow, Diefenbaker observed: "Under the irresistible dictates of geography the defence of North America has become a joint enterprise of both Canada and the United States. In the partnership each country has its own skills and resources to contribute, and the pooling of these resources for the most effective defence of our common interest is the essence of production sharing."[51]

From the American point of view, the Defence Sharing Agreement was a useful concession, greatly strengthening Canadian economic dependence on the United States. While tariffs and the Buy American clause were eliminated on Canadian bids for US military contracts, American policy-makers probably also saw in the agreement a check on any hypothetical bid by Canada for freedom of action in the foreign policy field. The Vietnam war was to bring this point forcibly home.

Elsewhere, I have dealt with the workings of the Defence Sharing Agreement in the 1960s, and Canada's increasing involvement in arms sales for Vietnam.[52] Here, it is enough merely to draw the implications of continentalism in defence production for Canadian defence and foreign policy.

Lester Pearson is himself the most damning witness in this regard. In his reply to the request by professors at the University of Toronto in January 1967 that Canada ban all further arms sales for Vietnam, Pearson made clear the overall continental framework within which Canadian policy operated:

It is clear that the imposition of an embargo on the export of military equipment to the United States, and concomitant termination of the Production Sharing Agreements, would have far reaching consequences which no Canadian Government would contemplate with equanimity. It would be interpreted as a notice of withdrawal on our part from continental defence and even the collective defence arrangements of the Atlantic Alliance.[53]

In the context of the Vietnam war this meant that Canada would continue to support the United States and abstain from any measures which might detrimentally affect her long-term relationship with the

United States, Pearson stated this on another occasion: "In concrete terms, and on the Canadian side, this means that we shall support the United States whenever we can and we shall hope that will be nearly all the time." [54]

Thus, the economic stake in continentalism served to reinforce the military one. The North American continent, one for purposes of defence since 1945, was no less one where defence production was involved. Canada could not disengage from integration in weaponry without grave consequences in the short run to her capitalist economy. Nor could she turn her back on the sophistication and expertise of the United States in military production, given her dependence for over twenty-five years on American research and development. The Swedish model of an independent industrial base and an independent defence industry was well-nigh unrealizeable in Canada in the late 1960s, short of a concerted national policy to Canadianize and socialize the economy. Despite Walter Gordon and the Watkins Report, the Canadian political and corporate élites were no more prepared now to support economic nationalism, even in a capitalist form, than they had been a decade or two previously.

It is here that we come to the roots of the whole process of continentalism in the post-war period, and to an understanding of Canada's position within the American empire. For unlike the sentimental nationalists who abound these days, not least within the ranks of groups such as the University League for Social Reform, I view the process of continentalism as having been unavoidable, once granted the premise of a liberal capitalist Canada.

Intellectually, Canadian liberals were incapable in 1945 of seeing liberal America, the source of their inspiration, as a rising imperial power. Economically, a capitalist Canada which was part and parcel of a world economic system dominated by the United States could not have developed on its own. The vision of its corporate élite was too narrow, its domestic market too small, to have a vibrant capitalism; only American capitalism, with its growing empire and dynamic military-industrial complex, could put to use the natural resources which became the basis of Canadian development. Politically, therefore, Canada's liberal élite had every reason to opt into the Cold War and to link Canada's interests to the American star.

To fail to see these connections is to blind oneself to contemporary reality. For the liberalism of a Trudeau can no more break with the American pattern than the liberalism of a C. D. Howe. The imperatives underlying foreign and defence policy are in Canada's case rational, not emotional. The interests of Canada's liberal élites continue to dictate an open capitalist society, closely linked to the United States. If here or there Canadian policy may show greater independence, on fundamentals her capitalist structure dictates junior partnership.

There is no point therefore in talking vacuously about an independent Canadian foreign policy* or neutralism in defence, unless one relates these structurally to the nature of Canadian capitalism. Nor does the "Americanization of Canada" mean anything unless one sees Canadian membership in the American empire and support for American imperialism as a reflection of her élites' liberal capitalist ideology.

The alternative to the empire, today as in 1945, is not sentimentalism but socialism. Only a socialist economy can avoid extreme dependence on the American market, both for trade and for capital. Without our underestimating the difficulties she would have faced, both within and from outside, a socialist Canada could none the less have laid the basis for economic independence, the necessary precondition for political independence.

Moreover, revolutionary socialism alone would have provided the rationale for neutralism in the Cold War. Rejecting capitalism on the one hand, Stalinism on the other, a socialist Canada might have been able to play a vital role in the easing tension between the two blocs, by unilateral disarmament of the North, for example. At the same time, she could have been much more forward in her support of the liberation of the third world from all imperialism, including Canadian capitalism.

Whether neutralism would have allowed Canada to reduce her overall defence expenditure is another matter. Much would have depended on the reaction of the United States. But armed neutrality in support of Canadian independence would have provided Canadian

---

*   The majority of essays in S.H.E. Clarkson, ed., *An Independent Foreign Policy for Canada* (Toronto, 1968), do precisely this, avoiding any mention of the capitalist basis of continentalism and colonialism in Canadian foreign policy.

defence policy with a *raison d'être* quite different from continentalism in support of the American empire.

The real threat to Canada since 1945 has come from the south, not the north. And it is our liberal capitalist élites, in their pursuit of continentalism, who have let American imperialism into the gates.

NOTES

1 Noah Webster, *Sketches of American Policy*, 1785 (New York Scholars' Facsimiles and Reprints, 1937), p. 47.
2 *Borden Diary*, Dec. 1, 1918, cited in Gaddis Smith, "External Affairs During World War I," in Hugh Keenleyside, ed., *The Growth of Canadian Policies in External Affairs* (Durham, NC, 1959), p. 57.
3 John Brebner, *North Atlantic Triangle* (Carleton Library Edition, Toronto, 1966), p. 244.
4 "Great Britain, the United States, and Canada," in Mary Q. Innis, ed., *Essays in Canadian Economic History* (Toronto, 1956), p. 405.
5 Department of External Affairs, *Statements and Speeches*, Ottawa, Jan. 13, 1947, p. 8. Referred to hereafter as *S and S*.
6 *S and S*, June 8, 1948. Address to the Kiwanis International, Los Angeles.
7 W. W. Rostow, "Guerilla War in Underdeveloped Countries," in M. G. Raskin and B. D. Fall, eds., *The Vietnam Reader* (New York, 1967), p. 111.
8 *House of Commons Debates*, 1947, vol. 1, p. 347.
9 General Henry, the Senior US Army member of the PJBD, at its June 1945 meeting. Cited in Stanley Dziuvan, *Military Relations between the United States and Canada, 1939-1945*, US Army History of World War II (Washington, 1959), p. 335.
10 There is a brief account of this process in the US Army history of Canadian-American military relations during the Second World War, *ibid*. But Canadian documentation remains under wraps, and the vital role played by such figures as Lester Pearson, A. D. P. Heeney, and Hume Wrong in fostering the Cold War defence alliance with the United States, is hidden from the public eye by External Affairs' fifty-year secrecy rule.

11 See Gar Alperowitz, *Atomic Diplomacy: Hiroshima and Potsdam*, (New York, 1965), and Isaac Deutscher's "Myths of the Cold War," in David Horowitz, ed., *Containment and Revolution* (Boston, 1967), to cite but two works, for an analysis of American responsibility for the origins of the Cold War.

12 Cited by James Reston, *New York Times*, Feb. 13, 1947.

13 Cited in Captain D. J. Goodspeed, *A History of the Defence Research Board* (Ottawa, 1958), p. 22.

14 "Canada Looks 'Down North,'" *Foreign Affairs*, vol. 24 (July 1946), p. 644.

15 In reply to a questionnaire in the *Financial Post*, Aug. 24, 1946.

16 *S and S*, 41/16, Oct. 7, 1947, p. 3.

17 *Ibid.*, 48/23, p. 8.

18 *Ibid.*, 47/20, Nov. 17, 1947, p. 9.

19 *Ibid.*, 48/3, Jan. 30, 1948, p. 7.

20 *House of Commons Debates*, March 27, 1954, p. 3339.

21 See the account in Dale C. Thompson, *Louis St. Laurent: Canadian* (Toronto, 1967), pp. 222-4.

22 George Kennan, in his *Memoirs, 1925-1950* (Boston, 1967), argues cogently against American use of the United Nations to legitimize its intervention, and scores the use of the word "aggression" in the context of the Korean Civil War.

23 Cited in F. H. Soward, "Have We Accepted Collective Security?" in *Twenty-Five Years of Canadian Foreign Policy* (Toronto, 1953).

24 *External Affairs*, Ottawa, vol. 2, no. 11 (Nov. 1950).

25 *Financial Post*, Feb. 3, 1951 (Italics not in original).

26 John J. Deutsch, "Recent American Influence in Canada," in *The American Economic Impact on Canada* (Durham, NC, 1959), p. 45.

27 C. D. Howe, cited in the *Financial Post*, March 14, 1953.

28 Irving Brecher, "The Flow of US Investment Funds into Canada since World War 2," in *The American Economic Impact on Canada*, p. 103.

29 *S and S*, April 10, 1951 (Italics not in original).

30 See R. J. Sutherland, "The Strategic Significance of the Canadian Arctic," in R. St J. Macdonald, ed., *The Arctic Frontier* (Toronto, 1966), and James Eayrs, *Canada in World Affairs, 1955-57* (Toronto, 1959), pp. 141-52 for an account of the construction of the lines.

31 Samuel Huntington, *The Common Defense* (New York, 1961), pp. 327-34.

32 *Ottawa Evening Journal,* Jan. 29, 1955.
33 Cited in Richard Stebbins, *The United States in World Affairs* (New
    York, 1955), p. 406.
34 Melvin Conant, *The Long Polar Watch* (New York, 1962), p. 88.
35 Charles Foulkes, "The Complications of Continental Defence," in
    L. Merchant, ed., *Neighbours Taken for Granted* (New York, 1966),
    p. 111.
36 House of Commons, Special Committee on Defence, *Minutes of
    Proceedings and Evidence,* Oct. 22, 1963, p. 510.
37 In an interview with the author, Aug. 13, 1968.
38 *S and S,* 59/22, June 7, 1959.
39 *Ibid.,* 59/27, Sept. 3, 1959.
40 Major-General W.H.S. Macklin, *Globe and Mail,* Toronto, Oct. 28,
    1958.
41 *House of Commons Debates,* 1958, vol. 1, pp. 1020-1.
42 Tom Kent, "The Changing Place of Canada," *Foreign Affairs,* vol. 35
    (July 1957), p. 581.
43 *Canadian Weekly Bulletin,* July 12, 1961.
44 *Financial Post,* March 25, 1967.
45 *Globe and Mail,* Jan. 13, 1963.
46 *New York Times,* Feb. 1, 1963.
47 *Winnipeg Free Press,* Editorial, May 28, 1965.
48 Paul Martin, *S and S,* Jan. 31, 1966.
49 *Ibid.,* 68/8, March 7, 1968.
50 Foulkes, "The Complications of Continental Defence," p. 120.
51 *House of Commons Debates,* 1959, vol. 2, p. 1223.
52 In my article "Canadian War Industries and Vietnam," *Our Generation,*
    vol. 5, no. 3, in particular pp. 22-6.
53 *S and S,* March 10, 1967.
54 *Ibid.,* 65/6, March 5, 1965.

John W. Warnock

An associate editor of *Canadian Dimension*. He teaches political science at the University of Saskatchewan, Saskatoon.

All the news it pays to print

When an advanced industrial nation plays, or tries to play, a controlling and one-sided role in the development of a weaker economy, then the policy of the more powerful country can with accuracy and candor only be described as colonial.

The empire that results may well be informal in the sense that the weaker country is not ruled on a day-to-day basis by resident administrators, or increasingly populated by emigrants from the advanced country, but it is nonetheless an empire. The poorer and weaker nation makes its choices within the limits set, either directly or indirectly, by the powerful society, and often does so by choosing between alternatives actually formulated by the outsider.

WILLIAM APPLETON WILLIAMS

The Tragedy of American Diplomacy

Much of the attention in recent years devoted to the role of the mass media has concentrated on the impact of television. There can be no doubt that television has had a more persuasive influence than earlier media; but the press and publications remain important. In Canada, most adults still read a daily newspaper; and most read one or more magazines or journals. There is also a continuing concern about the impact of the United States on all aspects of the Canadian mass media. How can there be any distinct Canadian identity, or a national approach to problems, when communications are so heavily influenced or dominated by a single foreign country? And why has this situation developed?

In order to understand the problems associated with press and publications in Canada, it is important to be aware of how these institutions behave in actual practice, as opposed to theory. First, it is crucial to keep in mind the fact that Canada, like the United States, is a liberal democracy, where the economy is based on private ownership of business. The press and publications industries are privately owned and operated as profit-making enterprises, rather than as institutions dedicated to public service. In contrast to other sectors of the economy, the ideology of early liberalism has prevailed and has protected them from government interference and regulation.

The traditional liberal view of the role of the press assumes that "In order for truth to emerge, all ideas must get a fair hearing; there must be a 'free market place' of ideas and information. Minorities as well as majorities, the weak as well as the strong, must have access to the press."[1] Concern that the press was not living up to this standard led to the creation in the United States of the Commission on Freedom of the Press, which released its report in 1947.[2] The Hutchins Report concluded that the American people "have not yet understood how far the performance of the press falls short of the requirements of a free society in the world today." Yet they concluded that the press should not be regulated by the government in the manner of other public utilities: it should regulate itself.[3]

In an attempt to adjust the earlier liberal standards, which they recognized could not be met, to the fact of monopoly newspapers controlled by business interests, the Hutchins Commission formulated a new set of standards. The new standards, commonly referred to as the "social responsibility" theory of the press, are as follows:

(1) a truthful, comprehensive, and intelligent account of the day's events in a context which gives them meaning; (2) a forum for the exchange of comment and criticism; (3) the projection of a representative picture of the constituent groups in the society; (4) the presentation and clarification of the goals and values of the society; (5) full access to the day's intelligence.[4]

If newspapers met these loosely defined objectives, then the public presumably would be satisfied.

If both the traditional liberal standard and the more recent "social responsibility" standard are applied to the daily press in Canada, it clearly does not live up to either. There is no radical press in Canada. There is no press which supports the moderate social democracy of the New Democratic party. The press does not even give adequate space to radical or socialist views. In ideological terms, it is a one-party press.

The basic characteristic of the press of Canada is monopoly. Most cities have only one newspaper. Some cities (like Vancouver, Calgary, and Winnipeg) have more than one newspaper, but they are so similar in content and ideology that there is no real choice. Only in Toronto and Montreal is there any real competition, and then it is only within the framework of liberalism.

Furthermore, the monopoly situation is not limited to localities. Newspaper chains dominate Canada and their strength is increasing. Today 55 of the 107 dailies in Canada belong to the three big chains, Southam, Sifton-Bell (Free Press Publications), and Thomson. With respect to circulation, the dominance is even more pronounced. In New Brunswick, one man, K.C. Irving, owns all five English-language dailies. In Vancouver, the *Sun* and the *Province,* the only two dailies, are jointly owned by the Southam and Sifton-Bell chains! Recently a new chain of French-Canadian newspapers has developed, which has inspired so much public concern that it has led to an investigation by the Quebec National Assembly. Part of this fear is due to the fact that control of the French-language newspapers may be leaving the province, and this may lead to an increase in English-speaking influence on the Quebec press. Gelco, a subsidiary of Power Corporation of Canada, has bought four of the seven Quebec dailies. Power Corporation is jointly owned by Paul Demarais, a Sudbury businessman, and Warnock-Hersey International, a financial holding company headed by Peter Thomson.[5]

The decline of competition and the growth of monopoly and oligopoly is, of course, the basic characteristic of the North American economy. Newspapers are businesses, operated so as to earn a profit for their owners. Like all capitalists, they do not believe that competition is of any special value, in itself. Stuart Keate of Free Press Publications argues that in the past when there was competition the newspapers were associated with political parties; today, the dailies are "independent" and can give the reader a "cross-section of opinion which enables him to arrive at a much more balanced judgement."[6] This view is shared by apologists for the monopoly press in the United States. One of the best-known American professors of journalism, for example, holds that the early period of competition "resulted in the establishment of more papers than were necessary to serve the public with either news or advertising." The "decline of partisan feeling" made it possible to eliminate "unnecessary competition."[7]

Ownership of the press in Canada is similar to that in the United States: it is concentrated in the hands of the small upper-class economic elite. There is a greater tendency in Canada to have ownership tied to families; present owners have inherited this wealth. As John Porter has shown in *The Vertical Mosaic,* the publishers of newspapers in Canada are similar to the economic élite in general: they have tended to go to private schools and the better universities, they belong to the same exclusive clubs, and they are almost all of British ethnic background. In both countries, the concentration of the press in the hands of the upper class has determined the conservative ideological orientation of their newspapers. This parallel situation has been recognized by studies done for the Hutchins Commission in the United States and by Wilfred Eggleston and Carlton McNaught in Canada.

William Ernest Hocking has reported that the press of the United States has become "an active factor in the industrial system of the nation, and thus a directly interested party in the well-being of that system. And the maxim of worldly wisdom applies to it, when looked at statistically, *that the public cannot rely on any interested group for disinterested truth.*"[8]

In a study of the press in Canada, Carlton McNaught noted some time ago that the "publisher often acquires a point of view which is that of the business groups in a community rather than of other and perhaps opposed groups; and this point of view is more likely than not to be reflected in his paper's treatment of news."* Wilfred Eggleston underscored this point in his submission to the Royal Commission on National Development in the Arts, Letters, and Sciences when he stated that nothing has changed since 1940 to invalidate McNaught's conclusions.[9] The class ownership of the press is reflected in the fact that all dailies either support the Liberal or Conservative parties, both strong defenders of "private enterprise," and seem to have no difficulty in switching support from one party to the other.

Both the early liberal justification for a laissez-faire approach to the press, and the newer "social responsibility" theory of the press emphasize the absolute necessity of providing the public with basic facts upon which to make political judgments. Louis M. Lyons, curator of the Nieman Foundation in the United States, writes that "there is only one function which justifies the exalted protection given the press in our [US] Constitution: that is as a common carrier of information."[10] Publishers, of course, claim that today's dailies fulfil this function adequately. Frank Swanson, publisher of the Calgary *Herald*, has stated[11] that "no citizen of this community or of this nation today can blame anybody but himself if he is poorly informed."† Nevertheless, most of criticism of the press today centres on this very question.

* *Canada Gets the News* (Toronto, 1940), p. 21. However, in reality it does not seem likely that owners of Canadian newspapers have had to "acquire" or "develop" the attitudes of the business aristocracy; they have been a part of the wealthy élite for a long time, and new ownership tends to come from individuals who are representatives of established wealth in other areas of business.

† If Canadians are well served by the daily press, why is it that in 1968 – the year of the now famous review of Canadian defence policy and the Soviet occupation of Czechoslovakia – only 52 per cent of the Canadian public could answer yes to the following question: "Do you happen to have heard or read anything about NATO – that is, the North Atlantic Treaty Organization?" See the release of the Canadian Institute of Public Opinion, Nov. 30, 1968.

The average daily newspaper today devotes over one-half of its space to advertising. Much of the remainder is devoted to "entertaining" the reader, which the industry calls "boilerplate." This, the publishers claim, is what the public wants, not news. Thus little space is left for news and serious comment. In addition, the quality of the news reporting itself is open to question. North American journalism has been unable to attract the most gifted writers, perhaps because of their notoriously low wages. But most criticism has been directed at the widespread use of wire services. For over three-fourths of the daily newspapers in Canada, the Canadian Press (CP) wire service is their only source of news from the rest of Canada.[12] This wire service is a co-operative effort of the publishers, based on the Associated Press in the United States. However, it is primarily a clearing house, rather than a news originator. Local newspapers send out stories which they feel might be of national interest. The selection and writing of these stories reflects the biases of local editors and publishers. National news stories, when the wire services are used, are usually identical, word for word, in all subscribing dailies. Furthermore, because the wire services are paid according to how much of their material is printed, their stories are designed to irritate as few people as possible and to appeal to the political sympathies of those who own the newspapers.

Perhaps the most significant development that has affected newspapers in North America is the rise of mass advertising. Today, between 60 and 85 per cent of the revenue of the daily newspaper comes from advertising. Nevertheless, circulation remains very important, for large circulation attracts more advertising. Entertainment sections have been introduced into the newspaper not because of reader demand, but to provide fill around certain advertising appealing to certain markets.[13] Because of the heavy dependence on advertising, the publishers and editors feel that they must not print material which might annoy their advertisers; they also believe that a non-controversial "independent" newspaper will have larger circulation. As one American publisher, J. David Stern has put it: "The monopoly newspapers present news which will offend no one, arouse no emotions, tread on no one's toes, offer soothing syrup for mankind's bellyaches."[14] In fact, the chief function of the daily newspaper is no longer that of reporting news. Instead, it has become an agent of business, selling commodities.

Why has the press of Canada – or more accurately, the press of North America – failed to live up to its professed standards? The reason is contained in a description of the press provided by the *Wall Street Journal:*

A newspaper is a private enterprise, owing nothing whatever to the public, which grants it no franchise. It is therefore "affected" with no public interest. It is emphatically the property of the owner, who is selling a manufactured product at his own risk. If the public does not like his opinions or his methods of presenting the news, the remedy is in its own hands. It is under no obligation to buy the paper ...[15]

Second, the daily press of North America has been subject to the same economic developments as other businesses. We have moved from a period of competition in the early nineteenth century to a period of monopoly capitalism. Free market competition has eliminated rival industries. The result has been monopoly on the local level and the rise of chains on the national level. Today's monopoly press cannot satisfy the traditional liberal criteria. Furthermore, there is no evidence that the newspaper monopolies, or other monopoly institutions, have abandoned maximization of profit and have become public spirited, benevolent, "soulful" corporations. They cannot live up to the standards of "social responsibility."

The other main function of the press in the twentieth century is to act as an agency within society which transmits culture, traditions, language, and other national values. This was recognized to be a prime function of the press by the Royal Commission on Publications, which stated that "communications are the thread which binds together the fibres of a nation. They can protect a nation's values and encourage their practice ... The communications of a nation are as vital to its life as its defences, and should receive at least as great a measure of national protection."[16] Ten years earlier the Massey Report argued that communications were essential to promoting national life.[17] Nevertheless, the sad fact remains that most of the reading material in Canada continues to be published in the United States, as is the case with periodicals, or else is heavily influenced by news, articles, and entertainment originating in the United States, as is the case with newspapers.

Few Canadians are aware that almost all the international news which they read in the daily newspaper is written by foreigners. Most of this comes from American sources, and the rest largely from British news services, particularly Reuters, the Economist Intelligence Service, the London Observer Foreign News Service, and the Guardian (Manchester) News Service. There is very little direct news-gathering by Canadians. This is true even of the Canadian Press (CP), the Canadian wire service. Most of CP's foreign news copy originates from their New York office, where a small group of editors rewrite the news releases they receive from Associated Press (US) and Reuters (Great Britain). This is to stress aspects which are of more interest to Canadians, but the actual gathering is still overwhelmingly foreign.

In addition, many of the larger Canadian dailies subscribe directly to the foreign wire services, Associated Press, Reuters, United Press-International, the Chicago Daily News Service, The New York Times News Service, and the Washington Post-Los Angeles Times News Service. Most of the French-Canadian dailies also subscribe to l'Agence France Presse. Furthermore, the use of the foreign wire services is on the increase in Canada. When the local newspaper uses a foreign news story, then the reader does not even benefit from the Canadian slant that the editors of CP might give the story.* And it is quite clear that the American wire services carry their own particular biases. They cater specifically to the preferences of the local American publishers who buy their services.

Why is there so little direct Canadian reporting of news events? It is widely believed, and probably true, that Canadian alternatives would be more expensive. George V. Ferguson, editor of the *Montreal Star,* defended the use of wire services, arguing that there is an

---

* One example might illustrate this point. On February 1, 1968, Robert McNamara, US Secretary of Defense, issued his annual report to the Senate Armed Services Committee on the status and plans for American defence. The *Globe and Mail,* Toronto, carried this story on the following day, using the New York Times News Service; it was oriented to the US market and concentrated on US-Soviet problems. The Canadian Press story on the same event, carried in the *Ottawa Journal,* stressed the major changes which applied to North American defence, including radical changes in Canada's role and contribution, which the New York Times news report did not mention.

advantage to having important facts widely and commonly known. "If those facts are fairly reported, there is a national, even an international, gain in having some corpus of common knowledge."[18] In principle this may be true; but the fact that there is a clear bias in wire service reporting, both on the national and international level, is beyond question.

It has already been noted that newspapers provide more space for "entertainment" than they do for news or information. For Canadians there is one additional aspect to this problem: most of the "boilerplate" found in the Canadian dailies has its source, once again, in the United States. This includes almost all of the comics, Heloise, Uncle Ray's Corner, Art Buchwald, Medical Memos, Tell Me Why, Billy Graham, Ask Andy, Dr Alvarez, the horoscope, Ann Landers, Jacoby and Goren on bridge, as well as the fashion reports, Hollywood, how to cook, and so on. This material is distributed by American syndicates: North American Newspaper Alliance, Newspaper Enterprise Associates, World Wide Press Service, Women's News Service, Copely News Service, and many others. They are, of course, oriented to serving American interests. More pernicious, moreover, are the reactionary values that many of them reflect, particularly the comic strips. Because the syndicates tend to be auxiliary operations of the large national newspapers, this is one area where competition still reigns, and their costs remain relatively low. Again, this is why the Canadian publisher chooses to use the US services rather than developing Canadian alternatives.

These syndicates also distribute political comment. Canadian newspapers even seem to publish more political columnists from the United States than from Canada. Those which appear in many newspapers include Joseph Alsop, Walter Lippmann, James Reston, Marquis Childs, Carl Rowan, and William R. Frye. They are also beginning to pick up the local columnists from the *New York Times,* the *Washington Post,* the *Los Angeles Times,* the *Chicago Daily News,* and the other newspapers that are developing syndicates. Newspaper Enterprise Associates, which is connected with the Scripps-Howard chain in the United States, even circulates editorials and political cartoons. It is not clear how many editorials written by such syndicates appear in Canadian newspapers, but it is easy to identify their political cartoons when they appear in the smaller daily newspapers that do not have their own regular cartoonists. Obviously, business economics is a major factor here. But there is also something else, for there are many writers in Canada who would be willing to write background articles and columns for Canadian newspapers. Part of it must be associated with the colonial mentality which has dominated Canada for so long. The well-known commentator from the metropolitan country, first Great Britain and now the United States, carries more influence. Moreover, the American columnists tend to share the same conservative ideology of Canadian publishers and editors.

On the whole, then, the newspapers of Canada are barely distinguishable from those of the United States. And there is no concern expressed by the press on this question. But this should not come as a surprise. The newspapers of Canada are owned by big business interests (all Canadian with the exception of the chain owned by Lord Thomson). As a whole, Canadian businessmen have not been concerned about US control and ownership of the Canadian economy. They seem quite willing, if not anxious, to sell out to US interests, particularly if the price is right. For them, national boundaries are an anachronism in the era of monopoly capitalism and the multinational corporation. Furthermore, the newspapers receive a great deal of advertising revenue from American business interests.

Among the English-language newspapers, only the *Toronto Daily Star* has felt that American economic domination of Canada is an important problem. Yet during election campaigns it traditionally supports the Liberal party, the party of big business, and the party which historically has been in the vanguard of those interests promoting continental integration. The situation has led Arnold Edinborough to conclude: "Indeed, it is possible for a pessimist in 1962 to say that the press generally may be at least partly responsible for a general easing of public opinion to the point where absorption of Canada into the United States is in the foreseeable future ..."[19]

In many other countries an alternative source of national information is provided by magazines and other publications. This is not so in Canada. There are no widely circulated equivalents of the political magazines like the *New Statesman,* the *New Republic,* or the *Nation* that one finds in Great Britain and the United States. There are no weekly Canadian news magazines or newspapers. There are no equivalents of the smaller literary magazines, such as *Atlantic, Harpers,* or the *New Yorker.* As the O'Leary Report noted, in 1959 over three-quarters of all magazines sold in Canada were American. No other industrialized country in the world tolerates such a situation.

What are the reasons for this? One of the major problems is the lack of sufficient advertising revenues for Canadian magazines. The O'Leary Report showed that in 1959 approximately 75 per cent of the revenue of magazines sold in Canada came from advertising.[20] Of the total amount, the two American giants, *Time* and *Reader's Digest,* absorbed about 41 per cent. The Maclean-Hunter Publications absorbed another 46 per cent, leaving only 13 per cent of total advertising revenues for all the remaining Canadian magazines.* But even Maclean-Hunter Publications are beginning to feel the pinch. In January 1969 *Maclean's* magazine adopted a new format, reducing its size to that of *Time* in order to be able to re-run a full-page *Time* advertisement without any redesign costs.

The advantages of *Time* and *Reader's Digest* are well known, but the Canadian government has refused to act. The Canadian operation of *Time* receives most of its copy directly from the head office in the United States. The basic magazine costs are absorbed by the US operation – the cost of the Canadian operation is restricted to the small "Canadian content" insert in the weekly. Therefore, with low general costs, *Time* can afford to charge only $2,700 for a full-page advertisement, whereas *Maclean's* has to charge $4,600 a page in order to cover the cost of its operation.†

A second major problem for Canadian publications is newsstand distribution. The national distributors in Canada are Curtis Distributing Company of Canada, Select Magazines, and Fawcett Publi-

---

* In 1959 the four major magazines published by Maclean-Hunter accounted for 62 per cent of all circulation of Canadian magazines. This carries over to French Canada as well, where the largest magazine by circulation is the French-language version of *Reader's Digest.* The next two largest publications by circulation – *Le Magazine Maclean* and *Chatelaine: La Revue Moderne* – are both owned by Maclean-Hunter.

† Gary Dunford, "Why Are This Magazine's Measurements Now 8¼ Inches Wide by 11¼ Inches High?" *Toronto Daily Star,* Jan. 11, 1969, p. 31. Dunford notes that by 1969 *Time* and *Reader's Digest* had increased their share of all magazine advertising to over 50 per cent of the Canadian market.

cations, all American firms. Because there are so many magazines published in North America, they are forced to limit the number they distribute to the local newsstands. Therefore, they give preference to those magazines which already have high sales, including necessarily those which they distribute through their operations in the United States. If a new Canadian magazine manages to corner a distributor, the costs involved are tremendous. The distributor takes almost all the income of the first few thousand sales, and a high percentage thereafter. Thus a new magazine, if it wants to sell on the local newsstands, must be prepared to undergo steady losses while it builds up circulation, and few can afford that. No other industrialized country permits foreign control of newsstand distribution. It is a major factor in the domination of American publications in the Canadian market.*

The effect on Canada should be obvious. In 1951 the Massey Report concluded (p. 4) that "a vast and disproportionate amount of material coming from a single alien source may stifle rather than stimulate our own creative effort; and, passively accepted without any standard of comparison, this may weaken critical faculties." Ten years later the O'Leary Report noted (pp. 5-6) that Canada, more than any other country, is naked to the force of the US communications explosion, "... exposed unceasingly to a vast network of communications which reaches to every corner of our land; American words, images and print – the good, the bad, and the indifferent – batter unrelenting at our eyes and ears." John Porter has described this as the ideological counterpart of the external control of the economic system.[21] This impact is multiplied by the American influence on radio and television.

There are a number of other small countries in the world which are exposed to the danger of overflow in press and publications from larger, more powerful, neighbours. Yet the staff of the O'Leary

* O'Leary Report, p. 16. The American newsstand distributors also control distribution of paperbacks. McClelland and Stewart of Toronto instituted the Canadian Bestseller Library, a series of Canadian titles in paperbacks, but were forced to abandon the series because the American wholesalers refused to distribute them to newsstands. William French, "Books & Bookmen," *Globe Magazine,* March 24, 1969, p. 20.

Commission found that these countries maintain strong national publications industries.[22] In all cases, too, these states had introduced legislation to protect their own mass media – it was not left to the whims of laissez faire and private profit. The governments of these countries had determined that "the political nature of the purpose for which the press exists and the political influence consequently asserted by its leaders necessitates the conferment upon nationals of certain privileges and priorities in publication and distribution accruing to them as part of their political right."[23]

The countries which are in a situation most similar to that of Canada are Ireland, Belgium, Switzerland, and Austria. They have large neighbours with a similar language and cultural background. They are all liberal democracies, with private enterprise economies, yet all have vigorous publishing industries. It is interesting to see what methods these countries, and others, have used to deal with the problem; for in principle the same methods can be applied to Canada.

There have been two basic approaches used by states to protect a national press and publications industry: regulation and assistance. Those regulations which are widely used are as follows: (1) prohibition of overflow advertising; (2) national control of distribution, with priority rights given to national publications; (3) discrimination against foreign publications through customs duties, foreign exchange regulations, special taxes, quotas, and required price differentials; and (4) requirements that all publishing firms, including newspapers, be owned and managed by nationals.

It has been felt that these defensive approaches are inadequate by themselves to insure that a national press and publishing industry will flourish. The giant firms, like Luce Publications, can still play a dominant role. Therefore, states have granted positive assistance to national publications through the following programmes: (1) special postal rates for magazines and newspapers; (2) enforcement of anti-combines legislation; (3) special tax concessions to struggling publications; (4) regulation of advertising even to the extent of taxation and distribution controls; (5) other indirect subsidies, such as free transportation, telephone, and telegraph services; and (6) direct public subsidy to cultural publications. Within the constrictions of the private enterprise economy, these programmes would go a long way towards developing a publications industry in Canada.

The problems posed by the daily press are more difficult. It takes a

significant amount of capital to start new newspapers, and to survive
they must be able to attract considerable advertising. Since the Second World War there have been three attempts to start new dailies in
Canada (Winnipeg, Montreal, and Vancouver) and they have all failed.
Some programmes might be introduced to help promote competition.
A few have been suggested by Douglas Fisher: (1) a moratorium on
corporate taxation on new dailies and old ones which are in financial
distress; (2) a moratorium on taxes if profits are all reinvested in the
newspapers; (3) a federal loan fund to lend capital to new dailies and
weeklies; and (4) a guarantee by the federal government of any debts
that the new newspaper might run up with the Canadian Press.[24]

Certainly the government needs to strengthen and enforce its anti-
combines legislation and to apply them to the press. But this would
not be enough. There is a need for a national news collecting and
distributing agency, and a need for more syndicated material of
national origin. If the privately owned press will not undertake such
a service, then it is surely appropriate for the government to do so. In
addition, it seems that the "Canadian content" rule that applies to
broadcasting should be applied to other areas of the mass media.

Another reform has been proposed by Kenneth McNaught of the
University of Toronto: the creation of a publicly owned national
newspaper.[25] This would be in the tradition of the Bank of Canada,
the CNR, Air Canada, and the general public role in other utilities.
Furthermore, we already have the National Film Board and the CBC
in the area of mass media. McNaught suggests that this national newspaper take the form of a new corporation along the lines of the CBC.
It could experiment with new publishing and transmission techniques
not yet tried. It could add greatly to the number of national corres-
pondents. It would provide competition for the other newspapers
and set a higher standard of journalistic excellence. In theory, it
would be able to provide a wider spectrum of political views than
the present monopoly press.

It must be recognized that it is not likely that any of these suggestions
will be implemented by the Canadian government.* The Diefenbaker

* In the spring of 1969 Senator Keith Davey announced that a special
Senate committee would investigate the press of Canada and make
recommendations for legislation. However, it is not likely that Sena-

government, which was the most nationalistic government we have had for years, made no attempt to introduce the very mild suggestions of the O'Leary Report. Pressures exerted by the US government forced the Pearson government to drop the half-hearted reforms that were included in Walter Gordon's tax bill in 1965. The two major political parties have no real reason to be dissatisfied with the present situation. Canadian newspapers and publications support them, though smaller papers and minority publications might dissent. The business aristocracy supports these parties, particularly the Liberals. That is probably one good reason why there is no attempt to enforce the anti-combines legislation that already exists. Today, "freedom of the press" is a mere slogan used to protect the monopoly situation in press and publications.

If, through some unforeseen event, the New Democratic party were to form the government, then we might expect some changes in this area. However, it is not likely that they would have the courage to undertake a proposal even as modest as that suggested by Mc-Naught. But even if all the reforms were instituted, and we had a publicly owned newspaper, would we really have a pluralist press, with a fair presentation of dissenting views? The CBC certainly offers no hope that the situation would be any better. Furthermore, because most Canadians are able to watch American television, and to buy American publications, it is doubtful if there would be any significant qualitative change: Canadians would still be captives of the North American market economy, where the mass media are an agent of the business culture, subtly manipulating people to buy more commodities, creating "perpetual scarcity."

It is much more likely that the situation with press and publications will get worse. Significantly, the only action taken by the Canadian government in recent years in this general area was the revision of the postal regulations by the Trudeau government in early 1969. The new postmaster general, Eric Kierans, a millionaire businessman and former head of the Montreal Stock Exchange, decided that the Post Office (or at least certain aspects of it) should be put on a profit-making basis. There was a small increase in second-class mailing rates,

---

tor Davey or his wealthy business colleagues in the Senate will propose anything significant. Even if they did, it is extremely unlikely that the Liberal government would support them.

which apply to commercial publications, like *Maclean's* and the daily newspapers. But a minimum charge was introduced, which fell hardest on the small periodicals. However, second-class privileges are now denied to publications "of fraternal, trade, political, professional or other associations, or a trade union, credit union, co-operative or local church congregation." The minister argued that "all publications appealing to minority groups should pay their own way." Publications of these organizations will now have to pay the much higher third- and fourth-class rates. For example, *Le Travail*, for forty-four years the publication of the Confederation of National Trade Unions (CNTU), found that its mailing costs for one year would increase from $26,000 to $200,000. They decided to close the newspaper, as was the case with the *Labor Statesman*, the monthly newspaper of the British Columbia Federation of Labour. Many other small publications are cutting back or ceasing operations.[26]

The chief beneficiaries of this move will be the daily newspapers and Maclean-Hunter Publications, who have the advantages of monopoly position in the market. It will tend to kill off the smaller Canadian publications. It will not affect US magazines mailed from the United States.* Association publications will have to pay 50 per cent more postage to reach their subscribers than similar publishers in the United States. It is a tremendous blow to Canadian-based labour unions, for the large "internationals," which are based in the United States, mail their publications from the United States and thus will avoid the postage increase. Thus the only government action in the area of press and publications in recent years will further increase the monopoly situation in Canada and American domination of the Canadian market.

Are there no alternatives to the present situation? The public is becoming more aware of the nature of the monopoly press in North America, and the need for a printed medium which is more objective, and which will print news and opinion that is now ignored. The development of the underground press in North America is one

---

* The public subsidies to the two major American magazines which are mailed in Canada, under the new regulations, are as follows: *Time*, $725,153; *Reader's Digest*, $851,636. Reply of Hon. E.W. Kierans to a question in the House of Commons by Barry Mather, reprinted in the *Commonwealth*, May 21, 1969, p. 11.

symptom of dissatisfaction with the regular press. It started out as part of the "hippie" drop-out cult, but it is becoming more and more political. There has also been a significant expansion of radical periodicals and this is continuing. Perhaps, as this dissent increases and spreads to other interest groups, it will be recognized that the only alternative for North America is a daily press which is subsidized by political parties or interest groups. It has been recognized for some time in Great Britain and on the continent that this is the only way that there can be any semblance of a pluralistic press within a monopoly capitalist society.

Nevertheless, the future is bleak for Canada. Undoubtedly US domination of the Canadian economy will continue, and the capitalist ideology of the United States will be forced on us by the mass media. It is very unlikely that there will be any significant change until the worldwide American empire begins to break up. And even then, Canada will be the last colony to be liberated.

NOTES

1 Fred S. Siebert, Theodore Peterson, and Wilbur Schramm, *Four Theories of the Press* (Urbana, 1963), pp. 3-4.
2 The Commission on Freedom of the Press, Robert Hutchins, chairman, *A Free and Responsible Press* (Chicago, 1947).
3 *Ibid.,* pp. 91, 97.
4 *Ibid.,* p. 102.
5 See John Porter, *The Vertical Mosaic: An Analysis of Social Class and Power in Canada* (Toronto, 1965), p. 463; J. Williams, "Too Few Controls – Too Many Information Outlets," *Canadian Labour,* IV (Nov. 1959), pp. 25-8; John Cartwright, "Who Owns Canada's Press," in Paul Fox, ed., *Politics: Canada* (Toronto, 1962), pp. 21-3; and Richard Dahrin, "Quebec's Press Monopoly," *Canadian Dimension,* V, no. 4 (Jan. 1969), pp. 13-14.
6 "Pressures on the Press," in D. L. B. Hamlin, ed., *The Press and the Public* (Toronto, 1962), pp. 15-16.
7 Frank Luther Mott, *The News in America* (Cambridge, Mass., 1962), p. 188.

8 *Freedom of the Press* (Chicago, 1947), p. 145 (Italics in original).

9 "The Press of Canada," in *Royal Commission Studies,* A Selection of Essays Prepared for the Royal Commission on National Development in the Arts, Letters and Sciences (Ottawa, 1951), p. 43.

10 Cited by James S. Pope, "On Understanding the Press," reprinted in George L. Bird and Frederic E. Mervin, eds., *The Press and Society* (Englewood Cliffs, NJ, 1957), p. 99.

11 Quoted in Donald Gordon, "The Press," *Saturday Night,* LXXIX (Oct. 1964), p. 34.

12 John Dauphine, "The Canadian Press ..." in the Montreal *Gazette,* Sept. 19, 1967, p. 40.

13 Arnold Edinborough, "The Press," in John A. Irving, ed., *Mass Media in Canada* (Toronto, 1962), p. 15; and Donald Gordon, "Measuring the Mythical Family's Needs," *Saturday Night,* LXXIX (Feb. 1964), p. 22.

14 Cited by Douglas Fisher, "The Case against Newspaper Chains," *Maclean's,* LXXV (Nov. 17, 1962), p. 98.

15 Reprinted in the *Commonwealth,* Regina, Jan. 17, 1968, p. 4.

16 Royal Commission on Publications, Grattan O'Leary, chairman, *Report* (Ottawa, 1961), p. 4.

17 Royal Commission on National Development in the Arts, Letters and Sciences, Vincent Massey, chairman, *Report* (Ottawa, 1951), p. 4.

18 "Freedom of the Press," in *Press and Party in Canada: Issue of Freedom* (Toronto, 1955), p. 11.

19 "The Press," pp. 27-8.

20 See the charts on pp. 176-81 of the *Report.*

21 Porter, *The Vertical Mosaic,* p. 465.

22 Appendix H of its Report is a commission study on the periodical press in other countries, based mainly on UNESCO surveys.

23 *Ibid.,* p. 214.

24 "The Case against Newspaper Chains," pp. 98-9.

25 "The Case for a Nationalized National Newspaper," *Saturday Night,* LXXXIII (June 1968), pp. 26-7.

26 See "What Do New Postal Regulations Mean?" *Commonwealth,* Dec. 11, 1968, pp. 1, 2; "The Ruthlessness of Eric Kierans," *Commonwealth,* Feb. 5, 1969, p. 3; and Terrence Belford, "Postal Rate Increases Forcing Periodicals to Trim Issues," *Globe and Mail,* May 20, 1969, p. B-7.

Frank Peers

For some years supervisor of public affairs on CBC radio and television.
He now teaches political science at the University of Toronto.

Oh say, can you see?

Two days before retiring as prime minister, Lester Pearson told
Canadian Press: "The industrial and economic and financial penetration from the south worries me, but less than the penetration of
American ideas, of the flow of information about all things American;
American thought and entertainment; the American approach to
everything."[1] This summing up at the end of a political career recalls
the warning by Eisenhower who, as he was about to leave office,
emphasized the "grave implications" of the United States military-
industrial complex. On both occasions the ordinary citizen might
have asked, "But where were you when all this was happening?"

In Canada as American domination of Canadian entertainment,
popular culture, and communications increases, we shall see the
world more and more from American perspectives. This is most
clearly demonstrated by television, which in the past two decades has
been the single most important influence on our customary modes of
perception. John Kenneth Galbraith was asked, as an expatriate
Canadian, whether his former countrymen need worry about economic domination from the United States. He replied, "If I were still a
practising as distinct from an advisory Canadian, I would be much
more concerned about maintaining the cultural integrity of the
broadcasting system and with making sure Canada has an active,
independent theatre, book-publishing industry, newspapers, magazines and schools of poets and painters. I wouldn't worry for a
moment about the differences between Canadian or American corporations."[2] But the facts of corporate life result in the subordination
of Canadian mass media to the American, particularly when Canadian
political authority has been so timid about safeguarding what cultural
autonomy exists. And time is running out. Unless we can establish a
viable system to produce and distribute Canadian information and
Canadian programming under present conditions, the new techno-
logies related to cable, satellite communication, and the electronic
video recorder (EVR) will so complicate our range of decisions that
the country's broadcasting system will literally be in pieces, and we
will find another one superimposed.

Nationality of ownership in the broadcasting media is not the key
question, though it is one that has preoccupied legislators in the past.
The uses to which broadcasting is put, the values of society which it
is allowed to reflect, the assertion of public rather than private
interests in fashioning and controlling the system – these are the
important issues, and ones which can make the difference between a

separate existence for Canadians in the last third of the twentieth century and a loss of their identity in the American melting pot.

Without overemphasizing the mistakes of the past, we must take a look at the system as it is: the methods of making governmental decisions, the Broadcasting Act of 1968, the regulatory board (CRTC), the public network and production agency (CBC), the private stations and the private network (CTV), and the cable-distribution companies (CATV); and we must ask, can these elements make up a system to serve Canadian interests? There is in our broadcasting system a dichotomy that results in ambiguity if not contradiction. From our belief in the market system, we have embraced a concept of broadcasting as primarily a market process, a subdivision of advertising; but at the same time we expect broadcasting to be a public service with national responsibilities as a medium for communication and enlightenment. To the extent that the first concept prevails, the Canadian broadcasting system will be subordinate to the American.

THE BROADCASTING ACT OF 1968

The present broadcasting act is essentially a modified version of that introduced by the Progressive Conservative government of John Diefenbaker in 1958. Under that act Canadian broadcasting had a troubled history, and it exhibited a less distinctive national character at the end of the ten-year period than it did at the beginning. The 1958 act had established the "two-board" system; the regulating and operating components of public broadcasting were administered by the Board of Broadcast Governors and the Canadian Broadcasting Corporation, respectively. The BBG then began to implement the government's policy of licensing two television stations in any "market" that could support them, in order to give viewers in the larger centres additional programme choice. Without any additional measures, this would clearly have had the effect of increasing enormously the amount of American viewing in each community granted a second licence, since the economics of the industry would dictate that the stations fill their schedules with easily procurable material from the United States.*

---

* The production agencies of New York and Hollywood, with big budgets at their command, can recover their costs in the United States market, and any additional sales in the Canadian and overseas markets

In a largely futile attempt to offset this tendency to rely on imports of American programmes, the BBG encouraged the formation of a private television network, CTV, with most of the "second stations" negotiating affiliation agreements. The BBG's authorization did not guarantee the profitability of CTV, however, or the quality of its service. While the individual stations, in the better bargaining position, began to prosper, the network ran into financial difficulty. Eventually, ownership of CTV was vested in the station affiliates.

The problems within the broadcasting system were intensified by rivalries between the two public boards, BBG and CBC, the BBG tending to assume the role of protector of the private stations and of CTV. It was not certain how much authority the BBG had over the CBC; each reported directly to Parliament, and in addition the act did not clearly define their relationship.

In 1963 the Liberal government tried the easy solution of asking the broadcasters themselves what modifications in the system were needed. A "troika" committee was formed, consisting of the chairman of the BBG, the president of the CBC, and the president of the Canadian Association of Broadcasters, Don Jamieson, as spokesman for most of the private stations. Their report to the secretary of state in 1964 showed very little agreement, and a more formal advisory committee was appointed under the chairmanship of Robert Fowler. Its report led to a government white paper on broadcasting in 1966; this in turn was studied by a House of Commons committee which reported in March 1967. A bill introducing a new broadcasting act was given first reading in October 1967, and after further committee consideration and much parliamentary debate, an amended Broadcasting Act was finally given assent on March 7, 1968.

It took Parliament six months to pass the Broadcasting Act. A

---

merely increase their profits. Their film and television properties are therefore offered to Canadian stations and networks at a fraction of what it would cost Canadians to produce similar programmes. Moreover, because of the promotional build-up that is given them, the imported American programmes are especially attractive to both audiences and sponsors. Even the publicly-owned network, the CBC, attempts to meet the competition by scheduling mainly American programmes in prime time. The result is, more American programmes seen over *both* channels.

number of Conservative and Social Credit members, and especially a
maverick Liberal MP, Ralph Cowan, acted as protectors of the private
stations and therefore of commercial TV, and their opposition resulted in the dropping of a section of the bill that would have allowed
five-year financing of the CBC, rather than annual parliamentary
appropriations. As a consequence the CBC is still unable to make
long-term plans with assurance, and the government can chop or
change the appropriation under the pressures of the moment.

At each stage in the generation of the new legislation, attention
was drawn to the vulnerable position of Canadian broadcasting with
respect to the commanding position held by the American industry.
This is the Fowler committee's assessment:

An adequate Canadian content in television programs is unlikely
to be achieved by a *laisser faire* policy of minimum regulations,
governing advertising volume, morality and the like. Economic forces
in North America are such that any substantial amount of Canadian
programs will not appear on television schedules unless room is reserved for them by regulation. The plea of private stations that they
would produce better Canadian programs if they were allowed to
concentrate the available money on fewer productions is not supported by the experience in radio, for which there are no specific
Canadian content requirements.[3]

The report of the Fowler committee was weakened by the subsequent
attacks of the private broadcasters, of their journalistic allies, and
even of the CBC and BBG, whose conduct of affairs had been criticized
severely in the report. Under this onslaught, the Pearson government
thought it prudent to dilute Fowler's suggestion for one governing
board (the Canadian Broadcasting Authority), and to modify the
two-board system of 1958, renaming and strengthening the regulatory
authority (the Canadian Radio-Television Commission) to establish
a certain primacy over the CBC board of directors. Nevertheless, in its
white paper of 1966, the government recalled that forty years earlier
the Aird commission had found unanimity on one fundamental question – Canadian listeners wanted *Canadian* broadcasting. The white
paper continued: "This strong mandate did not arise from any narrow
nationalism that sought to shut out the rest of the world or, more
appropriately, the rest of the continent, but rather from a clear
conviction that the destiny of Canada depended on our ability and

willingness to control and utilize our own internal communications for Canadian purposes."[4]

The House of Commons committee reviewing the white paper agreed that "in future, broadcasting may well be regarded as the central nervous system of Canadian nationhood." It asked that the new legislation recognize that airwaves are public property, and that broadcasters be assigned use of these on condition that they serve "the public interest as expressed through national policy." It also urged "a clear legislative declaration of the pre-eminence of the public sector," and a recognition that "the CBC is the principal agency for carrying out public policy through broadcasting."[5]

The Broadcasting Act of 1968 declared that all broadcasting undertakings, public and private, constituted a *single system*, and that "the Canadian broadcasting system should be effectively owned and controlled by Canadians so as to safeguard, enrich and strengthen the cultural, political, social and economic fabric of Canada." It stated also that "programming provided by each broadcaster should be of high standard, using predominantly Canadian creative and other resources," and that the national broadcasting service of the CBC should be "predominantly Canadian in content and character." A more disputed requirement was that the CBC's service should "contribute to the development of national unity and provide for a continuing expression of Canadian identity."[6]

With the new act proclaimed, much would depend on the vigour and conviction with which the CRTC sought to apply it.

THE CANADIAN RADIO-TELEVISION COMMISSION

Compared with its predecessors (the BBG, and before that the CBC) the CRTC in its first year showed amazing energy and strength of purpose. It served warning that it was going to watch the performance of stations more critically, and that it intended to prevent excessive concentration of ownership within the communications media in any one area. It refused to renew the licence of a small radio station in Nova Scotia because of its unsatisfactory programme performance; it required the Bassett and Eaton interests of Toronto (Glen Warren Productions, the *Telegram,* and CFTO) to sell their shares in one of the cable television companies serving the Toronto area; and, in extending the licence of radio station CHSJ, Saint John, for only one year, it implied that it was going to formulate a tough policy regarding concentration of ownership within the media serving a community. CHSJ is controlled by K.C. Irving, who also controls the Saint John television station and who is the owner of *all* English-language dailies in New Brunswick.

Two other cases tested the commission's (and the government's) intention regarding American ownership of Canadian broadcasting enterprises. The act of 1968 restated the general principle that "the Canadian broadcasting system should be effectively owned and con-trolled by Canadians," and an order in council issued in September 1968 (revised March 27, 1969) directed the CRTC to issue new licences only to Canadian citizens and "eligible Canadian corporations." Ex-isting licence-holders had until September 1, 1970, to conform to the Canadian-ownership requirements. Eligible Canadian corporations, it was said, must have Canadian directors, and four-fifths of the voting shares must be held by Canadians or by companies incorporated in Canada. To close loopholes in this last provision, the CRTC was given considerable latitude in deciding what was an "eligible Canadian corporation." The strictures applied not only to broadcasting stations (radio and TV) but to other undertakings requiring licences under the new act, including cable television companies.[7]

The first owner to be caught by these provisions was Famous Players, which sought to establish a new company, Teltron Com-munications Limited, in which Famous Players would hold less than 20 per cent of the voting stock but all the non-voting shares. Famous Players, which owned the largest chain of movie theatres in Canada, was in turn owned by two American corporations, Paramount Pic-tures and Gulf and Western Industries. Famous Players had additional interests in television and radio stations in Kitchener and Quebec City, and in cable TV systems in over thirty communities, including Toronto, Montreal, Ottawa, and Winnipeg. After inquiring into the implications of such ownership for Canada's "social, cultural and political development," the CRTC refused the application for the share transfers to Teltron, finding the terms relating to voting shares unsatisfactory. The chairman of the commission, Pierre Juneau, also noted that Famous Players over the years had used its theatres almost exclusively to show Hollywood films, and he expressed the fear that its cable TV system would be used similarly as a pipeline for American shows.[8] After the commission's rejection of its proposals, Famous Players prepared to divest itself of some of its broadcasting interests.

A Windsor radio station, CKLW, was next to feel the restrictive power of the commission. CKLW was owned entirely by a subsidiary of RKO-General Tire and Rubber of Akron, Ohio, which was also the owner of CKLW-TV and several American stations. The CRTC determined that 96 per cent of the radio station's programming consisted of popular recordings selected, for the most part, by American consultants. Sixty per cent of the advertising revenue was derived from Detroit, and two-thirds of the "public service announcements" were oriented to the United States. The station's request for an extension of time in meeting the Canadian ownership requirements was refused, and a similar decision was made for CKLW-TV. It is probable that the John Bassett interests in Toronto will buy the television station, if the CRTC allows it to schedule programmes from both CBC and CTV networks. Such an arrangement would increase the number of Canadian offerings in the Windsor area, but the departure from the ordinary terms of network affiliation may have to be weighed against this.*

It is, of course, necessary that Canadian stations be controlled by Canadians, but that is not a sufficient guarantee that the service they provide will be Canadian. Because of Canada's geographic position, its growing economic dependency on the United States, and methods used to finance and support private broadcasting enterprises on this continent, radio and television programming will largely be supplied from the United States. The American system, which Canada has adopted in part, assumes that programmes will be determined by owners and advertisers in the interests of advertising and the sale of consumer goods. These factors have a far stronger influence on programming than private ownership of newspapers has on their news content. Partly this is the difference between space and time. The newspaper reader can scan, or pick and choose, or ignore the advertisements if he wishes. In the American broadcasting system, advertising is an integral part of programming, and the broadcaster's aim is to get all the viewers all the time. The result, as numerous appraisers have found, is that programmes under the commercial system are bland, escapist, slick, entertaining, of and for the moment; catering

---

* In order to protect its programs and the interests of its advertisers, the CBC so far has not allowed its affiliates to receive direct service from another network. This was a factor in the dispute with the BBG over Grey Cup telecasts in 1962.

to the common denominator of popular tastes, intellectually timid
and uninventive, repetitive ... and essentially unrepresentative of the
national life and culture.

Parliament has said that Canadians should have a better service
than this. How have its agencies attempted to assure a more positive
result?

CANADIAN CONTENT*

The simplest factor that the regulatory authority can measure is the
"Canadian content" of the television service. The BBG established a
rule, which the CRTC has continued, that at least 55 per cent of all
broadcasting time (averaged over a thirteen-week period) on television stations must be reserved for programmes basically Canadian
in content and inspiration. There are no minima in "prime time," but
from 6 pm to midnight the Canadian content must be 40 per cent.

Although some special events outside Canada "of general interest
to Canadians" (such as the World Series) have been included gratui-
tously in the "Canadian content" category, the regulations in the
main have served a useful purpose. We can expect that at least a
modicum of programmes on each station and network will be Canadian, and that some of these will be scheduled in the evening hours.
The requirement, however, has not been extended to radio, with the
result that many stations serve an unending diet of popular music –
songs found to be in the "top forty" of American hits – interspersed
with advertising and snippets of news every hour on the hour.

What Canadian content regulations cannot measure is the quality
of the programmes offered, their variety or suitability to the needs
and interests of the audience. United States television also fails to
achieve such objectives. There is a sense in which any regulatory
body cannot ensure standards of performance, since creativity – and
conviction – must come from within. That is why the role of the CBC,
as the national programme service, is so crucial. Nevertheless, the
Fowler committee thought that something further could be done by
the licensing authority. It recommended the establishment of individual station standards of programme performance, which should be
made a condition of each station's licence and enforceable as such.
To allow this, a totally new section (s. 17) was placed in the 1968

* See note at end of paper.

Broadcasting Act. The CRTC has yet to apply such conditions. We will
know that it means business when it requires some of the larger and
more profitable stations (such as CFTO Toronto and CFCF-TV Montreal) to spend more money and effort on Canadian programming.

THE PRIVATE STATIONS AND CTV

Most people are not aware that in radio and television more money
is received by the private stations than by the CBC – about $20 million
more each year.* But far less is spent by the private stations in
original programming. Public consciousness of the CBC's expenditures
arises from its main source of revenue. The revenues of the private
stations are not so visible. In 1968 about 93 per cent of their
operating revenue came from advertising, paid for ultimately, of
course, by the consumer. The CBC received only 16 per cent of its
revenue from advertising; nearly all the rest was from government
grants. Taking television alone, the CBC does receive and spend more
than the private stations, because of the high costs of television
production. But we must remember that CBC programmes are provided not only to its own stations but to three-quarters of the sixty-
odd private TV stations in Canada.

For private owners, television is extremely profitable. There was
only a brief period when the stations showed an operating deficit. In
1968 their total operating profit was $17.5 million. The *average*
profit per television station in 1968 was over $250,000, and for the
sixteen largest stations the average profit was $942,000. Only the
smallest stations as a group showed a loss; fifteen such stations had
an average deficit of $3,000. The total profit of $17.5 million represents about one-sixth of total operating revenue ($100 million).[9]

Given the stated objectives of the Broadcasting Act, it is time that
the private stations be required to divert some of their profits into
original programming for their television audiences. In 1965 the
Fowler committee reported: "The private television stations used
much ingenuity to produce the few programs they did produce in
Canada at the cheapest possible price ... There are some notable

---

* In the fiscal year ending August 31, 1968, operating revenue for all
private stations, radio and TV, totalled $195 million, and for the CBC,
$175 million.

exceptions ... but for the rest the systematic mediocrity of programming is deplorable."[10] The situation has not changed noticeably.

Certainly CTV has not been the answer. From DBS figures we find
that all seventeen private stations in Ontario (including CFTO Toronto
and CJOH Ottawa – the two stations contributing principally to CTV
– plus CTV itself) spent only $1,100,000 in "artists' and other talent
fees" in 1968.* The booby prize for CTV affiliates must go to CHAN-
TV in Vancouver. All seven private TV stations in British Columbia,
including CHAN, spent exactly $4,446 on talent fees in 1967!

The result of this niggardly effort in Canadian production shows in
the programmes offered by CTV stations to their viewers in prime
time. In a typical week in the 1968-9 winter season, CFTO Toronto
had 5½ hours of Canadian programming between 7.30 pm and 11.00
pm – about 22 per cent of the total. 2½ of these "Canadian" hours
were devoted to hockey, 1½ to variety, and 1½ to public affairs. The
other 78 per cent was given over almost entirely to crime and private
eye programmes, variety, situation comedy, and feature films, nearly
all produced in the United States.

The Fowler committee looked at the habits of viewing in cities before and after the advent of private Canadian stations where the CBC
formerly had provided the only local service, and found a paradox:

In general, the addition of a private station has increased the viewing
of American programs ... It seems clear that the advent of private
television in Canada, instead of widening the scope of programs
(whether American or Canadian) available to Canadian viewers, has
merely increased the broadcasting of popular entertainment, mainly
of American origin ... Private stations import about twice as many
American programs as the CBC. This seems to be the most important
factor in the consumption of American programs by Canadians.[11]

This situation continues today, with two minor modifications. CTV
has slightly improved the quality of its Canadian offerings, particularly in news and public affairs. The other development, less happy,
results from the growing commercialization of the system, although
Fowler as a businessman was unprepared to admit that it would be
so. The Fowler committee recommended that the CBC vigorously

---

* This is considerably less than the amount spent by one private TV
station in Montreal (CFTM), broadcasting in French.

pursue its share of the total advertising revenues, setting as a target 25 per cent of the television market.[12] This was regarded as the CBC's share at that time (1964-5), but to maintain that percentage as more TV stations were licensed would in fact mean hotter commercial competition in the years to come. The government has gladly gone along with this expectation. So it happens that the CBC, in an effort to increase its revenues and to please its affiliates, has stepped up the American content of its schedules in prime time. Its 1968-9 evening schedule was more American than ever, with its best hours given over to "Green Acres," "The Mothers-in-Law," "Bonanza," and "Mission: Impossible."

The CRTC should be more demanding of CTV and its eleven affiliates which, situated in the principal cities of Canada, are the favoured outlets for national advertisers. For reasons of prestige, CTV may try to increase its coverage to approximate that of CBC and its affiliates.* The CRTC should not allow this costly expansion but should ensure that CTV's profits are used in production, to carry out the obligation Parliament has placed on these stations to "strengthen the cultural, political, social and economic fabric of Canada." And the government must not bow to commercial interests, or allow their backbenchers to be panicked by the private stations in their constituencies, as has happened on numerous occasions in the past.

THE CBC

It is the CBC's special responsibility to provide a "national broadcasting service that is predominantly Canadian in content and character." The Broadcasting Act of 1968 attempts to ensure that a measure of priority will be accorded the CBC by this general provision: "Where any conflict arises between the objectives of the national broadcasting service and the interests of the private element of the Canadian broadcasting system, it shall be resolved in the public interest but paramount consideration shall be given to the objectives of the national broadcasting service." The first draft of the act, Bill C-163,

* The English TV network of the CBC reaches 95 per cent of the English-speaking population of Canada (34 per cent through its private affiliates). The CTV network's potential is about 77 per cent of this population.

had been more specific: "Where any conflict arises between the objectives of the national broadcasting service and the interests of the private element of the Canadian broadcasting system, the objectives of the national broadcasting service [the CBC] must prevail." The changed wording was suggested by a Progressive Conservative MP, Robert McCleave, to overcome objections by other Conservatives (such as Bud Sherman, a private broadcaster from Winnipeg) that the public interest and the interests of the CBC might not always coincide.

The CBC television service reaches the public not only through its own stations (ten in English, five in French), but through some forty private affiliates. Not all of the Canadian programming in prime time on CBC-owned stations is carried by the affiliates, since a few of the programmes are local and some others are not in so-called option time – that is, time reserved for the network service on all stations. English-TV affiliates carry about 50 per cent of the network service, and French-TV affiliates carry about 80 per cent of the service available. In both cases, the inducement is the popularity of network programmes with local audiences, and also the share of commercial revenue accruing to the station from programmes that carry advertising. There is also an element of compulsion: if the area is not covered by the CBC or by another CBC network affiliate, the station receives its licence only on condition that it secure such affiliation.

In a typical week in the 1968-9 winter season, the CBC's Toronto station, CBLT, had ten hours of Canadian programming during the week between 7.30 and 11.00 pm – about 40 per cent of the total. The variety of Canadian programming was somewhat better than in the CTV evening schedule: 2½ hours of hockey, 3½ of variety, and 4 of public affairs, science programmes, and a current events quiz programme, "Front Page Challenge." But not all of the public affairs programmes were carried by the affiliates, and United States "specials" were carried frequently in certain periods normally allocated to Canadian productions. The CBC variety department is a shadow of its former self, and dramatic productions, on tape or on film, also are in decline. The reasons usually given for this are the increasingly high costs of production; the competition of popular programmes available much more cheaply from the United States; their greater attraction to advertisers for sponsorship or commercial "participation" by a group of advertisers; and the preferences of the affiliates for filmed or other programmes which are given American or "international" promotion.

But there are other reasons for the decline of the CBC English television service that are not so frequently discussed. First, the growing
number of television outlets has resulted in the fragmentation of
advertising revenues, leaving proportionally less for the CBC. Second,
some of the best production and performing talent that developed in
the early days of television in Toronto and Vancouver has gradually
disappeared – much of it going south – and the echelon of managers,
now middle-aged and tired, has not discovered and trained new talent
to replace the old. Then there has been the effect of the interminable
battles that have occurred within and around the CBC. Some of these
exhausting disputes arose from the uncertainties of the Broadcasting
Act of 1958; some of them were related to Parliament's irresponsible
behaviour in an atmosphere conditioned by private interests reaching
for new spoils; some of them were induced by weaknesses in CBC top
management. It appears that too much has been spent on production
facilities across the country (leading to continuing commitments in
staff, maintenance, and interest payments on capital advances), on
extension of service to areas that are costly to reach (at least through
public facilities), and on an inflated administrative apparatus.* Finally,
not only some production personnel but, more important, English-TV
network executives evidently have been persuaded by the commercial
competition, and particularly by the United States networks, that the
commercial model is the natural one for television; that every whim
of television production in the United States must be followed and
imitated; that ratings are the name of the game; that the revenue

* CBC accounting methods do not enable one to judge with any accuracy how much money truly is spent on programming. The 1968-9
annual report shows that the television programme service cost $98
million, compared with $18 million for network distribution and
station transmission. But the programme costs are cost-accounted
in such a way that they incorporate all sorts of "indirect" costs –
for example, the costs of administrative and other personnel only
dimly related to the production of particular programmes. The CBC's
desire to have a "presence" in each province and region has resulted
in establishments that could hardly be justified in any rationalized
system of programme production. The former CBC president was a
notable exponent of CBC self-sufficiency, and the programme towards that end may have gone forward too fast, weakening the
national claim on private-station affiliates.

from advertising is much more important, dollar for dollar, than the funds provided directly by the public through Parliament. All these influences have led to a schedule (and I am speaking only of English-language television) that is becoming more and more indistinguishable from that of ABC or CTV; the differences are in degree. Even some of the original Canadian programming finds itself caught up more intensely with American rather than Canadian subjects – American entertainers, American social problems such as race relations, or American poverty, if you please.

Still, the hunger for Canadian themes exists, and its manifestations surprise even those doing survey research. It is, of course, undeniable that the majority of "top-rated" programmes, on CBC and on CTV, are American in origin. But that does not say that many of the same people will not watch Canadian productions with interest if they are compellingly done. The major public affairs series attract nearly two million viewers if they are scheduled in option time; the afternoon programme "Take 30" is near the top of the "appreciation index"; and specials such as the national political conventions attract enormous audiences. The filmed dramatic series, "Quentin Durgens, MP," had an audience of over two million each week.

We need not expect Canadian television to do all the kinds of programmes it once did, because television has changed and, more important, Canada has changed. This country sustains much more activity in the arts on a community basis than was true ten or fifteen years ago – theatre, concerts, galleries and museums, and recreational programmes of other kinds. At one time CBC radio and television were all we had, and undoubtedly they played a part in stimulating and maintaining an audience for such institutions as the Stratford Festival, the large symphony orchestras, opera and ballet, the Manitoba Theatre Centre, and Le Théatre du Nouveau Monde. Now other public agencies have taken over this function at least partially – the Canada Council, the provincial arts councils, the National Arts Centre, and so forth. The CBC must now find a new role in co-ordinating its activities with such community enterprises, becoming more active in the newer fields of science, technology, urban development, and further education attuned to the post-industrial society. The CBC, in one of the less pleasant consequences of professionalization within the media (relying on professional performers and its own staff to develop and execute programmes), has severed many of its ties with the articulate members of the Canadian society it is supposed to serve. In general, they are no longer involved in network programming. Without retracing old steps, the CBC must re-establish its connections with the community or much of its public support will collapse, as it has shown signs of doing. And this means a renewal of faith in the things it can accomplish as a *Canadian* enterprise: not seeking to blot out influences from the outside, but helping Canadians to see them in relation to their own experiences.

With the government attempting to slow down inflation and cut public spending, the CBC is not likely to receive increased revenues at the rate it enjoyed in the past five years. Indeed, the Treasury Board is reported to have suggested that the CBC's operational revenues be held constant for five years beginning in 1969-70. This in fact would mean a very drastic cut, because of the built-in escalation in union contracts and so forth, together with the decreasing value of money. The CBC will be pressed to increase its share of commercial revenues by offering its news and public affairs programmes for "participation" spots, and by making its radio service as commercial as its television. These are self-defeating moves, for unless the CBC offers an image that is demonstrably different from that of private television and the American networks (and clearly oriented toward public service), public support for the CBC will retreat and eventually vanish.

US STATIONS AND CABLE TELEVISION

American programmes are seen in Canada *mainly* through their transmission by CBC, CTV, and Canadian private stations. But half the population has direct access to stations in the United States, and that proportion will increase with the rapidly expanding systems of cable television. There are approximately twenty-three US television stations lined along the border, some of them clearly placed strategically to bombard Canadians with American programmes. According to surveys by the Bureau of Broadcast Measurement in 1968, total Canadian viewing was distributed as follows:

	per cent
American stations	17
CBC English network and affiliates	35
CTV stations	19

per cent

Independent stations
(e.g., CFTM Montreal and CHCH Hamilton)   15
CBC French network and affiliates   14

Programmes from stations in the first category were practically 100 per cent American. And given the preponderance of American programmes in the next two categories (CTV and CBC English), especially in prime time, it is clear that most viewing hours were filled with American programme information.

The most dynamic element in the current situation is cable television (or Community Antenna Television – CATV). Essentially, cable systems furnish better reception and make available more programme choices. Undoubtedly the main impetus to their development has been the desire to receive American programmes with greater clarity than the average roof-top antenna can provide. But with the transfer of licensing jurisdiction from the Department of Transport to the CRTC, an attempt is being made to integrate cable into the whole broadcasting system. As noted previously, there is new emphasis on Canadian ownership, and on preventing too great a concentration of ownership in any one locality among all the communication media. Moreover the CRTC is encouraging cable systems to provide some programming of their own, and it is requiring them to carry Canadian television programmes as a matter of priority.

The CATV systems are now required to carry television programme services in the following order of precedence: (1) CBC French and English networks; (2) private Canadian networks; (3) independent Canadian TV stations; (4) local and educational programming; (5) non-Canadian television stations. If a system carries FM stations, it should carry all available Canadian FM stations as a priority.[13]

In encouraging the cable systems to initiate some programmes of their own, the CRTC has said: "CATV can assist in the development of a community identity through locally produced programs; they can also assist provincial and local authorities in the development of educational services [and] ... through the distribution of Canadian produced films, educational information, and other films of particular interest ... not normally available in that area." The president of the Canadian Cable Television Association told the press that in the future most cable systems will be telecasting their own news, weather, and educational programmes. He said that the cable operators could be more daring than commercial TV stations "because our programs will not be tied to popularity in the ratings."[14] Technically, cable can provide much more programme choice. But given the commercial development of CATV, and the overlapping of ownership with the private stations, it is doubtful whether greatly increased choice will materialize.

The television broadcasters who are not involved in cable companies look on this development with some misgivings, fearing that their audiences will dwindle as more programme services are provided by the cable companies. Their chief protection is the CRTC's statement that "at present" the commission will not license CATV undertakings that carry commercials other than those received in broadcast programmes. But how long will this restriction last? As the cable companies become more powerful and capture an increased share of the viewing by television homes, they will press for permission to sell their own commercials, arguing that additional revenues are necessary to sustain the programming they have begun. Private radio stations in the past made similar representations before Parliament and the governing board; their success is marked not only by the commanding position won by these stations in Canadian radio, but by the virtual freedom they enjoy from any effective regulation. The CRTC should be forewarned.

In any case, the public soon will be spending large sums to buy cable services. About 15 per cent of television households now have cable connections; in some areas, such as London, the percentage is as high as seventy. To protect television broadcasters whose enterprises are a bit precarious, the CRTC has refused to license some regions of the country. Even so, the number of systems is expanding rapidly. In a few years' time, half of the five million television households may have cable connections; if each household pays a fee of $5 a month, the gross revenues will be in the order of $150 million a year – as much as the parliamentary grant to the CBC in the fiscal year 1968-9. (In 1968 the total operating revenue for the CATV industry was reported as $31 million, and profit appeared to be about $5 million.) It is hard to argue that Canadians cannot afford the amounts now spent on Canadian programming when they are willing to spend so much on an often marginal increase in the variety of programme service.

Another possibility for the future is that large American interests

– networks, electronics companies, periodical and book publishers
(already companies in these fields are arranging mergers) – will provide programmes by film and tape which can be transmitted through
cable more cheaply than Canadian or local programming can be
produced. An FCC commissioner expressed an opinion to the author
that cable might not provide any more choice than the average
community now has; that big companies will find ways to dominate
viewing habits as they now do under the system of network delivery;
and that the precedents of radio broadcasting show that a multiplicity
of channels does not often result in an increase of real programme
choice, because of the follow-the-leader syndrome.

  Canadian networks would do well to anticipate the delivery of
programmes by means other than through-the-air transmission. In
particular, they should be preparing banks of programmes that can be
distributed by cable or otherwise to supplement the on-air network
services. Without such planning there will be no adequate Canadian
supplement to the influx of American packaged programmes, "educational" or otherwise. A new look should be taken at methods for
CBC-National Film Board co-operation; and educational institutions
should develop production or co-production arrangements with cable
companies serving the same areas. Under the CRTC policy, the cable
systems are at present licensed for two-year periods, and it may be
to their distinct advantage, when their licences are up for renewal, to
have initiated such programming.

AMERICANIZATION THROUGH THE MEDIA

The *quantity* of American programmes viewed in Canadian homes,
week in and week out, is fairly evident. It is harder to measure the
impact of such programmes. Given the present concentration of
United States media in the same hands,[15] we can reasonably assume
that the messages we receive from American films, magazines, news
reports, television and radio broadcasts tend to reinforce one another.
With 75 per cent of all Canadian sales, American magazines are clearly
predominant, as are American books in English-speaking Canada.
And the news sources for Canadian television, radio, and newspapers
are in large part American. Without presuming that there is any
conspiracy to present a uniform or homogenized pattern of information or message-symbols, one can at least infer that American media

will reflect their own national concerns and national interests; and that these will not always coincide with Canadian needs and interests.

Edwin R. Black, now director of research for the Progressive Conservative party of Canada, has deprecated the faith that has been placed in the nationality of ownership as an important determinant of the media's content, and he cites the marked similarities between private radio stations on both sides of the border as evidence that such faith is misplaced.[16] Under existing conditions his point is well taken, in so far as Canadians learn to share essentially American value systems, and in particular the myth that the real function of the media is to sell goods and that programmes are essentially a give-away in the marketing process.[17] If these are our values, we may as well surrender to the "private government" of the big corporations and forget about irrelevant political accidents like the Canada-US boundary. The real decisions will then be made in the boardrooms of corporate enterprise, and not in the capitals of our nation or of the provinces.

But these were not the ideas on which Canada was founded, and a Conservative like Mr Black should be aware of this. There have been discernible differences in the values customarily held by Americans and Canadians. We have seen these in the ways the two peoples respond to emergencies, in our differing attitudes to government and the public service, in the use of public enterprise and the intervention of the state even in cultural matters, and in our differing notions of community. The media may have blurred these and other distinctions, but they have not yet erased them.

Mr Black admits that the maintenance of political independence will depend on the "self-identification of her citizens," but denies that this will require "major distinctiveness in life styles." I am not quite clear what is encompassed by "life styles," but would argue that the viability of the Canadian political system will depend on our developing some common values among citizens of the two principal linguistic communities, and that at the very least such development will call for greater interchange of communication between those communities. These purposes can never be served by American media, or by Canadian media in a flat-out race to imitate the American model in selling the most goods.

The CBC has failed by not coming to grips with this central question of our national existence; and in spite of pious pronouncements by successive presidents, the corporation has given up even trying to maintain the dialogue between English- and French-speaking Canadians. The principal reason for this, in television at any rate, is to be found in its commercial preoccupations. We have been told recently that the CBC is going to revise its traditional policy of rejecting sponsorship or commercial "participation" in informational categories of programmes such as news and public affairs and a start has been made in selling spots in programmes covering special events and in documentaries. Presumably it is thought we should accept as commonplace documentaries that will be interrupted by commercials for a dozen products, as Robert Lewis Shayon recounts in connection with an NBC programme on Vietnam: in half an hour it was sprinkled with commercials for the sale of Peter Pan Peanut Butter, S & H Green Stamps, Geritol tonic with iron in it, Sominex pills for sleep, Johnson's foot soap for tired, aching feet, Lanacane for any itching problem, and Oceanspray Cranberry Juice Cocktail.[18] Up to the present, I have always been persuaded by the arguments that a dose of commercials was the price we had to pay for national programme distribution. The CBC says that in selling more commercials it is in effect buying time in which to present a few more Canadian productions during the evening hours. But if it is doing this at the expense of imitating the American system *in toto,* then I say the price is too high. It would be better to have an exclusively non-commercial CBC service, and if necessary pay the affiliates to carry part of it.

Our mass media, like our other institutions, exist to help us make the right choices and decisions. If the choices are reduced to those that serve the interests of large North American corporations, as the whole tenor of our entertainment programming would suggest, we may as well curl up and attach ourselves to the American marsupial pouch. As John Diefenbaker would say, that was not Macdonald's idea, that was not Cartier's idea, that was not Laurier's idea. Nor is it ours.

EDITOR'S NOTE Since the first printing of this book, the CRTC has revised its Canadian-content regulations for television. By October 1, 1971, the broadcasts by private stations in the evening must use at least 50 per cent, and by October 1, 1972, at least 60 per cent, Canadian content. The CBC is required to attain the 60 per cent level by October 1, 1970. A maximum of 30 per cent of programming can come from any one country by October 1972. Furthermore 30 per cent of the music broadcast on AM radio is to be written, composed, performed, or recorded in Canada.

NOTES

1 *Toronto Daily Star,* May 2, 1968.
2 Quoted by Mavor Moore, "America Leads and Canada (alas) Follows," *Toronto Daily Star,* Sept. 14, 1968.
3 *Report of the Committee on Broadcasting* (Ottawa, 1965), p. 63.
4 Canada, Secretary of State, *White Paper on Broadcasting, 1966* (Ottawa, 1966), p. 5.
5 1966-7 Standing Committee on Broadcasting, Films, and Assistance to the Arts, *Proceedings* no. 42 (March 21, 1967), pp. 2088-90, 2097.
6 Statutes of Canada, 1967-68, c. 25, s. 2.
7 CRTC public announcement, "Community Antenna Television," May 13, 1969.
8 See the *Toronto Daily Star*'s editorial, "Famous Players and a Vigorous CRTC," April 21, 1969.
9 Figures approximated from the Dominion Bureau of Statistics, *Radio and Television Broadcasting, 1968* (Ottawa, Oct. 1969).
10 *Report of the Committee on Broadcasting,* p. 30.
11 *Ibid.,* pp. 34-5.
12 *Ibid.,* p. 225.
13 CRTC announcement, May 13, 1969.
14 "Cable TV Operators Find a New Role," *Globe and Mail,* Toronto, July 23, 1969.
15 See "The American Media Baronies," *Atlantic Monthly,* July 1969, pp. 83-94.
16 "Canadian Public Policy and the Mass Media," *Canadian Journal of Economics,* May 1968.
17 See Dallas Smythe, "Five Myths of Consumership," *The Nation,* Jan. 20, 1969.
18 *Saturday Review,* June 7, 1969.

Gail Dexter

The former art critic of the *Toronto Daily Star*. She is now a free-lance writer and broadcaster.

Yes, cultural imperialism too!

Today, almost twenty years after its completion, the Massey Commission Report[1] still stands as one of the sternist warnings to Canadians about the danger of the Americanization of our culture. The commissioners perceived this danger as both real and imminent, so they wrote a cultural report in which military analogies set the mood:

On this continent, as we have observed, our population stretches in a narrow and not even continuous ribbon along our frontier – fourteen millions along a five thousand mile front. In meeting influences from across the border, as pervasive as they are friendly, we have not even the advantages of what soldiers call defense in depth ...

Our military defenses must be made secure; but our cultural defenses equally demand attention.

One remarkable aspect of the report is that, while it detailed the dangers of American cultural imperialism (to use a term beyond the political horizons of the commissioners), to our broadcasting, scholarship, and publishing, it did not recognize the danger to our plastic arts. Indeed, the commissioners wrote of the Canadian spirit manifest in the new abstract art of the 1940s: "Canadian painting no longer seeks to express itself through the Canadian landscape but for all that, it is maintained, it is nonetheless Canadian." Despite the facts that these new schools of abstract art, making their first appearances in Montreal, Toronto, and Winnipeg, represented a radical departure from the accepted romantic naturalism of the Group of Seven and that they were heavily influenced by European and American painting, and despite the fact that this new art told Canadians nothing of their traditions, politics, or aspirations, the commission accepted with a certain degree of pride an interpretation of Canadian abstract art as the manifestation of the Canadian spirit. And the comparatively careless attitude of the commission towards abstract painting cannot be attributed – as perhaps we would today – to the marginality of the plastic arts. On the contrary, the report notes time and time again the pre-eminence of painting among the country's arts:

Canada's reputation in the arts, both at home and abroad, is based mainly on her painting. All those who came before us recognized the importance of Canadian painting both as an art and as an expression of Canadianism ...

Painting, then, is generally regarded as the most advanced and at the same time as the most immediately communicable expression of the spirit of Canada.

The most obvious reason for the pre-eminent position of painting at that time was the relative renown in the European capitals of certain Canadian painters like James Wilson Morrice and Alfred Pellan. But a more substantive explanation is to be found in the commission's very concept of culture. It is a defensive concept, particularly characteristic of the ruling class in a semi-dependent country. The anti-American stance of the commissioners was not a political position. It derived from their valuation of American culture as commercialized and vulgar. Their exhortations that Canadians in broadcasting, publishing, and scholarship develop "Canadian" traditions carried the implicit assumption that these traditions were firmly planted in the aristocratic British and European past. Whereas the United States had developed a mass culture based on the imperatives of buying and selling commodities through advertising, Canadians should simply popularize ruling-class European culture – the rightful heritage of Canada's colonial élite. In promoting "Canadian" culture the commissioners were, in great part, defending their own cultural interests against the American intrusion.

Since at the time of the Massey Commission the plastic arts were hardly touched by this commercialism; they could be perceived as free from the vulgar influence of the United States. Painting, the most aristocratic of the arts, could emerge – no matter how abstract or downright meaningless it might appear – as the true repository of the Canadian spirit. This bourgeois notion of art as the objectification of some transcendent spiritual value divorced from content, style, and political consciousness has been linked to the naïve assumption that paintings painted in Canada will be "Canadian." The result of this idealism is that today, twenty years after the Massey report, Canadian painting is completely absorbed into mainstream American art – an imperial art which, as I hope to show, has much more than spiritual meaning.

The common response to this statement is neither anger nor disbelief. Artists and scholars tell me that art knows no nationality, that art is international in spirit. And perhaps their pronouncements articulate the measure to which the Group of Seven[2] failed to develop a national style by thrusting the Canadian landscape before the public eye. Through their hard struggles to gain recognition as Canadian painters, the Group succeeded in creating a national cultural consciousness. But the style they created, a mystical naturalism, became a burden to younger generations of painters who regarded the Group with some justification as parochial and backward-looking.

To the young artist working in Canada's urban centres today the problem of style is all-important. For when he reads the learned studies of bourgeois art historians and studies the glossy pictures in international art journals, it quickly becomes clear that the history of western art is the history of changing styles – a history that has been greatly "speeded up" in the twentieth century. It also becomes clear that the so-called great artists of our time have achieved success not by developing what was once called a personal style (as in the handling of landscape or figure conventions, say) but by innovating "new" styles. Quite understandably the young artist then attempts to gain recognition by making his contribution to the history of style.

Generally speaking, style is the way in which an artist or group of artists make visible, or represent, their reality. But style, if it is to be understood, must be seen as a *system* of representation; as a system, style can be reduced to definable patterns which can be reproduced and copied. It is through the reproduction and copying of this system that style is transmitted from one medium to another: from teacher to pupil, from magazine to studio, and from country to country. The more simple the system of representation, the more easily it can be analysed and explained, the more quickly can it be transmitted. Because the very process of mastering an art involves both copying and reproduction, the artist finds himself almost automatically participating in the endless elaboration of an existing style. The common expression "art is made of and about art" describes the practical situation of the artist.

There is one way out of this seemingly endless cycle. The artist might analyse the dominant styles of his time, find them bankrupt and worthless, and set about to make art on a completely new basis. There are many factors that militate against an artist taking this road in capitalist society. And, in a dependent capitalist country like Canada, it is all the more unlikely that a group of artists would take the path that would lead to the development of a national style.

The process of elaborating existing styles is largely unconscious. The creative process is so mystified by false purposes and phony definitions that the artist believes (as the rest of us believe in pursuing our own work) that he is freely expressing himself and solving important technical and aesthetic problems. Since capitalist society defines artistic work as value-free and non-political, the artist rarely

questions the assumptions of the technical and aesthetic problems he
inherits – let alone their relevance and meaning in the real world.
Ever since modernist painting solved the old conundrum of form
versus content by proclaiming the unity of the two and virtually
abolishing content, it has become increasingly difficult for anyone
(even the critics most anxious to point out that the emperor is
wearing no clothes) to see that art is political in so far as it serves
both economic and ideological functions.

As long as the Canadian economy is dominated by the United
States, Canadian culture will be submerged and Canadian painting will
bear the hallmark of the imperial style. This is surely not surprising
when most of the great international styles of western culture have
been the adaptation by European countries of the style innovated for
the use of the ruling class in the most powerful cultural metropolis.
What is perhaps remarkable about Canada's case is the singular lack
of national adaptation* and the recent lack of interest in the development of an art that will be meaningful to the Canadian people.

As long as Canadians define their artists as harmless if somewhat
irresponsible dependants of the nation's surplus, as men whose productivity is so marginal that they are permitted to live according to
the vicissitudes of the art market, our artists will never develop the
political consciousness necessary to struggle against the prevailing
stylistic tendencies. As long as our artists must compete in an art
market and art world dominated by US interests, they can do no
more than compete according to the standards established by the
Americans. When Terry Fenton, a Canadian art critic and assistant
director of the Norman Mackenzie Gallery in Regina, wrote in a
powerful American art magazine that Canadian art must be provincial
where it fails to match the achievements of the best art shown in New

---

* This point was most forcibly brought home to me early in October
1969 at the opening of a group show by five young Toronto artists
at Hart House. The exhibition was identical, stylistically, to one of
December 1968 held at a private gallery in Toronto and called "New
York Now." The artists I met seemed unconscious of the extent of
the American influence – yet it was as though they had picked up all
the mannerisms (the stripes, the free-form unstretched canvases, the
pastel colours) of the New York group.

York,* he was stating the political economy of Canadian art. As long as New York remains the world's art centre and we continue to accept its abstract and meaningless standards as criteria of artistic value ... Canadian art will remain provincial.

Recognizing this situation, ambitious Canadian artists eagerly pore over each new issue of the American art magazines, seeking out reproductions that will give them the key to mainstream styles. Many travel to New York to see the originals. Others go to the United States to live and study, often with the help of Canada Council grants.† It seems pointless to them to continue being provincial when they can go to the heart of the empire and the heart of the action.

What is happening in the heart of the empire today should give those of us who believe that art activity is central to human liberation some cause for concern. I would suggest that the often lauded achievements of New York art all point in the same direction: towards replacing aesthetic values by style values and thereby making art a more palatable commodity and propaganda tool within the structure of American capitalism. The so-called "revolutions" in style

* Terry Fenton, "Looking at Canadian Art," *Artforum,* September 1968. A further example from his article will emphasize the gravity of this situation. "In this latter sense, [Art] McKay and [Jack] Bush have certainly produced the most important works of art in Canada during the sixties. That they did so only after having radically redirected their art following contact with Americans from New York serves to confirm rather than deny the issue of provincialism as a problem facing the artistic imagination."

† Some of our talented artists who have taken this road are not particularly known for their progressive political views. Joyce Weiland, painter and filmmaker living in New York, is an avid Trudeau supporter. And Canada's prize-winning representative at Brazil's São Paulo Biennial, Robert Murray, a sculptor who has been living in New York for the past ten years, had this to say to a *Globe and Mail* reporter (October 27) about the various boycotts of the show: "Well, I refuse to take a political stand. I think it's a very bad situation if art is driven underground by the closing of a show ... Anyway, the military government doesn't run the São Paulo show. It's put on by an extremely wealthy man, a Senor Matarezzo. He's a kind of Rockefeller of South America."

that have marked recent decades of American painting have also caused the rapid extension of the American art market.

One technical innovation that has greatly contributed to this expansion is the production of the largest portable paintings in the history of art. These paintings are made by soaking paint into raw canvas which means that the canvas may be taken off its stretcher and rolled up for easy portability and storage. The style associated with this innovation – a style which has won ready acceptance in Canada* – is called post-painterly abstraction and it consists of stripes or romantic patterns of delicate spray colour paint on huge surfaces. These paintings have recently "grown" too large for the average middle-class home but they are the ideal decoration for office buildings and mammoth art emporiums being built by state and municipal governments. These paintings are priced by the running foot and have lead to the recent critical formulation that "scale" or size is a major criterion of quality – that is, the replacement of qualitative by quantitative values.

The fact that style has become an end in itself has also been a powerful force in the expansion of the "international" art market. The New York art season is short and fast, evolving at least one new style each year with a dozen "major" practitioners and the consequent rediscovery of a previously unheralded "old master" whose work must also be bought and preserved. Styles of five years previously become incredibly inflated in their value, making their acquisition by second-string collectors and provincial museums impossible. This spiralling inflation produces a pressure on collectors and small museums to buy styles while they are young and cheap ...

* Canadian painter Jack Bush fits into this school as do most of the five young painters at Hart House. So does Toronto painter Paul Fournier whose October exhibition was a sell-out and judged by the Toronto *Telegram*'s art critic as the most important of 1969. This school of art was given a prime position in the Metropolitan Museum's centenary exhibition, "New York Painting and Sculpture, 1940-1970." This exhibition was sponsored by $150,000 from the Xerox Corporation. It prompted the *Globe and Mail*'s art critic to remark (October 25, 1969), that David Mirvish, the young Toronto collector and gallery owner who has been exhibiting this art for the past four years, is Canada's most "astute" collector.

thus encouraging artists to produce something new and stylistically distinctive each year.* Style begets style. Each style is called a "revolution in perception." Each style promises to end the cycle by negating art itself. But art objects continue to be produced; collectors continue to collect; and museums, ever convinced of the social value of middle-class art, build new additions to house the burgeoning number of styles. These art styles have become commodities with attendant use value in the subtle and ever-changing visual world of advertising, television, and film. The styles innovated to feed the New York market and to inspire the American advertising propaganda machine would influence Canada anyway through the media were it not for the fact that our artists are forced to ape them.†

The vast scale of American painting and the huge projects envisioned by American artists as well as the increased technical know-how required to execute these projects means that artists are becoming more closely tied to corporate America. Only large corporations (or large museums on which directors of large corporations have great influence through various boards) can buy works, sponsor projects, and provide the technical aid artists are demanding. There is no reason to believe that artists have the controlling hand in their new partnership with industry.

An organization like Experiments in Art and Technology (EAT) is funded by industry in order to promote the collaboration of artists with technicians in the production of art works. A new art movement like "conceptual art"‖ (artists carry out projects like drawing mile-

* Re the style speed-up, count 'em – abstract expressionism, pop, op, post painterly abstraction, minimal, sytemic, earthworks, new realism, conceptual; and this list does not include subtler variations or general categories.

† American advertising in Canada not only encourages us to buy certain products but also makes the American world of dream commodities seem both easily accessible and desirable. To be effective, advertising must be visually stimulating; thus it borrows heavily from avant-garde artistic trends. American advertising is all the more effective in Canada because both our "high" and avant-garde cultures are identical with the American.

‖ An amusing example of the "national adaptation" of this new style is found in this capsule review in *Art News,* April 1969: "Richard

sized pictures on the surface of the Mojave Desert) has freed the artist from the necessity of selling his art as a commodity only to tie him firmly to large-scale sponsorship. The cost of materials for some larger projects also encourages dependence on industry.* The day is not far off when artists will be fully integrated into corporate America: creating art for advertising purposes, performing for quiz-gag shows, and testing new materials for industry. Art is no longer being produced in the interests of liberation but in the interests of domination and pacification.

There is a real sense in which this American art, to which our artists are bound in cultural servitude, can be seen as propaganda. For what kind of consciousness does it produce? The "revolutions in perception" that have surfaced in the art of the past decade – the art of stripes, of stripped-down objects to which people are expected to react as they would to a scene of industrial waste, the mammoth concepts that loom impressive for a day – have formal and aesthetic value only to that class of people which profits from the mystification of life experience: to that class of people which equates a marginal artistic licence with human freedom; to that class of people for which real life struggles for liberation are either irrelevant or dangerous. The art of the imperialist bourgeoisie therefore presents unity where real life presents class struggle; monumentality to hide the fact that their decadent institutions are cracking; and a dazzling succession of styles so simplistic that they can be copied by artists throughout the world who are bribed by false hopes for wealth and immortality in the American art market. There is little difference, except in sophistica-

---

Long is a talented 23-year old Englishman who showed photo-documents of some of his work since 1963 ... One piece consisted of inscribing an X in a meadow by snipping off the heads of flowers ... The new earth art is obviously not limited to US homegrown examples nor to bravado exploits; Long's work is gentle, *very English* and very good." (emphasis added)

* For student radicals who have not had time to look into the funding of fine art departments: "The art department of Southern Illinois University is being assisted by three large corporations: Inland Steel and Alcoa Aluminum are donating materials for the use of sculpture students and a boxcarful of Styrofoam is being presented by the Dow Chemical Company." *Art News,* October 1968.

tion, between recent American and British, Australian, Brazilian, and Canadian art.*

Questions of aesthetics in the age of imperialism are questions of politics. To take a non-political view of American art is to be dominated by it. Canadians are no longer in the happy position described twenty years ago in the Massey report when we had the choice for or against a national culture. English-speaking Canadians in particular face a situation in which our culture, especially painting, is completely submerged. It is important to understand American art because it is an imperialist art. And Canadian art, like Canadian industry, is no more than a branch plant of the American. Because American art is imperialist, Canadian art, if it is to evolve a national style, must be overtly anti-imperialist. In other words, it is my firm belief that the creation of a Canadian style of painting is nothing less than a political act.

What the new art will look like I do not know. Whether it will be representational, abstract, or environmental is up to the artists who will carry on the political struggle to create a subversive and truly living art. This is no small task. It means destroying an art that is propaganda for the American ruling class and replacing it with an art that is meaningful and functional for the Canadian people. This means that our artists must know Canada and all classes of Canadians. Then, and only then, will what our artists have to say (no matter how they may wish to say it) be relevant.

This process has already begun for a few artists in London, Ontario, who have tried to cut themselves off from American influences and locate themselves firmly in their region of the country. Their art speaks with a rare freshness and vigour and it has been encouraged by the National Gallery of Canada through purchases and exhibitions. But some of these artists reject a political perspective and for that reason they are always in danger of failing to accomplish the task they have set of creating a living regionalism. As more of our artists join those in London by identifying not with the metropolitan bourgeoisie but with the people where they work ... we will begin to see the emergence of Canadian art.

* Space does not permit me to describe the activities of artists, both in the United States and without, to change the art system. Some are forming Art Workers Unions, others are attacking public museums, and still others have given up the traditional artists role in order to use their creative abilities in radical political work.

NOTES

1 Report of the Royal Commission on National Development in the
   Arts, Letters, & Sciences, 1949-51 (Ottawa, 1951).
2 The actual achievements of the Group of Seven will be greatly clarified by the National Gallery of Canada retrospective exhibition to
   be mounted in Ottawa, June-Sept. 1970.

James Steele and Robin Mathews

Members of the English Department at Carleton University. Last year they edited *The Struggle For Canadian Universities: a Dossier,* which brings together letters and documents about the de-Canadianization of Canadian universities.

The universities: takeover of the mind

Foreign scholars are always welcome in Canadian universities. Nevertheless, it is a matter of concern that in recent years the proportion of Canadians on academic faculties has been diminishing rapidly. In 1963 approximately 539 university teachers immigrated to Canada; in 1965, 1,048 entered the country; by 1967 the annual number rose to 1,986, a figure which represented some 12 per cent of the total number of university teachers in Canada that year.* Of these, some 857 came from the United States, 457 from Great Britain, 100 from India, and the remainder from other countries. In 1968 Canadian universities employed about 2,642 additional faculty.† Of that number the vast majority were non-Canadians; 1,013 entered from the United States, 545 from Great Britain, and 722 from other countries. Thus it appears that only about 362 Canadians have been hired. Statistics describing precisely the cumulative effect of this influx on the citizenship composition of each and every Canadian university faculty do not exist. Nevertheless, certain related information may be considered roughly indicative of what has happened.

An analysis of 1961 census data has shown that of Canada's 8,779 male university professors, 2,238, or 25.5 per cent, were foreign born, and 6,541 or at least 74.5 per cent were Canadian born and therefore probably Canadian citizens.[1] Mr Max Von Zur Meuhlen of the Economic Council of Canada discovered through a survey of the 1967 arts and science calendars of fifteen Canadian universities‖ that, of

---

* Not every immigrant intending to be a university teacher would have found employment as such, but the Department of Manpower and Immigration affirms that the correlation is very high. Any discrepancy here would tend to be counterbalanced by other factors. For example, those who entered Canada to teach as "non-immigrant visitors" are not represented at all in these immigration figures. For an authoritative discussion of the reliability of this correlation see Louis Parai, *Immigration and Emigration,* pp. 95-7.

† This is our estimate. It includes the net increase of 2,287 reported by the Dominion Bureau of Statistics and an allowance for "turnover" owing to deaths, retirements from the profession, and emigration, at the rate of 2.1 per cent of the previous year's total faculty population of 16,378.

‖ Acadia, Dalhousie, St Francis Xavier, Memorial, Sir George Williams, Trent, McMaster, Waterloo, Western Ontario, Laurentian, York, Victoria, Calgary, Manitoba, British Columbia.

the two-thirds of those faculty members in non-professional disciplines for whom a first degree was listed, 51 per cent obtained their first degree outside of Canada. This percentage is a rough indication of the citizenship composition of those faculties.* Thus there is evidence for believing that the proportion of Canadians in Canadian universities has diminished by about 25 per cent between 1961 and 1968, a change which has probably occurred for the most part since 1965 when the number of scholars immigrating to Canada began to rise sharply.

Information from particular campuses has not been gathered yet in a complete or consistent way. But first studies bear out the gravity of the situation. A survey conducted at Simon Fraser University in 1967-8 shows that 68 per cent of faculty in professorial ranks were not Canadian citizens. A similar survey conducted by the University of Alberta[2] reveals that 60.8 per cent of full-time faculty in 1961-2 were Canadian. By 1968-9, the proportion had dropped to 47.2 per cent. In a study made by the University of Waterloo information services,[3] it is estimated that in 1964 about 68 per cent of faculty were Canadian. By 1968 the proportion had declined to about 57 per cent. The figures for the Faculty of Arts at Waterloo, however, are more alarming. In 1964-5, about 60 per cent of Arts faculty members were Canadian. By 1969 the proportion had dropped to about 49 per cent.

Intensive study of disciplines and departments throughout Canada must be undertaken if we are to gain a full understanding of the relations that exist between citizenship of faculty, citizenship of graduate students, course offerings in general, and attitudes towards Canadian information. But early studies here also give some indication of a relation between the paucity of Canadian material available and the heavy participation of non-Canadian scholars. A survey done

---

* There are several biases in the figure which would tend to cancel each other out. Foreign faculty members who took their first degree in Canada were counted as Canadians; Canadian faculty who took their first degree abroad were counted as foreign. The proportion of foreign faculty among the one-third of faculty members for whom no first degree was listed was probably larger than among those whose first degree was known, because the first degree or its equivalent is not as common in Europe as in Canada.

by Michael Kennedy[4] reveals that in 1968-9 at the University of Alberta, the Sociology Department, made up of nineteen non-Canadians and four Canadians by calendar count, offered seventy-nine undergraduate and graduate courses, only one of which is described in the calendar as pertaining to Canada. In the Political Science Department, with six of thirteen staff members Canadian, sixty-six courses were offered, seven concerned with Canadian matters. Only two of these courses dealing with Canadian particularities were offered to undergraduates.

At the University of Waterloo a similar situation was found.[5] An examination by calendar of the citizenship composition of the Departments of Economics, English, Fine Arts, History, Philosophy, Political Science, Psychology, and Sociology/Anthropology revealed that every chairman was a US citizen, that a minority of full professors were Canadian, while about half were US citizens. In the Sociology Department, with about six Canadians among the twenty members, sixty-two undergraduate and graduate courses are offered. None is described in the calendar as dealing with Canadian problems. In the Department of English only two courses in Canadian literature are listed among the ninety or so undergraduate and graduate courses offered.

In the Political Science Department of Laurentian University, Sudbury,[6] with one Canadian in five members, only a half course is offered on Canadian government. The English Department, with three Canadians of ten members, offers no Canadian literature. The Geography Department, with two Canadians of five members, offered no Canadian geography in the last two years but will begin to do so in 1969-70. The evidence indicates that the proportion of non-Canadians on faculty affects the offerings involving Canadian material.*

---

* At Winnipeg University, for example, the only Canadian on the Political Science Department there resolved to use two US and three Canadian texts instead of four out of five US texts for an introductory Political Science course in 1969-70. Professor Rodgers gave his department chairman written notice of the new list. In the fall some one hundred and twenty students unanimously approved of the change for their course. Professor Rodgers received a letter from the chairman of his department on September 15, "insisting I use the four out of five American texts or else face 'disciplinary steps.'" R. S. Rodgers, Letter to the Editor, *Uniter,* Winnipeg University, September 29, 1959, p. 13.

Departments of History, English, Political Science, and Sociology give some indication of departmental interest in matters pertaining to Canada, because they are able to offer courses with an ostensibly Canadian content. One can only speculate, however, about departments less observable. What, for example, is the interest in Canadian particularities of the Psychology Department at Simon Fraser University, which on January 1, 1969 had fifteen members, thirteen of whom were non-Canadian, ten of whom were US citizens?

Clearly the statistics of the issue are of critical importance. At the simplest level they suggest that too few Canadians are being urged to excellence, are being helped to continue study, or are being hired when qualified personnel are sought for positions in the universities. Wherever the failure lies, the decline in the proportion of Canadians reveals discrimination against Canadians, a failure to make opportunities available to them, and so a breach of public trust. But Canadians do not suffer discrimination in employment alone. The figures which suggest that Canadians are presently in a minority and that Canadians are being employed in a decreasing ratio indicate root and branch discrimination against able Canadian students and against the community which makes possible Canada's higher educational institutions.

That is another way of saying that there has been, in the last decade, a dramatic failure of planning, co-ordination, and administration on the part of departments of education, senior administrators in education, and national organizations concerned with the welfare and operation of the universities. Moreover, the statistics reveal a demoralized concept of Canada held by those groups; for no self-respecting country in the world would permit itself, willingly, to fall into the condition that Canada presently suffers in its institutions of higher learning. The situations described at Alberta, Waterloo, and Laurentian, for example, result in large measure from the diminishment of the number of Canadians on staff and the increase of non-Canadians who are often seriously ignorant of the Canadian fact.

The condition must be seen in the broader context of Americanization of the country on a number of levels. We know that Canadians suffer more invasion by US media than almost any other country in the world. We know that Canada is smothering from US economic takeover. We know that some US "international" unions have for decades been eating at the heart and spirit of Canadian unionism.[7] We know that Canadian students at all levels are strongly influenced by

US educational texts and materials.[8] And we know that studies of critical importance to the understanding of Canada – of critical importance, moreover, to the maintenance of academically self-respecting university communities – often are totally lacking or shabbily and superficially treated outside the mainstream of "important" material. We are presently conferring degrees upon Canadian students who are often so ignorant of their own country that they are a disgrace to it, and an indictment of the degree granting institutions from which they come.

More than in any other country, because of the proximity of the United States and its often oppressive influence on many aspects of Canadian life, studies in the Canadian experience should be available to every Canadian student in the fullest range and at the highest academic level possible.

It is sometimes argued that US citizens are present in the Canadian universities in a proportion of about 15 to 20 per cent, and so are not a significant part of the Americanization of Canada. Without for a moment underestimating the serious threat of concentration by any non-Canadian group in Canadian educational life, the unique quality of US participation must be seen clearly for what it is, in relation to the conditioning of the US academic himself and to the general deluge of Americanization in Canada.

As the examples from Laurentian, Waterloo, and Alberta show, the concentration of US citizens in certain disciplines affects course offerings. Moreover, it affects the disposition and direction of what superficially seem to be studies not necessarily related to national consciousness. One of the few examinations of work produced by students in an area of US faculty concentration is that of Professor J. Laurence Black. His information is frightening:

... let me cite a case referred to me by a marker for a first year course at my university, Laurentian (and I am using Laurentian University here simply as a typical example; I assume it is no better or worse than other Canadian universities in this regard). Some 260 students in this course were required to prepare a term essay on one of several topics. Of 50 students who attempted an essay on "race relations," almost half treated the problems faced by the American negro. Only 5 dealt with distinctly Canadian racial difficulties: three with the Indian in Canada, two with the negro in Halifax. Some, but not many, mentioned the French-English dialogue but only one felt this was important enough to treat it separately ... Most of those who wrote

on ethnic minorities and immigration limited themselves to studies
on large American cities. Of more than 100 essays on the family,
nearly all parrotted their American texts on the suburban family in
the United States – only four spoke of the Canadian family. A large
number described bureaucracy in the United States and gave the
impression that we cannot even develop our own ideology – in many
there were comparisons made with the bureaucracy in the Soviet
Union, often quite irrelevantly and inevitably to show that their
system was worse than the American one. The most devastating blow
to my Canadianism, however, was the fact that several Canadian
students used the terms "my", "ours", "us", when they were actually
referring to the United States. There are no Canadian faculty members in that particular Department.[9]

The attitude that invites Canadians to consider US information as
"universal," "non-nationalistic," "cosmopolitan," is a product of US
nationalism and "manifest destiny," linked intricately to the so-called
"objective" ideology of the behavioural sciences. Intensively precon-
ditioned to believe that US information is uncoloured by "petty
nationalism," some US citizens and intellectually colonialized Canadians come to the point of being able to say, as a US writer did
recently in *Canadian Dimension:* "The United States has a long past
in training university personnel, but American scholars are not bringing American culture with them but the accumulation of world
knowledge. If Canadians want home-grown propagandists, that is
their affair, but the ensuing result should not be called universities."[10]
This naïvely universalist attitude is characteristic of many, though
not all, US citizens exerting power or forming groups in the Canadian
university. The outcome is clearly observable.

The general flood of Americanization in Canada has resulted in
colonial-mindedness among many Canadians. They appear to believe
US citizens are superior administrators. How else, for instance, could
one explain the fact that in 1968-9, the dean of arts, the two associate deans of arts, and the deputy dean of arts at Waterloo University
were all US citizens? Colonial-minded Canadians, unfortunately, assist
US citizens to Americanize Canadian universities. American hiring
centres are visited; Canadian applicants lose out. American graduate
qualifications are applied; Canadian graduate students lose out. US
ideas of "significant" information are applied; Canadian studies lose
out. Even worse, through the failure to advertise openings consistently

and demonstrably in Canada Canadians have been automatically excluded. The failure is not simply one of carelessness or disorganization. It is to some extent an effect of psychological Americanization.
To go to the US hiring centres and procure US citizens, without regard
for Canada and Canadian needs, guarantees "excellence," "the highest
standards," "the latest information" – which many US citizens and
colonial-minded Canadians believe to be unavailable in Canada.

By far the largest proportion of foreign scholars recently entering
the Canadian universities have come from the United States. Canadian
universities are becoming Americanized in direct relation to the number of US citizens present, *the number of Canadians absent,* and the
increasing influence of Americanization in other sectors of Canadian
life.

Professor Allan Smith of the History Department at the University
of British Columbia, unequivocally describes the situation:

For Canada cosmopolitanism and internationalism mean, in fact,
continentalism. Opening our frontiers to the world means in practise
opening them to the United States. A policy of cultural laissez-faire
means, *not* that we subject ourselves to a wide variety of ideas
emanating from a host of different sources bearing in upon us with
equal intensity. Inevitably, owing to the sheer size and weight and
proximity of the American cultural establishment, it means that we
are subjected to one set of ideas emanating from one source. The
open door is acceptable, and even desirable, but to leave it wide open
would make Canada's cultural and intellectual life a mirror image of
the American, instead of the proximate reflection it is now. Canadians, like Holmes' man in the crowded theatre, are compelled to
apply their principles with circumspection, owing to the situation in
which they find themselves.[11]

Finally, a very clear indication of the kind of nationalism felt by
US scholars in Canada is revealed in the study by David Brown and
James MacKinnon. Their examination of political scientists in Canada
led them to make the following observations:

Presumably, non-Canadians who have come to Canada with the intention of becoming Canadians will gradually come to look at politics
in ways that are relevant to Canadian students. But our results show
that most immigrant professors do not intend to become Canadians.

Fewer than one-third are engaged in research on Canadian problems; two-thirds of Canadians are. Fewer than 30 per cent of the Americans who replied believe they will be teaching here in 10 years' time. Ninety per cent do not intend to become Canadian citizens. By contrast nearly half of those of other nationalities plan to become citizens.[12]

Americanization exists at a number of levels: in numbers and attitudes of faculty, in course offerings, in ideological orientation of studies, in hiring procedures and preferences, in the failure of concern about the limited opportunities for Canadian students. A change of heart is necessary in Canadian higher education. But it needs to be prepared for. Governments should take some first steps to set the Canadian university on the road to recovery, and Canadianization. They must pass legislation to ensure reasonable and consistent advertising in Canada of all new positions in Canadian universities. They must also insist, by legislation, that Canadian citizens administer the Canadian universities. To that end they should legislate that Canadian citizenship be made a necessary qualification for all new appointments to administrative positions from chairman to chancellor inclusive. They must strive more effectively than in the past to bring Canadians back to Canada. Complaints are continually made that Canadians of excellence are helped in no serious way to repatriate when they leave Canada to study or work. Moreover, in order to give greater incentive to Canadian scholars, governments must re-examine their policies of awards. And they must pass legislation of a hortatory nature, calling upon universities to strive as a general policy to employ Canadians of excellence in order to ensure that Canadians remain or eventually become a clear two-thirds majority of full-time faculty members in each department.

Such legislation would form the basis for the development of universities sensitive to the aspirations of the Canadian community. And with respect for non-Canadian scholars, Canadian universities would soon begin to demonstrate a full and proper regard for the Canadian student and a concerned awareness of the particular problems and needs of the Canadian community. Without such a change in direction, no one can hazard a guess as to what will happen as the university in Canada becomes increasingly irrelevant to Canadian life, and as the Canadian people become increasingly aware of its irrelevance.

NOTES

1 L. Parai, *Immigration and Emigration of Professional and Skilled Manpower During the Post-War Period,* Special Study No. 1, Economic Council of Canada (Ottawa, 1965), p. 224.

2 "Analysis of Full-Time Faculty at the University of Alberta – By Country of Birth," in Robin Mathews, Cyril Byrne, and Kenneth McKinnon, "The University of Waterloo: A Special Study," presented to the Minister of University Affairs *et al.,* Aug. 1969, Appendix, Item One.

3 "Waterloo's Faculty and the 'Non-Canadian Controversy,'" Waterloo *Gazette,* June 4, 1969.

4 "Number of Canadian Courses and Canadian Teachers in the Departments of Political Science, Sociology, History, and Psychology at the University of Alberta (1968-9)," in Mathews, Byrne, and McKinnon, "The University of Waterloo," Appendix, Items 2a and 2b.

5 Mathews, Byrne and McKinnon, "The University of Waterloo."

6 J. Laurence Black, "Americans in Canadian Universities, II," *Laurentian University Review,* vol. 2, no. 4 (June 1969), p. 111.

7 Charles Lipton, *The Trade Union Movement of Canada: 1827-1959* (Montreal, 1966).

8 Kenn Johnson, "This Courier Investigation Indicates the Extent of U.S. Influence on Canada's Schools," *Educational Courier* (May 1969), pp. 69-75.

9 "Americans in Canadian Universities, II," pp. 110-111.

10 David Rodnick, "Academic Chauvinism," *Canadian Dimension,* vol. 6, no. 2 (July 1969), p. 2.

11 "An Open Letter on Nationalism and the Universities in Canada," no date, distributed personally.

12 "Teaching Canadians the American Way," *Globe and Mail,* Toronto, June 18, 1969.

Ellen and Neal Wood

They teach political theory at York University in Glendon College
and the Faculty of Arts and Science respectively. Neal Wood has also
taught at Columbia and the University of California.

Canada and the American science of politics

The statistical "Americanization" of Canadian universities is a well-publicized phenomenon. The mass media have often enough in recent months cited figures testifying to the surprising number of Americans teaching in Canadian universities. There is, however, another aspect of the phenomenon of Americanization about which, in the long run, Canadians should perhaps be even more concerned: the *substantive* or cultural Americanization of Canada, the adoption by Canadians themselves of the "American way of doing things." This may be brought about, not simply by American immigration into Canada, but by a tendency of Canadians themselves to judge their own country's progress in terms of its conformity to American patterns. Sometimes, indeed, Canadians deliberately try to induce conformity when it fails to occur on its own. As evidence of this, one need only note the degree to which the formula "ten (or fifteen or thirty) years behind the United States" apparently has become an accepted way of describing Canadian development.

The tendency to apply this rather uncritical yardstick is particularly prevalent in many political science departments in Canadian universities. Ironically, at a time when Canadian political science is beginning to establish itself as a distinct and vigorous discipline, when new departments of political science are springing up everywhere in Canada and political science faculties are growing tremendously, when an excellent journal devoted exclusively to political science has for the first time been launched in Canada – at such a time some Canadian political scientists, particularly in the new universities, are applying this superficial standard and finding their discipline wanting directly in proportion to its lack of conformity to the "American way." Consequently they are attempting to "modernize" – or, to put it more precisely, to Americanize – departments of political science in Canada. The absurdity of the self-fulfilling prophecy that Canada will always be x-number of years behind the United States is most dramatically demonstrated by its effects in political science. Many Canadians are demanding the Americanization of their discipline precisely at a time when many American political scientists are beginning to question profoundly the direction of their own science. The Americanization of Canadian political science, then, is being fostered as much by Canadians themselves as by immigrant Americans, and may continue to spread even if the statistical problem is corrected. For this reason, it seems important to examine both the

number of American political scientists teaching in Canadian universities, and the *substance* of the American science of politics which is
being adopted by Canadians.

What is meant, then, by the Americanization of political science,
and in what sense is it a substantive cultural phenomenon, rather than
simply a matter of population statistics? In other words, what is the
"American way of doing things" in political science, and in what
sense might it be regarded as a manifestation of more general American cultural traits?

Non-Americans have been concerned about something called American civilization or culture for quite some time. Attempts to define
and characterize that way of life have as often as not been associated
with the menace of "Americanization." Canadians have perhaps only
recently begun to regard Americanism as a menace, but it has been a
favourite European *bête noire* for decades. In the late 1920s, for
example, in an article called "'America'—by Formula" John Dewey
commented upon the European fear of Americanization. Looking at
his characterization of Americanism as the worried Europeans saw it,
we are struck by how perfectly that Americanism has now found
an almost caricatured intellectual reflection in the social sciences.
Referring to a European analysis which he regards as the most reasonable and insightful of the many he has encountered, Dewey explains
the characteristics of the "American type":

Fundamentally, they [the characteristics] spring from impersonality
... Hence the "externality and superficiality of the American soul"; it
has no ultimate inner unity and uniqueness – no true personality. The
marks and signs of this "impersonalization" of the human soul are
quantification of life, with its attendant disregard of quality; its
mechanization and the almost universal habit of esteeming technique
as an end, not as a means, so that organic and intellectual life is also
"rationalized"; and finally, standardization. Differences and distinctions are ignored and over-ridden; agreement, similarity is the ideal.
There is not only absence of social discrimination but of intellectual;
critical thinking is conspicuous by its absence ...

Quantification, mechanization and standardization: these are then
the marks of the Americanization that is conquering the world ...

I shall not deny the existence of these characteristics, nor of the
manifold evils of superficialism and externalism that result in the

production of intellectual and moral mediocrity. In the main these traits exist and they characterize American life and are already beginning to dominate that of other countries.[1]

Whether or not one accepts this as an accurate description of the "American soul," or accepts even the notion that there is such a thing, there is no question that American social scientists have very obligingly created themselves and their science in this image. Many of them in fact seem to have projected this caricature of the American soul on to their subject matter, apparently making an externalized, depersonalized man their model of man in general. In other words, their science tends to reflect "American" externalism, superficialism, and dehumanization both in its method and in its content, its perceptions of the world it seeks to study.

It will, of course, be pointed out that the new political science was created in order to make the study of politics into a more precise *science.* Therefore, before outlining our critique in somewhat greater detail, and before we are accused of a reactionary aversion to precision and science – as others who have expressed similar objections have been accused – perhaps a preliminary explanation of our criticism is in order.

First of all, the objections are directed not so much at the idea of a science of politics as at the simplistic, restricted, and shallow conceptions of science and scientific method which are reflected so strongly in the "new" political science. These conceptions resemble notions abandoned by the natural sciences in the last century, and are even less appropriate to the study of human behaviour and social phenomena than they are to the study of natural phenomena. Again, it is often not because of its much-vaunted preoccupation with facts, but precisely in order to *rescue* facts, that many critics attack the narrow superficiality of much of contemporary political science. In a sense, the very conceptions of science and precision adopted by political science necessarily defeat the purpose of a precise science of politics – which presumably is to gain deeper insight into political phenomena. The new science of politics has come perilously close to being irrelevant to the study of politics.

Second, the study of politics, in the name of science, has become dangerously and unimaginatively parochial, abandoning virtually all other concerns for the sake of a narrow, formalistic professionalism, pursued almost solely for its own sake. The cult of professionalism has in many cases excluded all but the most fashionable concerns and approaches, at best tolerating them as quaint amusements and dilettantism. Moreover, this professionalism has more to do with form than with content, and the latter frequently suffers as a result. In short, the barren cult of professionalism is an obstacle to a fruitful science of politics.

From a somewhat different perspective, criticisms of the current American political science are perhaps analogous to those levelled by social critics against post-industrial society in general. The objection in these cases is no more against technology and industry as such than is ours against science and technique. The social critics are attacking the existence of a so-called "technological *a priori*" – the situation in which industry and technology have acquired their own momentum, their own conditions and demands to which men must conform, so that men become the instruments of technology instead of the reverse. In such a dehumanized situation, human goals are forgotten, and men paradoxically become objects and means for their own creations – creations originally conceived as means toward man's own ends. Leaving aside the original question of the inadequacy of political science even as a science, one might argue that the discipline has evolved its own dehumanized technological *a priori*. Not only is everything subordinated to technique, but here the techniques to which all other considerations are sacrificed are simply those of the science itself, its own internal methodology. Thus, the science of politics is even further removed from human goals, even more turned in upon itself. And finally, not only have human goals been forgotten but, ironically, very often even the content of the research itself has been sacrificed to technique and methodology.

Here, then, is one of the most striking characteristics of American political science, one which often is criticized and which admirably reflects the "Americanism" characterized by Dewey. This is the "universal habit of esteeming technique as an end, not as a means" to which Dewey refers. The elevation of technique to an end in itself, the cult of methodology, means that political science has forgotten almost all the other goals and concerns with which political thinkers have traditionally occupied themselves, including the humanistic concern for the quality of human life. What may be less obvious, however, is the fact that the cult of methodology has been practised not only at the expense of concern for human goals, but even at the expense of meaningful factual knowledge. Professionalism in political science apparently means neither the traditional concern for the "good (or just) society," nor even insight into political problems, but the acquisition of certain skills and techniques largely for their own sake. Evidently these skills and techniques are selected and judged as properly professional more in terms of their conformity to some abstract and simplistic conception of the "scientific method" than in terms of their usefulness in studying social phenomena. Since considerations of methodology are paramount, content must be adapted to methodology, rather than the reverse. Moreover, the methodology tends to be so restrictive in its demands for precision, standardization, or quantification that content often must be distorted considerably to accommodate it. Just as often, the researcher is reduced to applying his complex scientific terminology, his jargon, to the most trivial or truistic observations. (To describe the nature of the relationship between method and content, critics sometimes use the analogy of the drunk searching for a lost coin under a lamp-post, who, when reminded that he had dropped the coin several yards away, answered, "Yes, but this is where the light is.")

It would seem that a phenomenon is recognizable only if it can be either measured or standardized by subsuming it under one of a few generalized and undifferentiated concepts or models. Critics have commented often enough on the distortions of non-western societies required to adapt them to generalized social science models – models which, ironically, were made general precisely so that they could be applied to non-western situations. But students who have heard the problem of French-English relations in Canada dealt with in terms of the diluted and undifferentiated concepts of political science can perhaps comment as readily as anyone on the adequacy of such analytic "superficialism" and reductionism.

The standardization and quantification of American political science is certainly, to return to Dewey, characterized by an "attendant disregard of quality" – quality here referring to the unique and distinctive properties or significance of things. Now there is no question that the construction of general concepts and models, or "ideal types," can be useful as analytic tools or "heuristic devices" (a favourite social science phrase). But what is lacking in the use of such devices in current political science is precisely what Max Weber demanded to make it at all meaningful: a "sense of the significant," based as often as not on intuitive insight and sensitivity, an appreciation for distinctive qualities. The kind of "empathetic comprehension" which Weber felt could alone justify the "scientific method" in the social sciences seems to have become scientifically unrespectable and unprofessional. In fact, it is surprising how many studies are based more on a command of the methodology and manipulation of models than even on familiarity with the situation being examined, let alone "empathetic comprehension" or a "sense of the significant." Thus, the impression that political science is indeed becoming a science may be more an illusion fostered by the proliferation of "scientific" jargon and symbols than by any meaningful development in the substance of the science.

Perhaps it can be said that American political scientists tend to confuse scientific "neutrality" with *neutralization*. Let us leave aside for now the cogent arguments which frequently are put forward about the dangers of excessive neutrality in science, or even the suggestion that such neutrality is often bogus and self-deceptive in any case. The point here is that to maintain neutrality in the interests of scientific objectivity does not mean to neutralize the content of scientific knowledge. ("Neutralize: to destroy the distinctive or active properties of; to paralyze, destroy, or counteract the effectiveness, force, disposition, etc. of.") The problem, then, is twofold: first, as we have suggested earlier, political science with its methodology and jargon tends to obscure, or even to distort, the "distinctive properties" and qualities of social phenomena; and second, if it does not make them absolutely incomprehensible, it tends to *desensitize* them, to deprive them of their effectiveness and force, to act as an inducement to indifference and apathy. Neutralizing or desensitizing a phenomenon which cannot be experienced neutrally or insensibly distorts it; this method, therefore, is not scientifically objective. A description which fails to convey something of the quality of an experience, which even obscures that quality, is not an accurate, objective, or even neutral description; indeed, it seems designed to make social science irrelevant to social issues.

Perhaps this is the place to note the disturbing fact that it is very seldom "professional" social scientists who bring attention to the most glaring problems facing American society. More often it is non-academic writers and "dilettantes." There are no doubt many reasons for this, but perhaps one of them is this process of neutralization. Consider the problem of poverty. Is this problem really described by an account of the behaviour of the poor, particularly when behaviour is conceived in the most superficial and depersonalized way – something akin to the motion of atoms or machine parts? Or does it become a problem to be solved only when one can convey what it is like to experience poverty? The problem of poverty in America seems so obvious now that it is difficult to believe that everyone has not always known about it. Significantly, it was not academic sociologists or political scientists, nor all the hundreds of academic social scientists on the generous government payroll, but a "dilettante," Michael Harrington, in his more or less journalistic *The Other America,* who seems to have made it an issue for the American government. Now it is, of course, possible that government officials prefer to read straightforward journalistic accounts than to wade through complicated scholarly studies. Nevertheless it is undeniable that social scientists – and this is perhaps less true now of sociologists than of political scientists – have a way of ignoring social issues for the sake of methodology. When they do occupy themselves with such issues, they have a remarkable talent for making them either totally incomprehensible or lifeless and meaningless in human terms.

Another characteristic of American political science which may be another symptom of its "externalism and superficialism" – and which perhaps it shares with American culture in general – is its ahistorical quality, the tendency to ignore its history and tradition. The most "professional" of political scientists seem to regard history, and in particular the long tradition of western political thought, at best as quaintly irrelevant and at worst as dangerously "unscientific" (that is, humanistic?).

Aside from the obvious fact that one cannot truly understand a society without knowing its cultural and intellectual tradition, it should be pointed out that arbitrary isolation from one's tradition is as inherently reactionary, unproductive, and uncreative as a slavish conformity to tradition. In the first place, when the tradition is as rich as that of western political thought, confrontation with it can be progressive. At the very least, all encounters with great minds are incentives to creativity; but more important the insights of many traditional political thinkers are still meaningful and may save their readers the trouble of duplication, or inspire them to transcend those insights by building upon them. Second, exposure to the long humanistic tradition may help to inject an element of sensitivity which political science sorely needs. Then, too, historical isolation tends to breed stagnant complacency.

There is another more complicated consideration. This kind of historical isolation, founded more on ignorance than on conscious and informed rejection, is inherently reactionary and unproductive precisely because it can never be more than superficial. True freedom from tradition – perhaps it would be better to say freedom *in* tradition – belongs only to those who are in conscious possession of that tradition and who, knowing it, can control, transcend, or make use of it. The truly great revolutionary thinkers have been revolutionary, not in spite of their tradition, but precisely because they were consciously steeped in their tradition, had seized it, nourished themselves on it, and bent it to their will. For the philistine who, though inescapably conditioned by it, pretends to reject it without truly knowing it, the rejection is unreal, it is false consciousness. In short, the tradition tends to become *ideology,* as the sociologists of knowledge use the word.

In this sense of the word, the concept of ideology reflects, as Karl Mannheim put it, "the insight that in certain situations the collective unconscious of certain groups obscures the real condition of society both to itself and to others and thereby stabilizes it."[2] Although the concept generally refers to the collective unconscious of social or economic groups, interests, or classes, it can be applied just as well to an entire intellectual culture, to the ideology of culture as to the ideology of class. The participants in a cultural or intellectual tradition are subject to the ideology of culture in so far as they are conditioned by it in their thought-style without at the same time being conscious of it. Ideological thinking is intellectual enslavement; for to be unaware of one's mode of thought is to be directed by it rather than to direct it. And, of course, it is impossible to progress or expand in thought beyond the conditions it reflects because those conditions limit and determine the possibilities of thought and experience themselves. Thus, in so far as an intellectual world becomes petrified in ideology, that world ceases to be progressive and creative. The intellectual tradition then limits, determines, and enslaves, but cannot enrich.

Perhaps the problem of tradition can be summed up from a somewhat different perspective by a quotation from Igor Stravinsky, hardly the most conservative or least inventive of men:

Tradition is entirely different from habit, even from an excellent habit, for habit is by definition an unconscious acquisition and tends to become mechanical, whereas tradition results from a conscious and deliberate acceptance. A real tradition is not the relic of a past irretrievably gone; it is a living force that animates and informs the present. In this sense the paradox which banteringly maintains that everything which is not tradition is plagiarism, is true ... Far from implying the repetition of what has been, tradition presupposes the reality of what endures. It appears as an heirloom, a heritage that one receives on condition of making it bear fruit before passing it on to one's descendants ... "a tradition is carried forward in order to produce something new." [3]

It may be partly because Americans have tended to ignore tradition and because their tradition has thus petrified into ideology or become an "unconscious, mechanical habit," that they are in many ways so conservative with regard to social and political doctrines. Despite their vaunted freedom from a blind thraldom to tradition, and despite a grudging acceptance of some welfare state ideas, in their political culture they still have at least one foot in the eighteenth century – for example, with regard to opinions on the sanctity of private property and private enterprise, attitudes towards the poor and "creeping socialism," etc. Britain, on the other hand, complacently regarded by American observers as the more tradition-bound culture, has in many ways been the more progressive in the evolution of its social doctrines. In part this is because its tradition has been a living thing, constantly reabsorbed, carried forward, and made into something new by Britain's great social and political thinkers, the popular political culture evolving with it.

In any case, the tradition of western political thought – or at least that part of it called the "liberal" tradition – apparently has become ideology, or an unconscious, mechanical habit for many American political scientists. It has become ideology in the sense of being an integral part of their unconscious intellectual baggage, part of the very perceptual apparatus through which they "objectively" and "scientifically" observe the world. It should be emphasized, however, that this does *not* mean simply that political science is not value-free or that American political scientists often have a commitment to liberal democratic values, a liberal bias. This many of them are prepared to admit, after they have been criticized often enough for obscuring their implicit value-judgments. Indeed, one might welcome the fact that they have value-commitments. But the problem here is less a moral one than an epistemological one. An ideology is not simply a value-orientation. It is a more fundamental thought-style, a mode of ordering one's perceptions, a set of unconscious perceptual categories which give particular structure or meaning to one's experience. The ideology of the liberal tradition has thus infused the very perceptions of political scientists. It has affected their definitions of politics and of what constitutes a political phenomenon, even when such definitions produce distortions because they are inapplicable to political systems in which the nature of society is different from that upon which liberalism is predicated. For example, the definition of politics in terms of interest, the tendency to regard men as more or less reflexive functions of their objective roles in an independently existing social system, the inclination to reduce creative action to responsive behaviour and to confuse human *rationality* with mechanical *functionality,* even the passion for a particular kind of exact social science – all these can be traced to liberalism and can be found to secrete the values of liberalism in what purport to be purely empirical concepts. In fact, it can be argued that the very idea of a *social science* as conceived by American political scientists is made possible by liberal conceptions of social forces and of man's place in the social mechanism carried to extremes.

All these symptoms of externalism and superficialism, then, have united to produce a rather stagnant science of politics, one which has threatened to become increasingly divorced from the human problems with which it was designed to deal. If the phenomenon of American political science could not be accounted for anthropologically in terms of more general American cultural traits, it would indeed be tempting to explain it rather paranoically as a massive conspiracy of reaction. Nothing could more effectively have emasculated meaningful social criticism than the sterile formalism which has come to characterize so much of American political science. Professionalization of the discipline has neutralized what should have been a major source of responsible intelligent, and constructive social criticism. The attendant cult of specialization and expertise has had the effect of a policy of divide and conquer by carrying to extremes the view, already so prevalent in American society, that every aspect of every problem is the hallowed domain of its own professionals. The effect is that specialists tend to become irrelevant to each other, and even more irrelevant to larger social issues.

Paradoxically, the fact that academic political scientists are all too often on government payrolls as policy advisers is not grounds for altering the judgment about their distance from social problems. We already have referred to the effects of confusion between scientific neutrality and neutralization; but there is another even more disturbing aspect to the question of neutrality. All too often, neutrality seems to be interpreted as a licence to sell whatever one has to offer to the highest bidder, and even sometimes to tell him simply what he wants to hear. And the highest bidder always turns out to be the government, the think-tanks, or foundations, which have little to gain from serious social criticism. Often the neutrality or neutralization of the science makes it so flexible – or so devoid of meaningful content – that it can be used as apologetics or rationalization for any status quo; thus, at best it is irrelevant and at worst, opportunistic.

This charge has been made by at least one prominent figure in American politics. Senator Fulbright, in no less an organ than the *Congressional Record,* is quoted as having criticized the universities for their failure to form "an effective counterweight to the military-industrial complex" and for, instead, having "joined the monolith, adding greatly to its power and influence." He specifically charges the social scientists, "who ought to be acting as responsible and independent critics of the Government's policies," with becoming agents of these policies instead. "The surrender of independence, the neglect of teaching, and the distortion of scholarship" mean that the university "is not only failing to meet its responsibilities to its students; it is betraying a public trust."[4] Fulbright cites as a primary cause of this betrayal the access which academicians have to money and influence. To this, the article which quotes Fulbright adds the other factors which have been discussed above: "a highly restrictive, almost universally shared, ideology and the inherent dynamics of professionalization." The betrayal appears to be implicit in the very nature of the social sciences themselves.

What all this adds up to is that political science has tended to become irrelevant to political problems. The study of politics traditionally has been a humanistic endeavour concerned with human goals and their implementation. Contemporary political science belongs to an exceedingly rich, age-old, intellectual heritage that dates from the time of Plato and Aristotle. Political science in the past has referred to the systematic knowledge of politics, and the difference between the political world and the world of nature as objects of knowledge was supposed to exist in the idea of conscious, purposeful action. For the Greeks politics was a primary, creative, formative activity, instead of the almost reflexive, but in any case subordinate, function of social and economic forces suggested by later conceptions. The polis was thought to be the realm of the truly human where man transcended his determined biological nature and found freedom and justice; politics was the highest human activity, the search for justice, and political science was the highest moral science. Even later, when political theorists like the classical liberals, wary of moral absolutes, assigned to politics a less exalted role, political science was still a humanistic discipline concerned with the quality of human life; and its humanistic concerns were not considered incompatible with its scientific aspirations.

Our terms "act" and "action" are derived from the Latin verb, *ago*, which came to refer to the conduct or management of public affairs, to doing, discussing, speaking, deliberating before legislative assemblies and tribunals of justice. If we examine the English verb, "to act," we discover that like the Latin root, *ago*, it literally means to put in motion or actuate, and later to bring about, to produce, or to perform. The nouns "act" and "action" denote things done or deeds. Later "act" referred to a deed or thing done – a decree – by a legislative body or a court of justice. And of course, "to act" like *ago* designates a unique kind of doing, the performing of a part in a play.

From this brief etymological digression we note that the ideas of act, action, and actor entail highly self-conscious and purposeful movement, self-directed doing to bring about ends upon which the doer has reflected. Action involves the conscious creation of something new, the defence or the challenge of what already exists, or any combination of the three. Action, therefore, is inextricably bound up with values. Its primary condition is language, by which man can realize self-consciousness, can order his universe, and can begin to think and to act in moral terms. Thought and experience, conceptual ordering and sensory perception meet in and are fused through action, and through action man possesses a history, shapes that history, and is shaped by it in turn. This is the central implication of acting as discourse and deliberation, of legislative and judicial decisions, of performing a part in a play.

Our argument, then, is that political science in the past has been fundamentally concerned with this very kind of self-conscious and purposeful motion of human beings, in which deliberation and decisions about the goals of human happiness and well-being have had the crucial role. The objects of systematic political knowledge were thought to be far different from the objects of natural science or natural philosophy. To say that political science has treated man as a self-conscious and purposeful creature, as an actor, is to affirm that whatever else man might be or do, he can consciously formulate ends, and then attempt to attain those goals through carefully chosen endeavour. In other words, man is a being capable of rationality, even though he may normally act in other than rational ways. Implied by this potential of rationality is conscious creativity, self-knowledge, self-direction, and personal autonomy.

Traditionally, political science has been vitally concerned with three essential tasks: first, the exploration and assessment of human ends and values, and the actual prescription of the ends and values most conducive to human happiness and well-being; second, the systematic analysis and recommendation of the means – the institutional arrangements and procedures necessary for the realization of the prescribed ends and values; and finally, in conjunction with all of these, an exhaustive and meticulous examination of man, society, and governmental arrangements as they exist in the present and have existed in the past. The political scientist intended his prescriptions and recommendations for the world of concrete practice; hence, within the horizons of his own intellectual perspective, he had to marshal and order the facts of human life. Political science was itself action in the most significant sense, a creative leap of intellect and imagination from an empathetic understanding of the past through a perceptive critique of the present into the possibilities for the future.

Consequently, we emphasize that traditional political science represented a synthesis of three basic concerns: a *humanistic* concern with ends and values; a *practical* concern with the actual political conditions of a particular time, and how they might be changed and improved for the better; and an *observational* concern with the facts of human life. The practical and observational concerns were always energized by the humanistic concern. The political scientist's practical preoccupation with society, with social, economic, and political structure, his deep-rooted doubt about the efficacy and viability of the current features of that society, and his desire for change were informed by both his humanistic and his observational focus. Seriously disturbed by certain aspects of his own world of social reality, the political scientist began to reflect upon human values and ends from the standpoint of how his own society might improve human welfare, and to investigate systematically the actualities of his own and other societies, both past and present.

What has happened to much of twentieth-century political science, particularly as it has developed in America since the Second World War, has been the disappearance of the humanistic concern, followed by a withdrawal from the practical concern. The observational concern began to be treated as an end in itself, becoming almost co-extensive with political science. Alienated from its traditional humanistic and practical orientation, political science was no longer able to focus upon political action, since political action by definition was conscious, purposeful, and creative. Action in the political arena was now transformed into *behaviour* because of the new observational orientation of political science. At the heart of this view was the idea not that men were capable of shaping and reshaping their political and social environments in accordance with their conscious purposes, but rather that men responded externally in essentially measurable ways to impersonal social, economic, and psychic forces.[5] Men could now be manipulated as the objects of an observational science, just as the objects of a natural science were manipulated. Political order began to be treated as causal instead of conceptual. Just as natural phenomena lack a history, so the historical dimension was eliminated from the scientific study of political phenomena. In the long run, by jettisoning its humanistic and practical perspective, a purely observational political science was in danger of serving whatever the predominant values and the practical concerns of society as it existed at the time might be. In practice, the value neutrality and practical detachment of political science in the name of observational objectivity meant subordination to the status quo. No longer did political science serve men by offering probing social criticism and by suggesting a way out of their difficulties. Finally even the observational concerns were sacrificed to the imperatives of methodology. It is difficult to say how much further this process of atrophy can go, but surely it would be foolish for Canadian political science to join in the final stages, when it could be a source of regeneration.

Whatever direction Canadian political scientists decide to follow, it is clear that they must take a long, hard look at the American discipline which they are beginning to adopt. A country like Canada – profoundly concerned with building a viable nation out of diversity, very conscious of its newness and the need for creative, imaginative, and constantly evolving solutions to new and often unique problems; a country which, while sometimes dangerously complacent, is still not so consistently smug that it feels no need for constructive self-criticism – cannot afford to adopt an inherently reactionary mode of social and political analysis which, more concerned with form than with content, is divorced from pressing problems and militates against a sensitive and creative social concern. In any case, it would be absurd to adopt wholeheartedly a pattern which even its creators have begun to question.

Canadians are tremendously concerned about defining a culture of their own, and Canada may be in a unique position to evolve a new form of post-industrial culture. Inevitably, perhaps, it will have to define its identity with reference to the United States; but perhaps there is too much of a tendency to resign oneself to "Americanization" or to a kind of universal "Americanism" inherent in the development of all post-industrial societies. Certainly there is no reason to make that conviction of inevitability a self-fulfilling prophecy by assuming it, and particularly by creating social scientists in its image, when these are the very people who should be finding new directions, if they can be found. If it is at all possible to achieve a post-industrial society which is not in the American mould, certainly the method is not to deliberately model the social sciences on the pathological aspects of American development, producing social analysts who are nothing but fodder for that system and emasculating their potential for responsible, effective, and rigorous social criticism.

Western society has for some time been characterized by the uneasy coexistence of a long humanist tradition and a history of technological development which provides the means to implement its goals, while at the same time constantly threatening to destroy it. If the

contradiction between these two equally native, but often antagonistic, cultural factors can be resolved, if they can be fused into a new,
consciously created humanistic post-industrial culture, Canada is
perhaps in a unique position to find the new direction. Perhaps there
is a real advantage to being "thirty years behind the United States,"
in the sense that the United States can serve as a laboratory – or an
anti-laboratory – for Canada. No one can deny the restrictions on
Canadian autonomy or the limited extent to which conscious efforts
may be effectual, but there is no reason to strengthen the restrictions
and increase the limitations by pleading inevitability. Certainly there
is no reason why Canada cannot maintain a high degree of intellectual
autonomy, or why the universities should collaborate with the Americanization of Canadian post-industrial development by becoming
conscious and willing instruments of a self-fulfilling prophecy.

NOTES

1 Reprinted in his *Individualism Old and New* (New York, 1962),
   pp. 23-5.
2 *Ideology and Utopia* (New York, 1949), p. 36.
3 *The Poetics of Music* (New York, 1959), pp. 58-9.
4 J. William Fulbright, "The War and Its Effects – II," *Congressional
   Record,* Dec. 13, 1967, quoted in Noam Chomsky, "The Menace of
   Liberal Scholarship," in *New York Review of Books,* vol. XI, no. 12
   (Jan. 2, 1969).
5 For the distinction between action and behaviour, see Hannah
   Arendt, *The Human Condition* (New York, 1959), pp. 155 ff. See
   also the systematic treatment of this problem by Richard Taylor in
   Action and Purpose (Englewood Cliffs, NJ, 1966).

Melville H. Watkins

The principal author of the Watkins Report, a vice-president of the New Democratic Party, and teaches economics at the University of Toronto.

The dismal state of economics in Canada

"The voice of the economist is heard throughout the land." Harold Innis wrote these words in 1941, but their relevance today is clear. The concern of this paper is with the quality of that voice and whether there is, or could be, any Canadian content to it.

It might be agreed that there is a certain absurdity in the notion of mathematics for Canadians, but that it is hardly absurd to talk about Canadian art. In spite of its pretensions, economics is more art than science – in current American parlance, it is a "soft" rather than "hard" discipline – and therefore we can speak of *Canadian* economics in the sense of there being at least the possibility of an indigenous and distinctive national style. Indeed, the possibility became a reality in the writings of Innis and the so-called staple approach. In the main, however, Canadian economics means the application of universal technique, or at least free-world technique, to Canadian problems. Since Canada is better endowed with some problems than others – for example, resource development, international trade, foreign ownership – specialization will result, and with specialization, innovation and the potential for the export of ideas.

Similarly, to the extent that Canadian problems are unique, importation of ideas and technique will have its limitations: "Theories developed and perfected in relation to the economies of Britain and the United States, while perhaps intellectually satisfying, could not by themselves be adequate instruments for analysing the economic life and difficulties of Canada. Neither Marshall's *Principles* nor Taussig's *Principles,* nor, later, Keynes' *General Theory,* could be applied directly to a country where the price system, though no doubt ultimately dominant, was complicated and distorted by significant national peculiarities."[1] By way of example of the latter, Macpherson cites "political rigidities such as the tariff." It is symptomatic of developments in the decade since he wrote that the present stance of Canadian economists is to get rid of such distortions so that the principles will apply; nature copies art.

J. H. Dales has pointed out that, in fact, nearly the whole of modern economic theory was developed by scholars working in three countries, England, Sweden, and the United States.[2] His intent was to show the absence of Canada – about which there can be no debate – but he unintentionally raises the question of the legitimacy of the American contribution, an issue of some relevance to Canada given the present Americanization of everything, including economics.

In fact, there would be little disagreement with the statement that economics was overwhelmingly British, rather than American, in genesis until after the Second World War. Walter Heller has recently listed five significant contributions to economics since the 1920s:

(1) Keynes' "spectacular rescue ... of economics from the wilderness of classical equilibrium"; (2) Hansen's "Americanization of Keynes"; (3) Kuznetz' "seminal work on the concepts of national income and gross national product"; (4) Samuelson's "neoclassical synthesis"; (5) "computer-oriented economists whose qualitative work is increasing the scope and reliability of economic analysis and forecasting."[3] Although apparently intending to do the exact opposite, he implicitly raises serious doubts about the importance and significance of the American contribution, and anyone else since Keynes, for that matter. Hansen derives from Keynes; quantification and computerization are hardly first-order activities – and econometrics is more Dutch than American in origin; Samuelson's neoclassical synthesis is little more than a transparent attempt to impose order on his best-selling textbook. It would appear that the United States took the neoclassical economics of Britain, including Keynes, and mathematized, quantified, and computerized it. In the process, any indigenous roots, such as Veblen's institutionalism, were sloughed off.

At the risk of only slight exaggeration, it may be said that American economics, at present so dominant in the First and Third Worlds, is a fragment of British economics. The latter was predominantly liberal bourgeois, and the former more so; witness the greater intolerance toward Marxism in Cambridge, Massachusetts, than in Cambridge, England. Economics became respectable within the United States as Keynesian economics, demonstrating, incidentally, the inherent limitations of Keynesian economics. Once dismissed as the dismal science, economics has been riding high ever since. John Kennedy brought top economists into the White House. It is difficult to avoid the conclusion that the export of American economics reflects more the dominant position of the United States in the international economy and polity than innovation *per se*; the pen is not mightier than the sword. For reasons of power, that present American economics understandably ignores, the economics of the centre has become the economics of the margins.

The state of economics in general, then, consists of neoclassical and Keynesian economics filtered through American technocracy, and this has profound implications. Political economy, slowly dying in the hands of the British, was decisively transformed into quantitative economics. American economics is the quantification of quantification. In the process, the theory economists use has been emptied of the political.[4] The modern economist sees himself as concerned with allocating scarce means among competing ends. He sees economic theory as a set of techniques that gives the best solution to this "fundamental" problem. The answer invariably turns out to be the use of markets, and endless energy is devoted to discovering their minor imperfections and to fighting false battles with businessmen and civil servants openly committed to the free enterprise ideology.

In the process what is ignored is that the market economy is not a neutral mechanism that can be allowed free reign in a society without the most profound political and social implications which, in their turn, constrain the solutions which economists can put forward. The market economy creates the market society and thereby a set of institutions and values which are anything but neutral. Suddenly, important things like the distribution of income and wealth become sacrosanct, for to challenge them would undermine the incentives requisite for the operation of the market economy – that is, it would undermine the power élite which has most to gain from the operation of the market economy. Economists become, without quite being aware of it, rationalizers of the *status quo*.

Even that is not the end of the matter. Economics has become increasingly a technology characterized by great abstraction and high-powered technique. Jacques Ellul has written[5] about the triumph of technique and its increasing autonomy from social and human considerations. As he makes clear, economics is a leading example of this disease. If economists say sensible and humane things, as they sometimes do, it is in part by accident, by a process of random truth. In politics, we speak of the radical right and the radical left. Abe Rotstein has suggested that modern liberal economists belong to the radical centre. As intellectuals and citizens, they are usually in the centre of the mainstream, or at most slightly to the left. But as technocrats, using techniques increasingly developed out of the exigencies of economic theory or adapted from the physical sciences, they may build models and propose policies which are genuinely radical in the sense of the social disruption that would result from their serious application. A case in point is that, in a world of tariffs, there is an almost universal commitment of economists to free trade, including its unilateral pursuit. In this fashion, economists tend either to support the *status quo* by their irrelevance and absurdity, or to contribute to the further disruption of a world that is already out of control.

Consider poverty as a case in point. In the last decade it has suddenly become visible in North America. The only economist who played any significant role in this discovery was John Kenneth Galbraith, and he is not highly regarded within the guild. The oversight is not surprising, for economists for at least the past century have not had anything important to say about the causes of poverty. Unwilling or unable to diagnose, prescription becomes haphazard. Economists talk about the poor as if they were dealing with dropouts who need a little help in shaping up. The possibility that industrialization, at least under capitalism, creates the poor in the very process of creating the affluent – or, worse still, that the affluent owe some considerable portion of their affluence to their ability to exploit others at home and abroad – is rarely perceived. The absence of perception, combined with the technocratic bias, is fatal to policy. Elaborate proposals to reform tax systems[6] or apply cost-benefit techniques to poverty programmes,[7] mask the distinct possibility that liberal democratic societies, like Canada, are unable, because of their power structure, to do anything serious about correcting poverty.

If the economist is a technocrat, then what manner of intellectual is he? A distinction must be made between the expert as traditional intellectual and the expert as organic intellectual. The former devotes himself to a critique of the way it is. The latter devotes himself to working for the system, not only, or even primarily, by helping in his small way to solve its problems – which is largely legitimate and proper – but rather by rationalizing its operation; by developing theory which ends up proving that this is really the best of all possible worlds, by endlessly debating minor differences in policy so that everyone forgets, partly through fatigue, that there may be major alternatives that no one is ever taking the bother to try to conceptualize. The economist today, with rare exceptions – the latter notably being Marxists such as Baran and Sweezy[8] – is an organic intellectual; fundamental criticism is *passé*.

To perceive the nature of present-day economics yields insight on the state of economics in Canada. If economists exist to rationalize or justify the economy, then those in a branch-plant economy rationalize the neocolonial situation. The status of the Canadian economy is hardly in doubt. Its efficient functioning rests on the turning out of branch-plant intellectuals, or organic intellectuals twice removed from the seats of power. As the Canadian economy has become Americanized, it follows, with only a short lag, that its economics must be Americanized as part of the broader process of Americanizing the educational system, both as institution and technique. John Porter has shown[9] how the Canadian élites systematically neglected higher education so as to remove potential threats to their power; in the process they neglected even their own education and contributed to the drain of power outward to the United States.

It would appear, indeed, that they failed even to run the branch plants efficiently, much less to create any kind of independent economy with a capacity to generate growth on its own. The great educational push in Canada in recent years is intended to improve the efficiency of the branch-plant economy. The process has been abetted by the importation of American academics, particularly in the social sciences. Rhetorical support for reformist measures to improve the performance of the branch-plant economy without changing its structure has been offered by the Economic Council, itself an emasculated version of the United States Council of Economic Advisers, with its research often done by economists otherwise employed by the Canadian-American Committee, a lobby group for North American economic integration, that is, for Canada's political disintegration. Canadian economists have made their contribution by, with few exceptions, demonstrating that the benefits from foreign investment are large and positive and, to the extent they are less than they might be, should be increased by abandoning the Canadian tariff. As apologists for the American-based multinational corporation, they are outranked only by American economists in the employ of American business schools. The Canadian case is no exception to the rule that an economy gets the economists it deserves.

Separate departments of political economy did not emerge in any significant way in Canada until the last decade of the nineteenth century. The initial tendency was to import scholars. As J. J. Spengler observes in the preface to the only book-length study of Canadian economic thought, by C. D. W. Goodwin: "Not until after World War I did Canadian scholars begin to contribute to the progress of economic science in general."[10] Following Goodwin, an examination of the appointment of W. J. Ashley to the first chair in political economy at the University of Toronto is illustrative of persistent phenomena. Ashley was an economic historian, not a theorist. When he came to Toronto, economic theory, especially as applied to commercial policy,

was a source of bitter controversy in Canada consequent on Macdonald's National Policy in defiance of British free trade. Ashley was
interviewed by the provincial premier, and it was clear that, being an
economic historian, it was anticipated that he would not adopt a
doctrinaire position; in fact, he did not disappoint. Nor was it an
accident that economic historians were reliable protectionists, for
economic history, as born in Germany and England, was a reaction
to the laissez-faire bias of classical economics. In the event, Canadian
economics, particularly at Toronto, was biased for the long run
towards economic history. The occasional indigenous character of
Canadian economics can be seen as an unexpected benefit of the
tariff; when Dales refers to "the sad effects on Canada's intellectual
life of the duel in the dark between commercial protectionists and
their opponents," he is in the curious position of an economic historian created by the tariff and now attacking it.

Goodwin makes a number of useful observations on the effects of
the tariff, as symbolic of the economy, on Canadian economics. On
the one hand:

The widely-held conviction that orthodox political economy was
no more than laissez-faire propaganda became for more than half a
century the most powerful check on the development of Canadian
economics.

On the other hand:

After Confederation the Liberal party, in opposing the National
Policy of high tariffs treated political economy practically as revealed
truth. It is easy to understand why for most people there was no
distinction between the study of economics and a policy of laissez-
faire.

Finally:

In the 1880's and 1890's a combination of circumstances gave life to
economics. Industrialization, westward expansion, and a new national
consciousness resulted in unprecedented public awareness of economic problems; at the same time controversies over commercial policy
(which for fifty years had made economic science unpopular) abated,
and attention focussed on labour legislation, land taxation, industrial
combinations, and a government currency. By the turn of the century

powerful social groups which formerly had regarded economics with distrust as an obstacle to tariff protection came to view the science with approval because it provided arguments against trade unions and government intervention.

The tendency for economics to reflect the economy is clearly evident.

The implication, by Goodwin and Dales, that the tariff inhibited economic scholarship is fair enough, but the hopelessness of the dilemma needs to be understood. On the one hand, protective tariffs were inevitable in areas entering upon industrialization; for Canada, there were the powerful examples of the United States and Germany. On the other hand, the imperialism of British classical economics was the counterpart of British imperialism of free trade. Intellectual imperialism is real, but reactions to it in marginal areas typically produce mediocrity – though the judgment is largely internal and tautological.

The breakdown of the British empire in the interwar period permitted economics to develop at the margin. "Economics came of age in Canada in the 1920's" (Dales). The so-called Toronto school of economics, associated particularly with the work of H. A. Innis and to a lesser extent with W. A. Mackintosh of Queen's University, emerged as the first and last evidence of an indigenous Canadian economics. Dales has maintained that Innis' monographs on the fur trade and the cod fisheries are the only outstanding works in economic history that relate to a non-European country. The unifying theme was the emphasis on staple production for export in new countries:

Concentration on the production of staples for export to more highly industrialized areas in Europe and later in the United States had broad implications for the Canadian economic, political and social structure. Each staple in its turn left its stamp, and the shift to new staples invariably produced periods of crises in which adjustments in the old structure were painfully made and a new pattern created in relation to a new staple.[11]

As economics, it was necessarily political economy: "The so-called Staple Theory, which is commonly used to explain economic growth in Canada, is really a pseudonym for a kind of imperial relationship."[12] Innis was creating not only a new economic history that would go beyond the traditional constitutional bias to focus on the interaction of geography, technology, and institutions, but also a new history of Canada – *vide* particularly the writings of A. R. M. Lower, the early Creighton, and the so-called Laurentian school – and ultimately a new economics, at least in the negative sense, of dissent from the mainstream.

Innis, the Canadian Veblen, rejected both Marshallian equilibrium analysis and Keynesian short-run monetary analysis. He was able to exploit the already established bias toward economic history at Toronto, the peculiar weakness of economics generally as a discipline in the 1920s – its sterility between Marshall and Keynes, with the latter saving the discipline from the worst of all fates, irrelevance – and the momentary freedom as Canada moved from the British to the American empire. Briefly, novelty was possible.

Though after 1940 Innis was to turn from Canadian economic history to universal history, there are numerous trenchant observations by him on the consequences of American imperialism for Canada and an implicit recognition of the futility of Canadian economics. His death in 1952 ended a dominance over Canadian social science that was more than intellectual – he both chaired the Toronto Department of Political Economy and was Dean of the Graduate School – and facilitated an Americanization of Canadian economics that has virtually obliterated his own work. It is tempting to assign the blame to his disciples who too often paid him only lip service and dismissed his analysis with that great Canadian cliché, "anti-Americanism."[13] But Daniel Drache has recently demonstrated[14] an inherent weakness in Innis' work that is symptomatic of (non-radical) attempts to dissent within the American system. Innis was a liberal nationalist for whom Canada, having sprung from liberalism, must develop its own national version. He recognized liberal (American) imperialism, but he did not abandon his faith in Canadian liberalism. The resulting tension made him personally highly productive but socially increasingly irrelevant. His contemporaries, unable to accept his analysis of liberal imperialism, became continentalists. Significantly, a present revival of interest in Innis, of which Drache is the most relevant example, is found among young socialist scholars. Innis, convinced that the price system was the basis of liberal culture and a fundamental protection for the individual, was unwilling to recognize positive government and hence precluded the possibility of adequate defence against Americanization. For those without that conviction, Innis' anti-imperialism argues powerfully for the necessity of a Canadian nationalism of the left.

In the period since the decade of the 1920s, the key event in economics at the global level is, of course, not Innis but Keynes. The combination of Keynesian economics and American imperialism made economics relevant and choked off independent developments in peripheral areas such as Canada. Canadian economics in the wake of the Keynesian revolution returned to its historic mediocrity; Innis survived by transcending the discipline but at the necessary price of irrelevance and neglect. From a low point in the mid-1950s, Canadian economics has recovered via Americanization. Significantly, the critical discovery was that the Canadian economy was a miniature replica of the American economy, with its lesser efficiency attributable to inappropriate Canadian policy. To stress the commonality of the American and Canadian economies at a time when the latter is a satellite of the former is to offer the most convincing evidence possible of how the political has been drained out of political economy. Innis as doyen of Canadian economics gave way to Harry Johnson of the University of Chicago and London School of Economics, seats of the new and the old imperialism. Where Innis had resisted and Canadianized, Johnson promoted and Americanized.

That there are benefits, albeit of a second order, from being safely ensconced within the paradigm, should be obvious; the contributions of Canadian economists to the American-dominated discipline have been ably, even generously, detailed by Johnson, and the interested reader is referred thereto.[15] In the days of the British empire, Canadian insistence on a protective tariff inhibited the importation of British classical economics. The result was not creativity but backwardness and mediocrity. In the days of the American empire, the rhetoric of pro-imperialism may be less, but the reality in terms of economic policy greater. The inhibitions once imposed by the tariff have been transcended, directly by a spate of monographs both beating the tariff to death in its own right and attributing any alleged costs of foreign ownership – the new concern of the masses – to the tariff, and indirectly by opting in the American tradition for technique over relevance. Mediocrity has given way to competence, and the Canadian economist as technocrat has earned the respect of his American counterpart. By accepting the imperial rules of the game, he can, as in the case of the Carter Commission on Taxation, work out policies of a purity and rationality denied to those who work in the less tidy and more pathological seat of power.

But quantity and competence are not to be confused with creativity. If economics in Canada is to become something other than a rationalization of a satellitic economy, then, short of the liberation of the economy and the consequent liberation of economics – admittedly the reliable though improbable route – Canadian economists must begin the struggle of coming to grips with the power structure within which the economy is imbedded. By ignoring power, the economist, in Canada and elsewhere, claims to be apolitical. Unfortunately, he seems simply to be trapped in the existing constellation of power and ideology, and to be deeply political in a sense that only the innocent can be.

It must be conceded that the future of economics lies largely outside our hands, though the revival of Innis is a useful technique of resistance for the sake of a Canadian economics. The revival of interest within the United States in Marx, as the last political economist, is a more hopeful development, not only because of the immediate relevance of even a fossilized Marxism, but primarily because it implies a subversion of the present paradigm that is a prerequisite for a new synthesis and leap forward.

Ultimately, however, there can be no escape from the rule that economics follows the economy. The increasing contradictions of American capitalism and, less certainly, the mounting concern for Canadian independence, suggest the possibility that economics in the 1970s may at least return to the creativity it demonstrated, at both the centre and the margin, in the interwar period. Until that happens, however, the non-economist heeds us at his peril.

NOTES

1 C. B. Macpherson, "The Social Sciences," in Julian Park, ed., *The Culture of Contemporary Canada* (Ithaca and Toronto, 1957).
2 "Canadian Scholarship in Economics: Achievement and Outlook," in *Scholarship in Canada, 1967,* ed. R. H. Hubbard (Toronto, 1968).
3 *New Dimensions of Political Economy* (New York, 1967), p. 4.

4 The remainder of this section draws in part on the author's "Economics and Mystification," *Journal of Canadian Studies,* vol. IV, no. 1 (Feb. 1969), pp. 55-9.

5 *The Technological Society* (New York, 1964).

6 *Royal Commission on Taxation, Report* (Ottawa, 1967). For a detailed critique of the Carter report in these terms, see Stephen H. Hymer and Melville H. Watkins, "The Radical Centre – Carter Reconsidered," *Canadian Forum* (June 1967).

7 Economic Council of Canada, *Fifth Annual Review* (Ottawa, 1968).

8 See, for example, Paul A. Baran and Paul M. Sweezy, *Monopoly Capital* (New York and London, 1966).

9 *The Vertical Mosaic* (Toronto, 1965).

10 *Canadian Economic Thought* (Durham, NC, 1961).

11 H. A. Innis, *Empire and Communications* (Oxford, 1950).

12 C. W. Gonick, "The Political Economy of Canadian Independence," *Canadian Dimension* (May-June, 1967).

13 An important exception is Donald Creighton; see his *Harold Adams Innis: Portrait of a Scholar* (Toronto, 1957).

14 "Harold Innis: A Canadian Nationalist," *Journal of Canadian Studies,* vol. IV, no. 2 (May 1969), pp, 7-12).

15 Harry G. Johnson, "Canadian Contributions to the Discipline of Economics since 1945," *Canadian Journal of Economics,* vol. 1, no. 1 (Feb. 1968), pp. 129-46.

Abraham Rotstein

The managing editor of the *Canadian Forum*. He teaches economics at the University of Toronto.

Binding Prometheus

Of all peoples on earth, Canadians are least able to understand the process of Americanization. America is total environment: it envelops us as a mist, penetrating every sphere of our cultural, political, economic, and social environment. For that very reason we seem to feel powerless, unwilling and unable to achieve the perspective necessary for an appraisal of our situation. It sometimes seems as superfluous to ask what should be done about the Americanization of this country as it is to ask what should be done about the weather.

It may well be that an assessment of the ground that we have already lost and of the process which continues to overwhelm us would lead any objective observer to declare "game over" in the battle for Canadian independence. But there is a moment at which the purging of illusion and even the deepest pessimism can beget the firmest resolution to survive.

The global significance of this country's fate should not be overlooked. Americanization is today a worldwide process and Canada is both the sharpest example and the clearest early warning system to many countries who are still on the fringe of a universal process that is proceeding with enormous impetus. A global perspective may also offer a better focus on our own dilemma. A preoccupation with Canadian-American relations as a bilateral process tends to create a mood which is introverted and myopic. We are thus inclined to miss the salient features and forces that transcend this bilateral relationship while still having a substantial effect on it. I refer particularly to the political and social consequences of industrialization as carried forward by the present thrust of the multinational corporation. It is the latest episode of the interplay of society and the machine.

The global expansion of the multinational corporation, usually sired by an American parent, can be seen by the historian as the New Mercantilism. The older mercantilism (roughly 1450-1750), spearheaded by the innocent wares of trade, carried the first European global thrust to the shores of the outlying continents of the world. Europeans established small trading enclaves and engaged in a very restricted operation in relation to local host countries in Asia and Africa. (The Americas, of course, had a very different history.) The innocence of this relationship was lost by the latter part of the nineteenth century when the expansion of Europe had militated for a total political domination of Asia and Africa in the period of economic, cultural, and political subjugation of colonialism. Nevertheless, for periods approaching two hundred years, small coastal states successfully contained and regulated the European mercantilist enterprises and effectively preserved their own national independence.

The thrust of the New Mercantilism is not that of trade but of technology, and in that sense it carries the life blood of the emerging technological society. The nature of the threat which this poses to national independence is of an entirely different order than the earlier instance of trade. A different appraisal of the situation is needed and a number of new measures will be required for the containment of the process.

What we must consider the one most significant area of this threat to national independence is the virtual monopolization of new technological development in the hands of the American multinational corporation which has become the single most dynamic economic force of our time. The value of the production of all multinational corporations in countries outside their home base in 1967 exceeded $214 billion. This makes the aggregate production of these corporations abroad the third largest economy in the world, second only to the domestic economies of the United States and the Soviet Union. To throw further light on the magnitudes involved, this production exceeded the total volume of world trade in 1967 (according to figures from GATT) and exceeded as well the combined gross national products of the United Kingdom and Japan. One forecast by the International Chamber of Commerce suggests that multinational corporations abroad will grow at a rate of no less than 27 per cent per year.

Obviously this is the major challenge to the independence and national integrity of countries such as Canada.

This paper attempts to seek out what is in the industrial experience of western societies that may offer some basis for action and for hope without illusion in our present circumstances. Our itinerary roams far afield, our argument is condensed and elliptic, not to say arbitrary, and the possibilities that are sketched out for Canadian independence against the tide of Americanization are at best intuitive. An uncompromising assessment of the Canadian political psyche must go hand in hand with an appraisal of the chequered course of the industrial experience of the West. There are grounds for believing that no determinism whether economic, ideological, or technological can properly encompass or predict the social, political, and moral erup-

tions which we have already witnessed in the unexpected century
and a half of the machine age. Hope rooted in the tides of both
historical experience and historical uncertainty may be brought to
bear on the present impasse of an eroding Canadian independence.

I. THE FIRST INDUSTRIAL REVOLUTION

Americanization and industrialization today are closely intertwined
and require a historical perspective to appreciate the range of forces
at work. Discussions of the consequences of industrialization tend to
centre on the confining effects of the machine on social existence,
the tendency for a proliferating bureaucracy to force daily life into a
straitjacket. In backward perspective, however, other forces can be
discerned; some social effects veered in exactly the opposite direction.
Three main phases can be discerned: the immediate social consequences of the industrial revolution in Europe, the effects on the
colonies, and the larger tidal wave of moral forces that were released
later in the nineteenth century.

In the first stage of the industrial revolution, the institutional
requirements at the time centred on the regular provision of the
voluminous quantities of raw materials and labour to feed the new
industrial factories and machines. It appeared then that only a free
labour market, accompanied by a free market for raw materials and
land, could organize an automatic flow of a self-adjusting kind, for
the new industrial order. The social transformation which this implied was novel, indeed revolutionary. The removal of a centuries-old
system of social welfare at the parish level was required in order to
establish a free labour market, for example. The unrestricted faith in
labour as a commodity implied the most pernicious consequences for
social organization. Child labour, employment of women in the mines
for long hours, the disorganization and demoralization of the early
factory towns, all of these social phenomena are too well known to
be recapitulated here. (The full story of the social history of the
nineteenth century is best told in Karl Polanyi's *The Great Transformation.*) What was striking about the social history of that century,
however, was what we may call the "double movement." The extension of the free market system for genuine commodities was
accompanied by a simultaneous attempt to restrict the market for
such "fictitious" commodities as labour and land, neither of which

was originally "produced" for the market. This spontaneous counter-movement was the natural response of society to safeguard the two basic ingredients of social existence, man and his environment. What seemed to some in that century a conspiratorial attempt to restrict the nascent "free economy," was in reality the self-mobilization of society to safeguard the essential features of its existence. It is this social dialectic which is the most impressive feature of our adjustment to the first round of the industrial revolution. A network of social institutions arose whose primary aim was to restrict and to thwart the unrestricted effects of an automatic social order (the market economy) running along its own rules, grinding out production in response to maximum profit possibilities and the needs of the market. In the end, the market economy of the nineteenth century was indeed humanized: child labour laws, housing and zoning regulations, safety regulations in the factories, the whole trade union movement, as well as the rise of tariffs and monetary restrictions in the international economy. It was also the era of the birth of socialism. All of these institutional devices were designed to insulate and protect the social order from an attempt to crowd society into the confines and rules represented by the market economy. What characterized that century, we repeat, is the unexpected renaissance of social institutions that were meant to free society from the juggernaut organized to feed and extend the new industrial order.

The impact of the industrial revolution on the colonial areas of Asia and Africa had a different history. For the first centuries of European contact with outlying countries, the European presence was limited and strictly confined to trading enclaves in coastal areas. Numerous examples exist in West Africa and on the Malabar Coast of India. Local rulers maintained full sovereignty and jurisdiction even though Europeans were from time to time engaged in political and diplomatic intrigue in the areas in which they landed and traded. On the whole, this assertion of sovereignty, the creation of a body of restrictive regulations by local rulers in regard to foreign European merchants, safeguarded their societies from the disruptive effects which were to come later.

The collapse of indigenous regimes came in a great rush roughly after the middle of the nineteenth century. European powers seized political control of the Asian and African continents, each rushing to carve out a sizable empire. Complex political forces were at work, but certainly one of the features of this rush to colonial empire was the attempt to secure total control over land areas which were producing the growing volume of raw materials needed to feed the European industrial machines. Another consideration was the large markets represented in these areas for European manufactured goods which were forthcoming in a torrent of new production, following the widespread industrial organization of European economies. But it required the force of arms to achieve the end of local independence.

In the present period, in a second and much more powerful round of what we may call the New Mercantilism, the moral of this story should be apparent. The new multinational corporations threaten the survival of the indigenous cultures and political integrity of the countries which they penetrate. Again, a well-conceived programme of regulation and careful accommodation should go far to limiting and restricting these effects of the second round of global penetration, whose result is rapidly becoming the Americanization of the globe. The areas of economic regulation and control may range widely: the policies of these multinational corporations in regard to local management, the extent of domestic production facilities and export policies, the participation of local capital and entrepreneurs, policies in regard to expansion and new investment, and finally the protection of the local country from the extension of American law through extraterritorial legislation.

This type of broad approach may benefit from the lessons of the first round of mercantilism at the margin of Europe. There was in these areas a vigorous stand-off relationship whereby chartered companies and trading agencies were confined and restricted in their operations. They had specific rights and they were met by an existing legal and political containment, which was amazingly strong even in the very small African potentates and in the small principalities of India. Countries such as Canada and other Western European countries should be able to muster at least as much initiative and imagination in the protection of their own independence and cultural survival as was demonstrated over a century ago by much weaker and often semi-literate small countries.

The third important lesson to be drawn from this first round of industrialization concerns the unexpected release of new moral forces within Europe itself which resulted in the transformation of traditional societies to the beginnings of what we now call modernization.

In backward perspective it would appear that tidal forces of a moral and ideological character arose, which altered the most basic assumptions on which society was organized and had dramatic effects on institutions and life-styles at the grass-roots level. It seemed that a strange dialectic with the machine released these new forces to create the modern West. The institutional change was enormous: the rapid development of mass literacy, mass education, universal suffrage, the development of new forms of public opinion and communication such as the daily newspaper, and a much more democratic and responsive society moving forward from the control of the traditional aristocratic élites which had been at the helm of European countries for many centuries. It is at this level that the lasting effects of the first machine age can be perceived. New premises of democracy and freedom and new axioms of political theory became an unexpected heritage of industrialization.

Summing up, the social history of the first century and a half of the machine offers a curious perspective. It began in such areas as the early Manchester of the 1840s, with the gin mills, the shocking conditions in the factories, the disruption of local networks of welfare and protection in society. In turn, a series of counterforces emerged to the point where a new conception of life and society eventually burst the bonds of the confining elements of the market economy. This should offer some evidence of the strength of the inner resources which the human social response may bring to bear at the present juncture, as globe-girdling networks of computers and complex technological processes penetrate once more in a second global invasion under the aegis of the American multinational corporation.

II. THE SECOND ROUND: MESSIANISM v. DESPAIR

Two divergent faiths confront the new technology today: a fervent messianism and an absolute despair.

For the adherents of the first faith, the new global thrust of technology has become identified as the very essence of progress. This tradition rests on a curious marriage between a messianic strand long characteristic of western thought, and the feeling that technology itself is the main vehicle for the establishment of the good life which is embodied in our vision of "the end of days." The feeling is widespread today that any new discovery in science or technology and any mechanical or electronic advance that promises a greater degree of efficiency can only bring us closer to that future. The notion abounds that as we ride the crest of an ever-proliferating technology, we ride the light and the progress which is the promise of our civilization. In a world of growing urban chaos, ecological devastation and pollution, and the nuclear threat, such a view needs no lengthy rebuttal.

The second group regards the stringencies of the new technology with the deepest pessimism. At stake is not only the independence of individual countries but the survival of the major values of western society. Modern bureaucracy, necessary for co-ordination and control of technology, has become a network of anonymous tyranny, the chief threat to the continuity of a tradition of freedom. The institutions which are the spearhead of this technology, such as the multinational corporation, easily displace and shatter indigenous cultures in the course of the technical onslaught.

Simplistic answers fail to meet the situation. The trite observation that "man has created technology, and so he can control it" does justice neither to the complexity of the accompanying social organization nor to the stringency with which we have committed ourselves to ongoing technological change. Technology is not born naked in the world but in a social context. There are questions of who controls technology, how technological change is co-ordinated, how technology expands and renews itself, and how its costs and benefits are distributed. These questions require an institutional solution, for they deal with the social cocoon in which technology is nurtured. Technology, in short, comes in a social and political package which necessarily will determine its consequences. The demands for proper co-ordination of the various inputs, raw materials, information, and the proper ordering of society in order to accommodate complex mechanical and electronic systems produce a stringency of their own. The feeling arises of man encompassed in a bureaucratic network running away on its own tracks.

Realism is needed in appraising the depth and complexity of the problem, but total despair may be premature. In so far as we find that the new technology is clothed in the laws and values of the Stars and Stripes, we are still able to counter and to contain, even if only in the near-term, the special effects and political thrust of the multinational corporation. The creation, at least through close regulation, of the equivalent of the old enclave for the multinational corporation is still possible. But it is sentimentality of the first order to pursue a policy, as has recently been followed in Canada, of enlisting the corporation in a set of "guidelines" for good corporate behaviour on a voluntary basis. This is only the latest example of the consistent history of uncertainty and vacillation in regard to the question of the multinational corporation. We have been preoccupied with only one set of consequences, namely the economic boon which these corporations offered to the development of the Canadian economy.

It must appear to be the greatest of paradoxes for a foreign observer to note the passive and quiescent way in which Canada has dealt with the penetration of its economy up to the present day. To take one example, the popular book, *The American Challenge,* by the French author J. J. Servan-Schreiber, rang the alarm bells in France when the level of foreign ownership of industry had hardly reached one-tenth the level in Canada. The fact that this country vacillates in a lethargic discussion of this issue, is a mark mainly of the impotence of the Canadian political culture, the weakness of the "will to survive" in this country.

III. THE "WILL TO SURVIVE"

The greatest weakness in the set of requirements for preserving Canadian independence is the peculiar intellectual and political tradition that forms the present basis of the Canadian political culture. In brief, we are the legatees of a transplanted political tradition stemming from classical English liberalism. While we have gained the legal trappings of sovereignty and independence, we are unable to muster the symbols and the political vocabulary necessary to understand the vital interests of this country and to act for its preservation. The essential weakness of the Canadian political culture lies in its derivative liberalism. This is the heritage of an intellectual colonialism whose concepts and symbols are inadequate to our dilemma and bypass the major problems surrounding Canadian independence.

Stepping back for a moment to view the question of the political culture which liberalism in general has produced, let us examine several contemporary problems and the liberal pronouncements about them. Centred as it is on a philosophy of nurturing and granting freedoms to the individual, liberalism has glossed over or failed to recognize some fundamental issues which relate to society as a whole and to the structure of its institutions. In the first instance we may examine, for example, the question of "the nation" as seen in liberal philosophy. The "nation" *per se* has no specific or recognized place in this outlook. It becomes in practice the source of obstruction to the free flow of goods and of capital through instituting tariffs and restrictions. It is further regarded as a source of chauvinism and of parochial and irrational ideas which obstruct the free flow of natural good will and disembodied "ideas" from man to man across the globe. The nation in its own right has no recognized existence as an aggregate or collective entity. There is consequently almost no way to mobilize liberal opinion in defence of the nation except in cases where either civil liberties or direct military threat is involved. The threat today however is from a different direction, and consequently unrecognized in a liberal perspective. The modern phenomenon of nationalism is totally incomprehensible and can only be seen by liberals as a demonic force.

A second major issue is the question of poverty. In this case, classical liberalism simply proclaims that in a free society (organized as a market economy) each individual has an equal opportunity to seek his just reward on the market. Thus poverty, at least in this formulation of the philosophy, remains a problem for which the individual himself must accept responsibility. Having been given equal opportunity to make his way among his fellows, there is no responsibility in principle accruing to society for the fact that he has not been successful.

A third illustration is provided by the problem of race. Liberal philosophy indicates only that "we look at the individual and not his 'background.'" The problem of race, in short, is abolished by a focus which necessarily begins with a view of society and its components as an aggregate of the individuals of which it is composed and their rights. There is a basic non-recognition of a vital problem which in its essence cannot be understood within the confines of an individualistic philosophy, but can only be seen as that of a collective entity.

These three issues, nation, poverty and race, curiously enough are the ones that have come up with a vengeance in the twentieth century, at the same time as they are the central blind spots of the liberal philosophy. One of the reasons that we have failed so badly to cope with them is that fundamentally we are unable to understand them because of ideological myopia.

The paradox is all the more striking since the questions at least of poverty and race are as old as mankind itself and have been problems ever since the existence of recorded history; the nation as we conceive of it today is certainly several hundred years old. It is therefore worth reflecting on why they have remained so deliberately obscured in the political theory fostered by liberal tradition. Today, moreover, these problems carry with them an urgency and a demand for virtually overnight solutions. The very fierceness of the claims made upon us may derive in part from the obscurity with which these problems were viewed previously. Add to this the fact that Canada has never had a historical moment of the actual creation of its national existence, and we may begin to understand why the combination of a colonial mentality (in the intellectual sense) and a quiescent history have together created no firm bases for an independent political culture in this country.

The only two issues which succeed generally in creating popular and vigorous reactions are on the one hand territorialism (viz. the public uproar in regard to sovereignty in the Canadian North) and in a second instance extraterritoriality. Both of these issues which are alive in the popular imagination are, however, nineteenth century in their essential importance. For the issue which mainly confronts us today, in the sense of being of vital national interest, is necessarily rooted in the major features of twentieth-century life, namely, technology, computers, electronics, all of which find their home in the economy. And it is the economy, of course, over which Canadians have lost virtually all control and with which they demonstrate only a sporadic and very partial concern.

In the absence of a vision of our nationhood and of a political culture possessed of symbols to evoke and protect our independence, it is no cause for wonder that the ideological pull of the United States has been strong and attractive throughout our history. We have found no alternative vision to sustain us in terms of our own political culture.

As a result, our social policy has also been largely derivative. It is a fact that most Canadian innovations and public policies, virtually since 1840, have been imitative of the United States: the building of the canals, the railroads, the land-grant system which was necessary in the settling of the Canadian West, anti-combines legislation (imitating the anti-trust philosophy of the United States) and finally the "war on poverty" – all have been derivative of American legislation. The seal of approval in Canada has derived from the earlier attempts at such legislation by the United States. This has both minimized the risk and created a source of legitimacy sufficient to endorse equivalent policies in this country. Admittedly, this legislation has often responded to similar problems, but it is true nevertheless that our sense of social innovation has been substantially restricted and fearful because the premises of our national existence have essentially been derivative and inadequate.

What we understand least is the nature of power, particularly as it applies to the economy. Power has generally been treated with deep suspicion and arm's-length reservation in English political philosophy culminating in Lord Acton's famous *obiter dicta*. We have relied instead on a faith in the built-in harmony of the market society growing out of Adam Smith's maxims about the individual pursuit of self-interest. The effect has been to gloss over or to negate the importance of the locus of economic power.

Thus when the power to make decisions shifts out of the country by virtue of foreign ownership of the economy, we are barely conscious that anything of importance has happened. We are unable to meet the challenge of the new technological thrust centring on huge economic and bureaucratic systems and external control. The world of atomistic individualism has faded away everywhere but in our minds.

IV. STRAIN AND TRANSFORMATION

The global strains of the technological society are becoming apparent everywhere. There is not only the contradiction between affluence and poverty (both domestically and internationally) but also the contradiction between nominal independence and real independence of nation states. The heritage of colonialism is being restored by technology, but the urge to attain genuine freedom continues unabated in many countries.

There are other strains as well that centre on the social constrictions of the great bureaucratic networks. We have never been more passionate or more militant in the attempt to awaken the counterforces for local control.

We can already see the signs of what appear to be volcanic forces arising as a countermovement to this global extension of the technological network. We are witnessing the most important feature perhaps of this new round of technological penetration, namely the second eruption in the great dialectic between the machine and the moral forces which are induced and released by its extension. If we can contain and channel the effects of these immense moral passions which are rapidly expressing themselves in continuing and seemingly mysterious waves of unrest, we may witness a new institutional transformation.

In France the student rebellion of May 1968, in the United States the eruptions against racism and militarism, and unrest and dissent in many other countries – similar political upheaval seems present everywhere. Even in Canadian politics, the weak whisper of the slogan "participatory democracy" has become a theme of our political life. These internal moral tides have begun to disestablish all our major institutions, religious as well as secular, churches as much as universities. Global forces, often blind and unfocused at first, have penetrated throughout the political processes of most countries. It may be too early to discern whether creative and lasting institutional change will result from this political eruption. Nevertheless, it should give pause to those in despair about the effects of technological change, who prophesy only an increasing erosion of democracy and freedom.

I have attempted in this paper to set the problem of Americanization and Canadian independence within a global perspective. I have also attempted to show that there are good reasons for avoiding premature pessimism or indeed capitulating to the spread of the technological society as spearheaded by the multinational corporation. The essential features of the history of the machine from the beginning have been the remarkable countermovements on both the institutional and moral levels which have transformed human society. I do not doubt that in Canada these forces will operate – as they will elsewhere – as the technological society continues its advance. The political forces which have been let loose are of enormous power; no established institutional force (and this includes the multinational corporation) will remain exempt from their effects.

It is apparent, however, that I have made no particular case for the survival of the nation-state within the context of these changes. In fact, the question may well be asked, "why do I see major institutional change everywhere except here?" The nation-state has become synonymous in our own day with the protection of the indigenous culture, institutions, and traditions of a particular society. It possesses the major political power and the means to resist, to modify, and to humanize the technological process. I fail to see how the nation-state can become obsolete and merged in a larger international setting as is sometimes predicted, when the additional functions and responsibilities which we attach to it increase almost daily. One need only list the tasks of economic growth, full employment, education, housing, control of pollution, and the number of other tasks continually thrust upon the nation-state, to see that it can hardly become obsolete at this time. If it remains a suitable agency for the performance and realization of these tasks, it will needs survive and assume a more democratic (and less class-ridden) role in carrying out these objectives.

The nation-state remains, in the end, the central locus of power and authority in our society and, until such time as transcending institutions have been created, we may envisage that it will remain to protect its members by moderating the intrusion of such technological forces as the spreading American corporation. For this reason, I remain a conservative in regard to Canadian survival and a radical in regard to the emergent institutions necessary to achieve this task.

Prometheus, the god who brought fire and the technical arts to mankind, was chained to a rock by Zeus where he remained during the greater part of human history. Now that he has freed himself in the century and a half of the machine age and tried to render the earth as his own, it will be necessary for man to chain him once more.

Larratt Higgins

An economist and a part-time lecturer at Atkinson College, York University. He has contributed articles to the *International Journal* and other periodicals on the management of Canadian water resources.

The alienation of Canadian resources:
the case of the Columbia River Treaty

Canada's presence on the international stage has been fading for the past fifteen years or so, especially in its dealings with the United States. During this period there has been also a noticeable decline in the power of the federal government in relation to the provinces. There is a connection between these two processes. The erosion of federal power in both respects stems in great part from a view, held widely in Ottawa, that the federal government is little more than an agent of the provinces on the one hand, and little more than a province of the United States on the other. A corollary of this view is that the government at Ottawa has no prerogative to exercise initiative or to take decisions in international negotiations concerning matters which come under provincial or divided jurisdiction. The result has been to reduce the federal government to something resembling a secretariat, whose function is but to implement decisions taken at other levels. The decline of Ottawa's power and influence in these terms can be seen clearly in its dealings with the United States and British Columbia in the Columbia River dispute.

The dispute was resolved finally on September 16, 1964, when the Columbia River Treaty of January 17, 1961, came into force.[1] Under the terms of the treaty, Canada undertook to build three storage dams in British Columbia at a cost then estimated at $410.6 million. In return Canada was to receive $274.8 million on the ratification date, with other payments totalling $70 million to follow.* The operation of these dams was to be under international supervision by a Permanent Engineering Board consisting of two members designated by each country. The two American members are Washington officials; on the Canadian side one member represents Ottawa while the other is a British Columbia nominee. The Canadian operating entity is provincial – the BC Hydro and Power Authority.

After thirty years Canada might receive a small but undefined amount of electric energy. In exchange for other unspecified energy

---

* This arrangement was touted as giving Canada a "profit" of $52 million on the assumption that the funds received could be invested at 5½ per cent interest until they were needed to cover expenditures. However, operating costs were omitted, most of the money was invested in the United States at 4¼ per cent, and the cost estimates took no account of inflation. *The Columbia River Treaty, Protocol, and Related Documents,* p. 138.

benefits which would accrue to a Canadian corporation, Canada is also required to make available, at its expense, some seventeen thousand acres of land in British Columbia for flooding by a dam to be built in the United States. The treaty can be terminated after sixty years upon ten years' written notice. Certain provisions relating to Canadian operation for flood control do not expire with the treaty.

The Columbia River Treaty, in its effect, is revolutionary.[2] The previous law and the institutions for administering the Columbia basin are swept away. In place of co-operation by national entities, the Canadian portion of the Columbia basin has been placed under international control, which is to be based upon the greatest good for the basin as a whole. The American portion of the basin remains under American control. This means that, in cases of conflict, Canadian operation must give way to the majority interest with no compensation for lost opportunity. In other words, the costs of co-operation are to be borne by Canada while the benefits will be reaped by the United States wherever a divergence of interest arises. The Columbia River Treaty is not for co-operative development and operation; it integrates the smaller but vital Canadian part of the basin into the whole.

One result of the Columbia River Treaty is that there are now two quite different sets of legal principles in force governing relations between Canada and the United States in water questions. The Columbia is governed by the continental resource concept of integrating Canadian resources into the economy of North America. This concept does not recognize the possibility of conflict in that all actions are dictated by the majority interest.

Other watersheds are still governed by the Boundary Waters Treaty of 1909,[3] which rests upon a premise of development of North America by separate national entities. The principle behind this treaty recognizes the possibility of conflict, and accordingly provides for its resolution. It provides also for international co-operation where both parties stand to gain without sacrificing more favourable alternatives. A set of rules and a mechanism were provided whereby disputes between Canada and the United States could be settled equitably within an agreed legal framework. The International Joint Commission was set up consisting of two national sections, each with three members headed by a chairman, as the machinery for resolving conflict between the two countries.

Two legal doctrines were embedded in the 1909 treaty. The first, and the more important, was the Harmon doctrine, which asserted that the upstream country has an unfettered right to "exclusive jurisdiction and control over the use and diversion ... of waters on its own side of the line which in their natural channels would flow across the boundary or into boundary waters."[4] In addition, the downstream state is prevented from "construction ... of any works in waters at a lower level than the boundary the effect of which is to raise the natural level of the waters on the other side of the boundary"[5] without the approval of the International Joint Commission.

The Harmon doctrine favours the United States both vis-à-vis Mexico and the eastern parts of North America, which were of concern when the treaty was being negotiated.* However, in the western part of the continent, the doctrine favours Canada on most of the trans-boundary rivers of significant size and potential. The doctrine was asserted most recently by the United States in 1952. Canada sought permission on behalf of the Consolidated Mining and Smelting Company (Cominco) to construct the Waneta dam on the Pend d'Oreille River, a tributary of the Columbia which flows from the United States into Canada. The Waneta dam would raise the level of the river at the boundary by a matter of inches and thus cause slight flooding of two and a half acres of US territory. The United States reiterated its claim to upstream sovereignty in a manner designed to preserve its future freedom of action to divert the Pend d'Oreille. The Order of Approval issued by the International Joint Commission in July 1952 stressed: "... the right of the United States recognized in Article II of the Boundary Waters Treaty to construct such works as it may consider necessary or desirable for making most advantageous use reasonably practical on its own side of the international boundary by diversion for power purposes or otherwise." The order carried with it the concurrence of both countries, and consequently is a valid precedent.

---

* Prior to 1909, the United States had diverted the Allagash River in Maine into the Penobscot, thereby depriving a small Canadian lumbering operation of the water for log driving that was necessary for its survival. The diversion of Lake Michigan into the Mississippi basin is a similar assertion of the Harmon doctrine which continues to this day.

The second doctrine embedded in the treaty is that of prior appropriation. This doctrine is not as explicitly stated in the treaty as is the Harmon doctrine, but it was asserted by the United States in a protocol to the treaty.*

Within the International Joint Commission, many of the words used were strong, and most of the positions taken were firm; but for the most part, the resulting actions provided harmonious and equitable lawful solutions. Canadian diplomats, who tend to assume that under no circumstances can Canada afford to offend Uncle Sam, were often made nervous by the proceedings. Nevertheless, in the process of sharp debate, much misunderstanding was cleared away, and an impressive body of precedent was created within the international law derived from the Boundary Waters Treaty.[6]

Part of the reason for the success of the International Joint Commission in the past undoubtedly was that, in most cases, the disputes were not international confrontations. Conflicts over problems such as the Great Lakes, the Niagara River, and the St Lawrence were for the most part between functional interests such as navigation, power, conservation, and riparian owners on both sides of the boundary. Canadian interests were not pitted against American interests, as such. For example, the Chicago diversion reduces the power potential of the Niagara and St Lawrence rivers in both countries. Conflicting interests within each country prevented each national section of the International Joint Commission from taking an extreme view, and tended to promote a greater reliance upon legal precedent than otherwise might have been the case.

Another reason for the original success of the International Joint Commission, at least from a Canadian point of view, was the willingness of the government to support a vigorous assertion of Canada's rights under the Boundary Waters Treaty. This included a sufficient

---

*   The following is an example of the doctrine in action. After the First World War the Canadian government wished to settle veterans on the Cawston benches in the valley of the Similkameen River (also in the Columbia basin). The entire low season flow of the river had already been taken into use in the United States, and any diminution of this flow would probably give rise to a claim for damages under the provision in Article II. Canada therefore built a dam to capture unused flood flows to provide irrigation water for these lands.

delegation of authority to the Canadian Section. The United States
has been hampered by a tendency to make the chairmanship of the
American Section a political appointment, and thus in effect to
relegate it to a somewhat less important status than that of its
Canadian counterpart. Very often, this has worked to the advantage
of Canada.

The initiative for joint development of the Columbia River basin
had come originally from the United States when the us Army Corps
of Engineers realized in 1943 that the full potential of the river within
American borders could not be achieved without the provision of
storage for flood flows in Canada, and for their release during the
low-flow season. The Corps of Engineers was directed to make a new
study of the American portion of the basin. In March 1944, at the
request of the United States, the two governments referred the matter
of co-operative development of the Columbia basin to the International Joint Commission.[7] The ijc set up the International Columbia River Engineering Board (ICREB) to investigate and report.

The United States had an early advantage because a great deal of
work had been done already on the American side. Two of the largest
dams in the world were generating power on the main stem of the
Columbia at Bonneville and Grand Coulee. In Canada, on the other
hand, little was known about the basin, and there were no developments on the Columbia. Topographical maps had to be prepared and
streamflow records had to be accumulated for at least a decade in
order to provide adequate information of the dimensions of water
supply before engineering proposals could be made. Thus the American plans were formulated before the Canadian alternatives emerged.

The Corps of Engineers issued a comprehensive report on the
American portion of the basin in 1949.[8] This report was important,
not only for the detailed information it brought together, but also
for a thesis it sought to establish according to which the benefits of
storage decline over time.* This fallacy was never challenged at the
official level by Canada, and ultimately it led to serious defects in the
Columbia Treaty as it applied to Canada.

* This is a fallacy on any watershed where development is taking place.
  It is true that the benefits of additional increments of storage at any
  one time do decline, but the benefits derived from a given amount of
  storage increase over time as development proceeds. See J.V. Krutilla,
  The Columbia River Treaty (Baltimore, 1967), chap. 3.

The final report of the ICREB was published in 1959. Long before the report was issued, the United States had begun to exert pressure on Canada through its early advantage in knowing its own requirements. Canada was able to resist these pressures, in part because they were blatantly premature and in part because the government of Canada was prepared to act upon the advice of the chairman of the Canadian Section, General A. G. L. McNaughton.

American pressures created two issues. One thrust came from the private sector. The Kaiser Aluminum Company approached the British Columbia government with a proposal to build a small dam at the outlet of Arrow Lakes on the main stem of the Columbia, a short distance upstream from Trail. The dam would yield $14 million annually to the United States corporation; Premier Bennett of British Columbia had agreed to accept an annual payment of $2 million with the dam to be built at Kaiser's expense.[9] The power generated in the United States during the low-flow season from released water was to be used to produce aluminum behind the American tariff to supply the market there in competition with Alcan's Kitimat project.*

The government of Canada intervened by passing the International River Improvements Act in 1955,[10] under which a federal licence is required for works which would "increase, decrease, or alter the flow of an international river." The policy of the Canadian government was set forth at the time by Jean Lesage, minister of northern affairs: "According to the Canadian constitution, works built on rivers in Canada having an effect outside the country fall under the jurisdiction of Parliament even if they are located in one province."[11] He went on to say that any projects, to be approved, must be compatible with optimum development of the resources by Canada, and that benefits from any downstream utilization must be commensurate with the resources made available.

The Kaiser deal had important implications. In the first place, it constituted recognition by downstream interests of the fact that storage dams in Canada would provide benefits in the United States,

---

* There was another private proposal by a syndicate of private power companies in the United States. They proposed to build the Mica Creek dam at a cost of $425 million, and turn it over to the province in return for timed releases, for a period of a hundred years. The economics of this proposal are considerably better than the Columbia Treaty arrangements, but Premier Bennett turned down the proposal.

and also recognition that these should be shared. Although the trans-
action was between private interests and a provincial government, it
provided a useful precedent. Second, the passing of the International
River Improvements Act demonstrated the power of the federal
government to impose its veto on a development with international
implications, even though the resource was otherwise under provincial
jurisdiction.

The other thrust of United States pressure on Canada was the
proposal of the Corps of Engineers to build a dam near Libby, Montana, on the Kootenai River in the Columbia basin.* Because this
dam would cause flooding into Canada for forty-two miles, putting
over seventeen thousand acres under water of depths up to 150 feet,
Canadian consent was needed under Article IV of the Boundary Waters
Treaty. The Libby dam was suggested by the Corps of Engineers as
early as 1948 and approved by Congress in 1950. The application was
made to the IJC in 1951. Within the IJC, the Libby and Waneta applications were under consideration simultaneously.

In the face of the Libby application, the American action in re-
confirming the right to divert the Pend d'Oreille in the Waneta order
was a major blunder; for construction of the Libby dam, the key to
United States control of the Columbia, required a repudiation of the
Harmon doctrine. Moreover, while the Americans lacked firm plans
to divert the Pend d'Oreille, the Canadians were developing their
plans to divert the Kootenay to the Columbia. It happens that as the
Kootenay River flows south in British Columbia, it passes within a
mile of the headwaters of the Columbia, and at the same elevation.
In fact, some of the waters of the Kootenay actually find their way
into the Columbia via a shallow canal that joins the two rivers. It is
therefore a simple matter to increase this diversion to the Columbia.
The waters of the Kootenay could be put to good use in Canada,
either to produce power on the Columbia (and perhaps the Fraser),

___

* The name of the portions of the river in Canada is Kootenay; in the
United States it is spelled Kootenai. The river flows south from
Canada, past the source of the Columbia, into the United States.
Then it loops to the northwest and flows back into Kootenay Lake
in Canada. Thus Canada is alternately the upstream state and the
downstream state on this river. The United States is first a downstream state, and then an upstream state.

or to provide water for irrigation on the prairies by diversion across the Rocky mountains. Indeed, the Kootenay-Columbia diversion was required for Canada if best use was to be made of the huge reservoir to be built at Mica Creek. To add force to the Canadian position, the diversion plan was cheaper and more efficient than the Libby proposal. Moreover, there was no downstream interest in the United States that would suffer damage from the diversion: on the contrary, it would provide needed flood protection.

The plan to build the Libby dam was controversial, even in the United States, because of its poor economics, and also because many Americans suspected that it was merely empire building on the part of the Corps of Engineers. In Canada the federal government opposed the application on the advice of General McNaughton, who had conceived the Canadian plan of diverting the Kootenay to the Columbia on the basis of his experience in the area many years previously. Local interests in the Kootenay valley where the river re-enters Canada tended to support the United States application. Among these was Cominco, which expected to receive a windfall gain in the order of $3 million a year from the operation of upstream storage at Libby.*

Cominco's support of the US proposal undoubtedly was based on self-interest. The company's attitude probably would have been more in tune with Canadian policy objectives if it had been made plain that it would not reap any windfall gains from Libby; there was no reason why these should not have accrued to the province of British Columbia on payment of an equitable rental for Cominco equipment used. Apparently, however, Cominco feared that the Canadian diversion plan would reduce its power output; and in this case, the government should have ensured that these fears were dispelled. The Duncan Lake project was proposed primarily to compensate Cominco for the flows that would be diverted. It is not possible to document any part that may have been played by Cominco in Premier Bennett's subsequent decision to veto the Canadian diversion plan; but the influence could have been considerable.

---

* Cominco seems not to have been concerned with the timing of releases from upstream storages, because it has been able to trade power to its satisfaction in a deal which is of enormous benefit to the Americans.

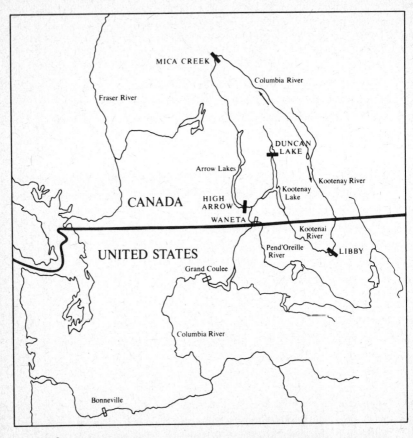

The first application for the Libby dam was withdrawn by the
United States on April 8, 1953, because of opposition by US railway
interests; under the plan, there would be extensive flooding of track.
Another reason, not stated publicly, was that the Americans entertained hopes that pressure from Cominco would cause the removal of
McNaughton from the IJC. They were anxious to get rid of him after
he had sprung the trap they set for themselves in the language of the
Waneta order; the Waneta precedent, coming during the Libby proceedings, completely deprived them of a legal case. After the local
opposition had been mollified, and after it had become evident that
McNaughton would retain the confidence of the Canadian government, the Libby application was resubmitted on May 22, 1954. It was

never disposed of by the International Joint Commission, but became a part of the political negotiations on the Columbia Treaty in which the IJC was not directly involved.

At one point, early in these political negotiations, the United States abandoned its demand for Libby and acceded to the Canadian diversion plan, which would provide the needed flood protection downstream in Idaho. Then the Bennett government, for its own political reasons, vetoed the Canadian diversion plan, much to the astonishment of the Americans. It was this action and, incredibly, its acceptance by the government in Ottawa that transformed the development of·the Columbia from a triumph of common sense and international co-operation into the wasteful disaster that has integrated the Canadian Columbia into the United States economy. There was no stand-by Canadian plan. Not only was the Libby proposal included in the Columbia Treaty, but the vested interest so created was reinforced by a clause which effectively prevents Canada from making a significant diversion.

When confronted with the British Columbia veto, the federal government could have broken off negotiations with the United States, or it could have given the Americans the option of continuing discussion within reduced terms of reference, excluding development on the Kootenay. There seems little doubt that the United States would have elected to continue the discussions because 80 per cent of the power benefits, and virtually all of the flood protection could be achieved without the Kootenay; in any event, the Kootenay plan could have been implemented later as no options would be closed off. But the Canadians had permitted themselves to be convinced that the value of storage declines over time, and therefore concluded that any treaty was better than no treaty.*

Diefenbaker's decision to go ahead with the signing of the Columbia River Treaty on January 17, 1961, was undoubtedly made on the advice he received, although there is ample evidence to indicate that

---

* This was the view of Davie Fulton, Canada's chief negotiator. The Americans were never taken in by this fallacy; and they protected themselves against it in the terms of sale by inserting a clause which permits them to determine the real benefits for purposes of resale in the United States, while still retaining the decreasing benefits in dealing with Canada.

this advice should have been conflicting. In Ottawa McNaughton was bitterly opposed, and he seemed to have the support of External Affairs Minister Howard Green. There was no binding agreement with British Columbia: on the contrary, the storm warnings were flying. Bennett had expressed serious reservations about the draft treaty in letters to Donald Fleming, minister of finance.[12] He had also referred the whole matter of the feasibility of the Columbia and Peace rivers to the BC Energy Board for detailed study in December, 1960.

Diefenbaker described the decision curiously to the House of Commons the next day:

May I say that in the signing of this tremendous treaty the course followed was one that gave emphasis to the importance of the occasion. The fact is that it was the last major official discharge of responsibility on the part of the President of the United States. That fact gives it emphasis. During the course of our stay there the Minister of Justice, myself, and several representatives from the two countries were entertained at luncheon at the White House, the last function of the kind that will take place during the presidency of Dwight D. Eisenhower.[13]

Like so many Canadian prime ministers before him and after, Diefenbaker seems to have been overawed by the experience.

The Columbia River Treaty was a disaster beyond the confines of the Columbia basin. In order to justify its action, the Diefenbaker government put forth a view of federal-provincial relations which was the antithesis of the position taken by Jean Lesage in 1955. Specifically, it claimed that the role of the federal government in any international dealings concerning matters under provincial jurisdiction was merely to satisfy the niceties of protocol in the international arena while acting as an agent of the province. In other words, it was an abdication by the government of Canada from its over-riding jurisdiction in external affairs. Such a view inevitably would destroy the credibility, relevance, and consequently the power of the Ottawa government.

In the two years that followed, the dispute between Ottawa and Victoria over the financing of the Columbia and whether to sell the power benefits added almost as much frustration to relations between Canada and the United States as did the Bomarc question. The news media were preoccupied with the Ottawa-Victoria squabble, and permitted it to steal the limelight from the important discussion which concerned the merits of the treaty.

Public discussion of the merits of the treaty was opened up when Diefenbaker abruptly retired General McNaughton as chairman of the Canadian Section, IJC, in April 1962 because of McNaughton's bitter opposition to the Columbia Treaty. As leader of the opposition, Lester Pearson took advantage of McNaughton's dismissal to create the impression that a government led by him would seek a renegotiation of the treaty to meet the objections of critics in Canada to the Libby project. As he fought his way to political power, Pearson intimated that before any decisions were taken there would be public hearings to ventilate the objections of the people in the affected areas, and to hear the recommendations of such critics as McNaughton.

During the election campaign of 1963, which brought Pearson to power, even George Cady, his Liberal candidate in the heart of the Columbia valley, was persuaded that Pearson intended to renegotiate the Columbia Treaty. Part of the confusion was due to a series of articles published in the Vancouver *Sun* under the byline of Jack Davis, MP. Davis was the author of the energy study for the Gordon Commission on Canada's Economic Prospects, and had been director of research for BC Electric. In Parliament Davis had been appointed chairman of the power study group of the Liberal opposition caucus, and he was widely regarded as the official Liberal spokesman on Columbia matters during the election.

His "Plan for Action on the Columbia" advocated immediate conclusion of an interim agreement on principle, under which early construction could start on Mica Creek. It was an ingenious proposal; it satisfied the political need for something to be done; it left open the option of whether to scrap the Columbia Treaty or modify it; and it would produce approximately 80 per cent of the benefits to be had. It carried the support of most of the critics and during the election Pearson gave no indication that he did not support Davis.

It was a shock to those who had been taken in by the Davis election promise when the new prime minister quietly and promptly accepted the demands of both British Columbia and the United States for ratification of the Columbia Treaty. Pearson had proposed his protocol to the Treaty when he was in Washington to attend President Kennedy's dinner for Nobel prizewinners in April 1962, a year before the Liberals came to power.[14] The crucial action was taken within twenty-one days of Pearson's coming to power, and the intention to negotiate a protocol appeared in the communiqué of May 13, 1963, issued at the conclusion of his two-day meeting at Hyannis Port with President Kennedy. It was confirmed by an agreement signed with British Columbia on July 8.[15]

Pearson's betrayal had made Davis look silly. The new prime minister was brutally frank in putting his defeated candidate in Trail into the post-election picture. On July 23, 1963, he wrote to Cady: "While the financial and other terms embodied in the present draft treaty will be improved, the physical plan will not be altered to any great extent."

During this time Paul Martin, who had become minister of external affairs and had been put in charge of wrapping up the Columbia, was busy picking the brains of the critics, including General McNaughton. This was not, however, participatory democracy; Martin intended to convey the impression that the critics had been consulted in order to allay public fears, and to give the government time to prepare answers to the critical arguments.

These answers were pathetic. The government of Canada even went so far as to admit its own ignorance of what it was selling: "The actual benefits purchased [by the United States] are unknown."[16] The government of Canada was attempting to tell the Canadian people that the Americans were about to lay out $275 million for a package of unknown benefits! The Americans know what the benefits are worth, and so do the Canadian critics. A billion dollars is a modest estimate. It will cost Canada about $100 million to give the Columbia away,[17] to say nothing of the cost of losing the International Joint Commission as an effective means of protecting Canadian rights elsewhere.

During the debate in Parliament on the Boundary Waters Treaty, Sir Wilfrid Laurier described the merits of the arrangement incorporating the Harmon doctrine: "At the same time, we shall have the same power on our side, and if we choose to divert a stream that flows into your territory you shall have no right to complain, you shall not call upon us not to do what you do yourselves. The law shall be mutual." Laurier's hopes were not justified. What had been done was described by D. S. Macdonald, parliamentary secretary to the minister of justice: "The governing law under the Boundary Waters Treaty as it applies to the Columbia is being set aside by agreement and an entirely new regime of law governing the river is created."[19] Under the old law, Canada could divert rivers subject to claims for damage. Under the new law, Canada's right to divert waters from the basin probably has been lost.

The Saskatchewan government was of the opinion that the Columbia River Treaty, if ratified, would foreclose the possibility of moving Columbia water to the Saskatchewan river, and it opposed ratification on these grounds. The language of the treaty supports the Saskatchewan contention. The government was unable to refute the argument, other than by unsupported denial based on a unique claim to higher wisdom on the part of Paul Martin.[20] The Pearson government, assured of support in the House from the Conservatives, paid no attention to Saskatchewan.* The Columbia Treaty was debated half-heartedly in Parliament between harangues on the flag debate. The Liberal party used a public flogging of the moribund British lion for public entertainment while it went about the flagitious business of selling out to Uncle Sam.

Pearson's protocol was a signal to the United States that Canadian water was for sale at distress prices. The reaction was swift. It came from the Ralph M. Parsons Company of California in a form described as a concept labelled somewhat pretentiously the North American Water and Power Alliance, complete with syncopated title – NAWAPA.[21] It was a scheme to divert vast amounts of Canada's water southward and eastward; as far as Mexico and the Great Lakes, with extensions to Labrador and the Gulf of Mexico. Mexico's share of this Canadian water would be slightly greater than Canada's, with almost two-thirds reserved for the United States.

The proposal was described by Trevor Lloyd, professor of geography at McGill, as "an exercise in sophomore civil engineering which has received far greater attention than it deserves."[22] General McNaughton minced no words in branding it as "... monstrous not only in terms of physical magnitude, but monstrous in another and more sinister sense in that the promoters would displace Canadian sovereignty, and substitute therefor a diabolical thesis that *all* waters

---

* Saskatchewan had not elected any Liberal members federally. During the hearings, the Liberals were returned provincially and apparently did not pursue the objections of the CCF to the Columbia Treaty.

of North America become a shared resource of which most will be drawn off for the benefit of the United States."[23]

The scheme is pure fantasy, but it has already become a factor in continental politics – not so much because it has been taken up by Senator Frank Moss of Utah, but rather because of the implied and open support it has received from high and influential quarters in Canada. As a result of this continentalist support from within Canada, Senator Moss undoubtedly was assisted in setting up in the US Senate his Special Subcommittee on Western Water Development. This was important because it provided a means of issuing NAWAPA propaganda at government expense and with the *imprimatur* of the Senate.

Three examples of utterances by continentalist-minded Canadians of some influence will serve to illustrate why Senator Moss has concluded that Canadian resources are ripe for picking:

1.   The Merchant-Heeney Report[24] (whose Canadian author, Arnold Heeney, succeeded McNaughton as chairman of the Canadian Section, IJC) advocated a continental approach to energy to be negotiated behind closed doors.

2.   A statement by the Western Canadian-American Assembly held at Harrison Hot Springs, BC, in August 1964 under the joint auspices of the University of British Columbia and Columbia University. The report is described as "aimed at presenting the consensus of opinion expressed during the discussions." This is an extract of the report: "Canada and the United States are moving in the direction of a new and significant policy for the development of energy resources, particularly water power, on a continental scale. Recent technological advances which have made the border increasingly irrelevant have brought about in both countries a willingness to consider an encouraging degree of integration ..." The report went on to recommend that the IJC undertake long-range continental plans for water resources. Senator Moss later suggested that all of Canada's water be brought under international study.[25]

3.   A statement on television during the 1965 election campaign by the Right Honourable Lester Pearson, Prime Minister of Canada:

The United States is finding that water is one of its most valuable and is becoming one of its scarcest resources ... the question of water resources ... is a continental and international problem. We have to be careful not to alienate this resource without taking care of our own needs and we will be discussing this with the United States who are very anxious to work out arrangements by which some of our water resources are moved down south. This can be as important as exporting wheat or oil.

It was like an echo of a statement made by an American financier and NAWAPA supporter a few days before: "Every Canadian knows Canada needs exports. Water can be their most important export."[26]

NOTES

1 Departments of External Affairs and Northern Affairs and National Resources, *The Columbia River Treaty, Protocol, and Related Documents* (Ottawa, Feb. 1964), pp. 58-81. Referred to hereafter as *Documents.*

2 For a detailed statement of this view, see International Journal (Canadian Institute of International Affairs) – Larratt Higgins, "The Columbia River Treaty: A Critical View," *International Journal,* Autumn 1961. See also C. Bourne, "Another View," *ibid.,* Spring 1962; A. G. L. McNaughton, "The Proposed Columbia River Treaty," *ibid.,* Spring 1963.

3 *Documents,* pp. 7-16.

4 *Ibid.,* p. 8, Article II.

5 *Ibid.,* p. 9, Article IV.

6 L. M. Bloomfield and G. F. Fitzgerald, *Boundary Waters Problems of Canada and the United States: The International Joint Commission, 1912-1958* (Toronto, 1958).

7 *Documents,* p. 17.

8 United States 81st Congress, 2nd Session, House Document, 531.

9 *Electrical Digest,* Toronto, July 1955, pp. 34-50.

10 RSC, 3-4 Elizabeth II, c. 47.

11 *Electrical Digest,* July 1955, p. 48.

12 Premier Bennett wrote to Fleming on Jan. 13, 1961, regarding the Columbia: "... assuming of course that it is proved feasible from engineering and financial standpoints. I must tell you that British Columbia entertains serious doubts ..." about the cost of energy delivered to Vancouver. The letter appears in the *House of Commons Debates,* Feb. 2, 1961, p. 1652.

13 *House of Commons Debates,* Jan. 18, 1961, p. 1159.
14 George Bain, "Liberal Ideas on River Treaty Not McNaughton's, Pearson Says," *Globe and Mail,* Toronto, April 30, 1962.
15 *Documents,* p. 100.
16 Departments of External Affairs and Northern Affairs and National Resources, *The Columbia River Treaty Protocol: A Presentation* (Ottawa, April 1964), p. 93
17 *Financial Post,* May 28, 1966; Vancouver *Sun,* June 2, 1966; *Financial Times,* Montreal, Oct. 24, 1966.
18 *House of Commons Debates,* Session 1910-11, vol. I, p. 912.
19 D. S. Macdonald, MP for Toronto Rosedale, in a letter to the editor, *Globe and Mail,* Feb. 19, 1964.
20 House of Commons, 2nd Session, 26th Parliament, Standing Committee on External Affairs, *Minutes of Proceedings and Evidence,* no. 25, May 14, 1964, p. 1249.
21 Ralph M. Parsons Company, *NAWAPA Brochure* (Los Angeles and New York, 1965).
22 "A Water Resource Policy for Canada," *Canadian Geographical Journal,* July 1966.
23 "Canada's Water," an address to the Royal Society of Canada at Sherbrooke, Quebec, June 8, 1966, mimeo.
24 *Principles for Partnership* (Ottawa, June 1965).
25 *Congressional Record,* United States Senate, Sept. 1, 1965, p. 21788.
26 E. O'Toole, "Vast Diversion Plan is Pressed to Trap Canadian Rivers," *New York Times,* September 12, 1965.

Lynn Trainor

A leading member of the Committee of Canadian Concerned Scientists. He serves on the Executive of the Canadian Association of Physicists, is a member of the Physics Advisory Committee of the National Research Council of Canada, and teaches physics at the University of Toronto. He was recently elected chairman of the North York Board of Education.

Science in Canada–American style

The impact of American values upon scientific development in Canada is particularly difficult to assess. American influences are so widespread and pervasive in Canadian science that they seem both natural and inevitable, and are widely accepted without critical analysis of their underlying value system. Moreover, the American technological dynamic has achieved a certain universality which makes it difficult to distinguish what is simply modern and inevitable in scientific development from what is characteristically American.

It is sometimes argued that science knows no national boundaries, that it is the objective description of nature, at once universal and politically neutral. But science is not just a collection of facts, it is also a practice, a human activity which is motivated and which has values within the context of any particular society. Moreover, science does not stand apart from its applications; its practice affects and is affected by a host of economic, social, and political factors. From this point of view, not only is it possible to study national and international influences on scientific activity, but it is essential to do so.

At the national level, science policy has been recognized explicitly as both an instrument and a concern of government by every major industrialized country in the world. In particular, the government of Canada has established several new advisory bodies on science policy, principally the Science Secretariat and the Science Council. The council comprises a broad spectrum of scientists, engineers, and industrial representatives, and is charged with advising government on long-range science policy. The council's fourth report, *Towards a National Science Policy for Canada,* is a remarkable document[1] - remarkable in the sense that it is idealistic and venturesome, and emphasizes for the first time the possible "role of science in helping to solve several of the important social and economic problems that now confront the nation." But it is even more remarkable in that it dwells on the central problem of Canadian science – the lack of an adequate research and development (R & D) base – without identifying the primary cause, the foreign ownership of Canadian industry.

Report no. 4 of the Science Council also fails to identify and to acknowledge the degree of disillusionment with science and technology which is felt among the public at large, particularly the younger generation. This disillusionment has developed over a long period of time and represents the lack of fulfilment of the prophecies of scientific liberalism, that discovery and technical innovation would liberate mankind once and for all time from the sufferings of poverty and disease. But to many, progress in these areas has been more than offset by the creation of new and seemingly more dreadful problems for mankind, such as the threats of nuclear annihilation and ecological disaster. The sense of ultimate security and purpose, common to the value systems of former times, has been swept away in wave after wave of technological change. Small wonder, then, that disillusionment exists.

It may be argued, of course, that all this has little to do with the Americanization of Canada, that it is a process of modernization that is largely inevitable and only incidentally American. There is some truth in this; in fact, there is no quarrel with modernization as such – it is a part of human progress. The real quarrel is with the degree and the intensity of modernization, driven by mindless economic forces and selfish interests. The excesses of science are largely American excesses. Servan-Schreiber has described forcefully how American management skills and corporate capitalism threaten the economic and cultural fabric of Europe by intensive exploitation of technology in the science-based industries.[2] The Canadian situation is even more precarious in this regard.

To a considerable extent one can describe Canadian science as merely an extension of American science in the continental framework of corporate capitalism. In some respects the extension is an emptiness of purpose and activity. One example is the almost total lack of an industrial research base in Canada, a direct result of the massive foreign ownership of our science-based industries. Not only does this mean that Canadians exercise almost no control over the direction of the R & D activity which so profoundly affects them; it also means that Canadian scientists and engineers have to emigrate to the United States if they are to pursue careers in the most interesting and vital areas of industrial research.[3] Under such circumstances, it is not surprising that many Canadian scientists regard themselves as part of the American milieu and accept the value system of the American scientific community with its emphasis on technical élites, commodity consumption, and the vigorous pursuit of short-range rather than long-range goals.

Even when the American value systems are rejected in theory, they are largely accepted in scientific practice because they appear inevitable and because there are no organizational means for challenging their validity and relevance to Canada. American wealth enables the United States to attract the best scientists throughout the western world by offering higher salaries, more hardware, and prestigious and influential research positions.[4] Even the heroes of science, such as Albert Einstein, become Americanized. Because of the apparent advantages, bright young Canadians also tend to go to the United States for graduate and post-doctoral training. Many factors encourage this trend: nearly all science textbooks used in Canada are written by Americans and are published in the United States; the most prestigious scientific journals are American; the most numerous and physically attractive scientific magazines are American-organized, American-owned, and American-dominated. It is the American science community that largely sets the goals and standards by which Canadian scientists judge the value and the relative excellence of their own scientific work. Even the aspirations of Canadian science are largely American aspirations, projects fashioned to compete with American projects rather than to serve primary Canadian conditions and concerns.

An excellent example of this is provided by the proposed Canadian participation in the high energy accelerator project at Batavia, Illinois, which we shall refer to as the Batavia project.[5] This project concerns high energy physics, a frontier field of research probing the ultimate constitution of matter. Activity in this field involves two kinds of research: one in mathematical theory, which is relatively inexpensive; the other in experimentation on huge and technically sophisticated particle accelerators. The latest generation of such accelerators will cost somewhere between $200 and $300 million. A consortium of countries is building one of these in Europe, while a second, the Batavia project, is under active construction in the United States. Largely because of the costs involved, Canada does not possess a high energy accelerator, even of the "previous generation." Canadian participation consists at present of "users groups," which carry out experiments at US accelerators and bring back data on photographic film and on computer tapes to be analysed in Canada.

Supported by a National Research Council grant, a six-man study group submitted a report in March 1969 calling for direct Canadian participation at the 8 per cent level in the Batavia project. Specifically, the group recommend a $20 million expenditure over a five-year period as a direct contribution to the capital costs of the US accelerator. Proponents argued that this gave Canada the opportunity to buy directly into the world's largest particle accelerator. They also argued that Canadian users should pay their own way and should not continue to depend upon the generosity of American high energy research groups for access to accelerator laboratories.

Here is a clear case of Canadian scientists sharing American aspirations and expecting the Canadian taxpayer to foot the bill. Opponents of the report argued that such large sums represented a serious threat to other fields of Canadian physics already in jeopardy through a shortage of research funds. Moreover, Canadian users groups have the assurance that access time to foreign accelerator laboratories depends upon the scientific merit of the proposed experiment and not at all on contributions to capital costs. In any event, Canada already contributes very substantially to the support of American science and technology, both directly through the "brain drain" and more indirectly through the support of research in American industrial laboratories by Canadian-based subsidiaries of American corporations.

A second example of the curious influence of the United States on the direction of Canadian science is the story of the Queen Elizabeth II telescope.[6] In 1964, on the occasion of the Queen's visit to Canada, the government of Canada, accepted a proposal from a group of Canadian astronomers to build a 157-inch reflecting telescope on Mt Kobau in British Columbia at a cost somewhere between $10 and $12 million. A road was built to Mt Kobau, a mirror and a grinding machine purchased, a design team established, and plans laid for a large optical shop at the University of British Columbia. After inspection of the Canadian design in 1967 by an American group, who were impressed with what they saw, a proposal was made for a joint Canadian-American telescope in Chile. There is no reason to suspect the intentions of the American proponents; but in fact the suggestion led initially to deep dissent within the community of Canadian astronomers, whether to proceed with the Mt Kobau telescope or to abandon it and place a telescope in Chile instead. In 1968, after four years of planning and the expenditure of $4.5 million, the government of Canada withdrew its support from the Mt Kobau telescope. The project was kept alive only by a determined effort on the part of four western universities.

A telescope in Chile has strong scientific points in its favour: the site chosen is said to be the best in the world from the point of view of observing conditions and also because of particular astronomical interest in southern skies. On the other hand, the Mt Kobau project was well on its way, and it was a distinctly Canadian project which would have provided a national facility of outstanding quality for Canadian astronomers. For the United States, which has several high quality telescopes at home, the Chilean venture is a natural aspiration; even so, American astronomers have failed to find the necessary funds. Canada does not have a single optical facility at this time which is both well situated and of high quality. The Mt Kobau project was a natural step in laying the foundations for a new generation of Canadian astronomers. The point is that legitimate American aspirations are not necessarily legitimate Canadian aspirations, particularly where large sums of money are involved; but the Americanization of Canadian science is so thorough that the point is not clearly recognized by many scientists in Canada, who tend to regard Canadian science as a simple extension of the American effort.

A third example of the "American presence" in Canadian thinking is our choice of the American (NTSC) system of colour television despite the evident advantages of the French system (SECAM III) and the German system (PAL). Except for France, Western Europe has opted for PAL while most other countries have chosen SECAM III. The advantages of PAL and SECAM III are set out clearly in the answers of James A. Byrne, parliamentary secretary to the minister of transport, to questions put to him in the House of Commons by R. J. McCleave, MP for Halifax-Dartmouth[7]:

Question No. 57   Mr. McCleave, MP
1 What colour television systems were considered for use in Canada?
2 What were the comparative cost factors of each system and of colour television sets which receive each?
3 Which of the systems is more readily recordable on video tape?

Answer (Text)
By Mr. James A. Byrne, Parliamentary Secretary to the Minister of Transport:
1 The following colour television systems were considered:

N.T.S.C.   (USA)
SECAM III   (France)
PAL   (Federal Republic of Germany)

2 (a) The system cost factors considered for the three systems were:
Network transmission and distribution;
Station transmitters;
Video tape recording
The N.T.S.C. system, due to its more stringent technical require-
ments, is the most costly in terms of the three factors above. The
SECAM III system is the most tolerant of deficiencies in the perfor-
mance of systems and equipment and can, therefore, utilize less costly
facilities for recording and distribution. PAL is intermediate in the
above respects between N.T.S.C. and SECAM III.

(b) The cost factors of colour television sets for the three systems
relate solely to the techniques of recovering colour information from
the composite colour television signal. N.T.S.C. receivers are the least
costly to manufacture, SECAM III costs slightly more, with PAL being
the most costly.

Signals of one colour system can be transcoded into another system. Due to the costs involved, transcoding can be achieved only at
the studio, along the transmission network, or at station transmitters.
Receivers designed specifically for one colour system cannot successfully receive colour TV signals from another system.

3 SECAM III colour signals are most readily recordable on video tape,
utilizing standard black and white recording machines. N.T.S.C. and
PAL colour signals require auxiliary colour equipment for recording.
A video tape recorded from one system can be used with another
system by the use of transcoding techniques.

It appears evident that in the matter of colour television, as in so
many other technical matters affecting Canadians, an inferior system
was adopted primarily on the grounds of compatibility with American systems. This example is particularly disconcerting because the
superior SECAM III system would have provided a natural barrier to the
flood of American television programming and a natural encouragement to economic and cultural exchange with France. (In fact, the
barrier would not have been insurmountably large, since signals from
the American system can be transcoded at the studio into SECAM III.)
Even when technology and economics favour an independent Canadian cultural stance, the Americanization of Canada persists.

American influences on Canadian science are particularly strong in
the area of military research. This is somewhat surprising since the
organization of military science in the two countries is radically

different. In the United States a large fraction of the total budget for all scientific research and development falls under the umbrella of military spending, and American scientists have come to accept such arrangements for funding as normal. The frightening power of the military-industrial complex in the United States is well known, but less well known is the extent to which scientists and technologists have been integrated into this complex;[8] certainly a large fraction of US scientists and engineers are employed in the so-called defence industries. By contrast, all classified research in Canada is done directly by the Defence Research Board, a civilian arm of the military establishment, and the total expenditure on military research is a modest fraction of the total research budget.

On the surface the Canadian situation seems rather satisfactory; a closer examination shows that it leaves a lot to be desired. The Defence Research Board apparently does not possess the resources to assess properly the national interest in the cold-war maze of military-scientific stratagems. The result has been a serious and continuing American penetration into the decision-making apparatus of the Canadian military research establishment. This penetration is justified by the policy-makers in terms of a simple and convenient creed, that Canadian and American national interests coincide.

A realization of the extent of American influences in the Canadian military-science establishment was brought home dramatically to me by a personal experience in 1963 during the public debate over nuclear warheads for the Bomarc missiles. In the aftermath of the Cuban crisis the Diefenbaker government was divided on the question of equipping the Bomarcs with nuclear weapons. Washington took advantage of divided Canadian loyalties on this issue to openly embarrass the faltering government in Ottawa. For reasons best known to himself, Lester Pearson reversed his stand on the issue of nuclear arms for Canada, going on to win the federal election and bringing the dramatic Diefenbaker years to an inglorious close. To the great relief of the Canadian press, Howard Green, the architect of Canada's resistance policy to US pressures on the nuclear arms issue, suffered humiliating defeat at the polls.

Proponents of Pearson's policy, including the former Conservative Minister of Defence, Douglas Harkness, claimed that a "small" nuclear warhead on the Bomarc (small meaning several times larger than the Hiroshima bomb) would be effective in *cooking* the larger hydrogen bomb carried by an attacking bomber. Opponents generally argued that by accepting nuclear arms Canada would lose much more politically than she would gain militarily. But many scientists in their private conversations went a good deal further and regarded the "cooking theory" as a public hoax.

I was a member of a group of eight physicists at the University of Alberta which decided to take public issue with the extravagant claims of Mr Harkness for the effectiveness of the cooking theory. We prepared a brief statement, setting out in laymans' terms the basic facts about Bomarcs, hydrogen bombs, and ICBM's and distributed it to the four national party leaders and to all candidates in Alberta seeking election to the federal Parliament.

The Alberta statement made little stir during the election itself, but the whole question of nuclear arms came up again in the late summer of 1963 before the newly appointed Defence Committee of the House of Commons. Paul Hellyer, the defence minister, and Dr G. S. Field, chief scientist for DRB, defended vigorously the government's acquisition of nuclear arms, largely on the basis of the supposed "cooking power" of the nuclear warheads on the Bomarcs. The following exchange between Gordon Churchill, a former Conservative defence minister, and Dr Field is revealing of Canada's acceptance of a satellite role in defence matters:

CHURCHILL: My second question is this: you explained the effect of neutrons from a nuclear explosion penetrating the nuclear bomb. Has this actually been tried out in an experiment or is this based on theory?

FIELD: We understand from our American sources that this has been theoretically and experimentally confirmed.

CHURCHILL: In other words, there has been a nuclear explosion where an anti-aircraft nuclear-tipped missile hit a nuclear bomb and the result was that the nuclear bomb failed to explode?

FIELD: We have not been given details on what was actually done because of the nature of this information. We have been told that the Americans have carried out work on this problem and are fully convinced that this is what happens. We have been informed of this.[9]

Informed by whom? We are left to wonder. Harold Winch, the NDP defence critic, then entered the discussion and after one exchange the following occurred:

WINCH: And we in Canada are expected to make our decisions without having full information?

HELLYER: I think on this subject the information we have and the verification which has been done by our own scientists is sufficiently adequate for reaching a decision.

What verification? The Canadian nuclear experts at Chalk River were never consulted on this issue! Moreover, the US secretary of defence, Robert McNamara, in lengthy testimony before a US congressional committee, referred to the Bomarcs as already obsolete; his testimony also implied that the alleged cooking powers of the nuclear warheads were never put to the test, even in the United States.

In testimony before the Defence Committee,[10] three members of our Alberta group argued on the basis of published information on the Bomarcs that these weapons were ineffectual at best. At worst, they did more harm than good; the enemy, knowing that the Bomarcs packed nuclear warheads, could easily arrange a gamma ray sensor to set off the hydrogen bomb payload before it could be destroyed by the neutron burst from the warhead on the Bomarc. The net result would be hydrogen explosions over inhabited areas of Canada instead of over their intended targets in the United States. Two DRB scientists, Drs Field and Keyston, gave counter-testimony before the Defence Committee and referred rather patronizingly to the Alberta group's "theoretical" arguments and their lack of classified information. Faced with these opposing views, the Defence Committee resolved the issue, not by appealing to further nuclear expertise in Canada (two of the three Alberta witnesses were nuclear scientists), but by appealing to the views of "U.S. officials at NORAD and Washington." In retrospect, it seems probable that the DRB scientists were never vitally consulted by the Canadian government on the Bomarc issue. To the extent they were consulted, they seemed to have accepted the advice of US officials without bothering to consult with any of the many Canadian experts in the nuclear field.

In more recent times, in the area of chemical and bacteriological warfare (CBW), the evidence again suggests that research done in Canada is a minor extension of work done in the United States, rather than an autonomous national activity. Spokesmen from DRB have admitted Canada's role in the four-power Technical Cooperation Program (TTCP) through which Canada provides the United States and Great Britain with an open-air laboratory at Suffield, Alberta,

for sampling and measuring biological materials. Dr A. M. Pennie,
deputy chairman of DRB, has emphasized the defensive nature of
Canada's research effort in CBW, claiming that it is consistent with
Canada's ratification of the Geneva Protocol in 1927 outlawing
chemical and biological agents in warfare.[11] The consistency is at
least questionable in view of the facts that the United States has not
ratified the Geneva Protocol and has used defoliating agents and
nerve gases extensively in the war in Vietnam. If Canada's role is
entirely innocent and defensive, and motivated entirely by national
interest, it is difficult to understand why CBW research is not carried
out under the auspices of the Department of Health and the results
disseminated widely among members of the medical profession.

Canadian expenditure on CBW research is estimated at $6 million,
or roughly 12 per cent of the total expenditure by the federal government on basic research in Canada in all fields. Despite the appearance
of DRB spokesmen before the Special Senate Committee on Science
Policy under Senator Lamontagne,[12]* this research was neither discussed nor questioned. (It was, however, brought to the attention of
the Senate Committee, after formal hearings had terminated, by
spokesmen for Canadian Concerned Scientists† at the University of
Toronto.) Failure to discuss CBW research was a serious but unin-
tended omission on the part of the Senate Committee; it is however,
symptomatic of the attitude that we cannot question military research because it is an extension of American efforts, and we do not
know what they are up to in any case.

Another example of our resignation to American expertise and
American interests in military matters is provided by the anti-ballistic
missile (ABM) issue. Public debate in Canada was meagre compared to
that in the United States, although the issue has as vital consequences
for Canadians as for Americans. Although the Commons Defence
Committee received testimony from a number of witnesses, notably
from DRB and the Department of National Defence, it did not pro-

---

* The Special Senate Committee on Science Policy under Senator Lamontagne held almost continuous hearings between March 12, 1968
and June 1969. A final report is expected by about Jan. 1970.

† Canadian Concerned Scientists is an ad hoc organization of staff and
students at the University of Toronto concerned with the social responsibility of scientists.

mote public debate on the issue, nor did it seek an independent
assessment from the Canadian science community at large. It is at
least questionable how much Canadian expertise was brought to bear
in an attempt to formulate a national viewpoint on this important
issue. It seems reasonable to conjecture that DRB spokesmen were
transmitting primarily American views rather than reporting on the
conclusions of an extensive Canadian analysis.

The Defense Committee's conclusion needs no further elaboration
as a comment on the pusillanimous attitudes of Canadian élites with
respect to military issues involving the United States: "The Committee has received conflicting evidence on the desirability of establishing
an ABM system for the protection of the U.S. nuclear deterrent or U.S.
cities against nuclear attacks. In view of the uncertainty of Congressional approval for the ABM system and the uncertainty of the extent
to which Canada might be asked to participate, if at all, the Committee is unable to make any recommendations concerning Canadian
involvement in such a system."[12]

In short, we have no independent view on this subject and we
intend to take no initiative one way or another. If the Americans
decide (in their wisdom or folly, as the case may be) to go ahead with
an ABM system and ask us to participate, we shall worry about the
whole business at that time. We shall declare ourselves in danger if
our American friends and advisers tell us we are in danger. Our
primary concern is not to determine Canada's vital interest in this
issue, but only the extent of our involvement with the Americans in
whatever they decide.

If we accept that there is a wholesale Americanization of Canadian
science, two principal questions arise: is there anything wrong with
this? And if so, can anything be done about it? In order to answer
the first question, whether there is anything wrong with wholesale
Americanization, it is essential to distinguish between the long-range
and short-range points of view. If one concentrates on the short
range, the rational choice is our present course of comfortable conformity, each of us pursuing individual goals within the continental
framework. This option is particularly appealing to the Canadian
scientist, since he can combine the comfort and convenience of a
more liberal social and political life in Canada with the prestige and
satisfaction of wheeling and dealing on the grand stage of American

science. And why not? It is even possible to convince oneself that relentlessly pursuing one's own scientific ambitions also happens to be good for Canada: it brings Canadian standards of "good science" to more respectable levels and thus contributes to the common good.

But what of the long-range view? Are Canadians serious about establishing a distinct political, cultural, and economic unit with a large degree of control over their own values and their own destiny? And what of American science and the value system on which it is based – what kind of future does it offer mankind? There is reason to believe that Canadians do want to preserve their history and establish a separate identity. There is also reason to believe that most Canadians, and in fact many Americans, are not happy with the organization, aims, and objectives of scientific activity in the United States with its emphasis on resource exploitation and military objectives. There is a growing concern about the perversion of science in serving anti-human ends – billions for space travel, nothing for rat control; expensive heart transplants while children die unattended; endless freeways, supersonic jets, pollution, the threat of ecological disaster – all in the name of progress and modernity.

The basic difficulty arises out of a conflict between what appears to be rational behaviour in the short view and a rational approach to long-term problems; the former involves a perturbation approach – you fix things up in small ways without essentially disturbing the system; the latter is more difficult to do, because it requires a certain degree of determination and a certain degree of short-range sacrifice.

One cannot drastically change the face of Canadian science without the simultaneous introduction of sweeping economic and social reform, but a start can be made by consciously emphasizing Canadian concerns in scientific activity. Even the awareness that it is possible to put a rather different emphasis on the purpose of scientific activity, as Sweden has done,[13] would be an important step towards a better Canadian attitude on science. The centennial stir aroused a latent sense of national purpose, and certain trends towards distinctive Canadian science organizations[14] and distinctive Canadian science magazines[15] offer some measure of hope. There is a vital need in Canada for in-depth studies of a socio-scientific nature,* to discover

* Unfortunately, Canadian social scientists have largely ignored the relationship of science to society in Canada.

what are the special problems of our society and how our scientific community can be organized to help in solving them. Special Report no. 4 of the Science Council is a step in the right direction, but any analysis which fails to take into account the special problem of Americanization is still playing at charades.

NOTES

1 *Towards a National Science Policy for Canada,* Report no. 4, Science Council of Canada (Ottawa, 1968).
2 J. J. Servan-Schreiber, *The American Challenge* (New York, 1969).
3 "Brain Drain Gain," *Canadian Research and Development,* Jan.-Feb. 1969, p. 11; "Brain Drain Worst in Years," *ibid.,* July-Aug. 1969, p. 7.
4 Ruth Jorin, "Wealth Attracts Talent," *Nation Magazine,* April 3, 1967, pp. 425-7; Lord Bowden, "How Much Science Can We Afford?" *Nation Magazine,* Jan. 2, 1968.
5 "A Particle Physics Programme for Canada," report to the National Research Council of Canada, March 1969.
6 A brief history of the Queen Elizabeth II telescope appeared in an article by Dr G. J. Odgers, project director for the Mt Kobau project, in an article in the Vancouver *Sun,* Sept. 24, 1968.
7 I am indebted to Dr E. H. Richardson of the Dominion Astrophysical Laboratory in Victoria for bringing my attention to the discussion in Hansard. *House of Commons Debates,* June 7, 1967, pp. 1250-1.
8 "Research Probe: Rickover broadsides the military-science complex," *Science Magazine,* vol. 161 (1968), p. 446.
9 *House of Commons Debates,* Special Committee on Defence, July 2, 1963, pp. 35-6.
10 *Ibid.,* Aug. 1, 1963.
11 "Canada's Role in Germ Warfare," as reported in the *Globe and Mail,* Toronto, July 3, 1969.
12 *House of Commons Debates,* June 26, 1969, p. 1252.
13 "World Datelines: Stockholm," *International Science and Technology,* Dec. 1965, pp. 86-7. The degree of independence which Sweden exercises in scientific affairs is also illustrated by the recent decision not to support research in high energy physics, despite its "popularity" in other European countries.

14 Krista Maeots, "Canadian Scientists Debate Their Role," report to
the *Ottawa Citizen,* Aug. 11, 1969.
15 *Science Forum,* a Canadian journal of science and technology edited
by David Spurgeon, has a unique format and is devoted to an intelligent discussion of Canadian science policy.

Bruce Kidd

Canadian distance runner, member of the National Advisory Council on Fitness and Amateur Sport. He has contributed articles on sport for *Canadian Dimension* and other periodicals.

Canada's "national" sport

Canada does not have a distinctive sports culture. Virtually every aspect of Canadian sport has been conditioned by American influences. Our sports heroes, with the exception of our hockey favourites, are mostly Americans – not surprisingly when our media constantly bombard us with as much American sporting news as Canadian, and when our sports commentators consider "American" to be the standard of excellence. Our best professional athletes seek their fortunes in the United States and our best amateurs seek the semi-professional status and the specialized coaching and facilities that are available through US athletic scholarships. Canadian sport impressarios – from track and field to tennis and golf – depend upon the "drawing power" of US athletes to attract spectators to their events. Canadian physical educators rely upon their American counterparts to prepare their teaching manuals, conduct their coaching clinics, and so on. Even our fitness fads are imported. Lloyd Percival has preached the benefits of jogging for more than twenty years, but it was an American Airforce major, Dr Kenneth Cooper, who fathered the present jogging boom. Canadians in search of a distinctive national culture get no help from sports.

To be sure, not every Canadian sport has been Americanized in the same fashion. In track and field and swimming, for example, the lack of adequate year-round facilities and the scarcity of good coaching has forced many Canadian athletes to go south: as a result, half the members of our 1968 Olympic team in these sports attended university in the United States. In football, on the other hand, opportunities for professional employment in the Canadian Football League have encouraged many American athletes to come north. This essay confines itself to one sport – hockey, our national game.

The Americanization of Canadian hockey is the direct outgrowth of the commercialization of hockey that occurred first in the United States and then in Canada, at the turn of the century.* Social conditions at the time – growing urbanization, shorter working weeks, the

---

*   "Strangely enough, professional hockey as such did not begin in Canada, but in Houghton, Michigan, during the winter of 1903-04. A dentist, Dr. J. L. Gibson, introduced paid Canadian imports ..." Nancy and Maxwell Howell, *Sports and Games in Canadian Life,* p. 206. As I shall explain shortly, in North America "professional" hockey invariably means commercialized professional hockey.

popularization of the press – were ideally suited to the promotion and sale of sport as a spectator attraction, and hockey was one of the most exciting games available for sale.* Ever since the British garrisons, which had been the focal point of most Canadian sport before Confederation, were sent home in 1872, Canadians had crossed the border to compete and exchange sporting ideas.[1] And hockey, which had always flourished in Canada, quickly caught on in the United States. By 1926 six of the ten teams† in what was generally recognized as the best Canadian hockey league, the National Hockey League, were located in the United States and owned by Americans.[2]

Although few US-born athletes have demonstrated outstanding skill at hockey, American entrepreneurs have been able to stage first-class hockey by importing Canadian players, coaches, and managers. Neither country has ever raised barriers against the free flow of hockey talent between the two countries.‡ Enjoying generally a

---

*   The special economics of commercial sport has been described by the commissioner of the National Football League as follows: "On the playing field, member clubs of a professional sports league are clearly competitors – and every effort must be made to promote this. But in their business operations, member clubs of a league are less competitors than they are partners or participants in a joint venture ... What sharply distinguishes member clubs of a sports league from ordinary businessmen joined together in a trade association is their predominant identity of interest. Whereas the ordinary businessman may view the business failure of a competitor with equanimity or even satisfaction, the members of the sports league cannot. This wholly alters the fundamentals of their relationship ... Every sports league must come to terms with this recognition. In the NFL there are innumerable recognitions of this partnership principle." Peter Rozelle, "A Commissioner Comments on Anti-Trust in Sports," *Virginia Law Weekly,* June 4, 1964. Essentially the same case is presented as an economic model in J. C. H. Jones, "The Economics of the National Hockey League," *Canadian Journal of Economics,* Feb. 1969.

†   The six teams were the Boston Bruins, the Chicago Black Hawks, the Detroit Red Wings, the New York Americans, the New York Rangers, and the Pittsburgh Yellow Jackets.

‡   I am aware of only two such barriers in sport. In the Canadian Football League each of the nine commercial clubs has agreed to play no

more lucrative market – larger population, higher incomes – than their
Canadian counterparts, American hockey entrepreneurs have been
able to pay higher salaries and attract the best Canadian players away
from the Canadian teams that employed them. Complete statistics
are difficult to obtain, but it appears that since the turn of the century there has been a general increase in the number of hockey teams
operating in the United States and a general decline in the number
operating in Canada. It is difficult to avoid the conclusion that
American capital has put Canadian hockey out of business in Canada.
Today, all but five of the forty-five North American commercial
hockey teams are located in the United States and all but six are
owned by Americans.* With ownership comes control: ten of the
twelve directorships of the NHL, which rules over both commercial
and non-commercial hockey in the two countries, are held by
American corporations.† The players may all be Canadian, but as
NHL president Clarence Campbell said recently, "The NHL has never
been a Canadian organization." § Not surprisingly, this non-Canadian
organization has rarely acted in the best interest of the Canadian
community.

　　It makes no sense to blame the Americans for their control of
hockey, distasteful as that control may be. Given the commercializa-

———

more than fourteen American players on its team at a single time. In
the National Collegiate Athletic Association in the United States,
foreign athletes over the age of twenty-three are ineligible for official
competition.

* The five teams are the Montreal Canadiens (NHL); the Montreal
Voyageurs (American Hockey League), a Canadiens farm team which
began operation in 1969, the Quebec Aces (AHL); the Toronto Maple
Leafs (NHL); and the Vancouver Canucks (Western Hockey League).

† The ten US NHL teams are the Boston Bruins, Chicago Black Hawks,
Detroit Red Wings, Los Angeles Kings, Minnesota North Stars, New
York Rangers, Oakland Seals, Philadelphia Flyers, Pittsburgh Pen-
guins, and St Louis Blues.

§ "Kidd Attack on Pro Sport Called Off Track," *Telegram,* Toronto,
Sept. 9, 1969. In a subsequent statement Mr Campbell said that the
NHL only continues to operate from Canada to avoid harassment
from congressional investigation in the United States. "U.S. Legal
Climate against NHL Moving," *Globe and Mail,* Toronto, Oct. 14,
1969.

tion of the game, its Americanization is inevitable. The particular characteristics of the takeover are unimportant. If the sport had not been exported almost entirely to the United States, control might have been acquired just as easily through the outright purchase of successful Canadian hockey corporations by American interests. No, there has been nothing out of the ordinary about the Americanization of hockey. What is difficult to explain, however, is its commercialization; or specifically, why Canadians have allowed – in fact encouraged – the sale of hockey to go unregulated for so long.

Commercial hockey in Canada is called "professional" hockey, but strictly speaking the two terms are not synonymous. In "professional" hockey the players are remunerated for their hockey efforts and thus can be distinguished from "amateur" players who are not so remunerated. The term "commercial" refers to a different aspect of the game altogether, the ownership and control of the game. In "commercial" hockey, team owners enjoy complete property rights in the players and the right of admission to actual contests, and they operate the hockey enterprise to make a private profit.

It has been the commercialization of the game, not its professionalization, that has harmed Canadian hockey. There is nothing dishonourable about professionalism in sport, for without a regular income, most highly skilled athletes would not be free (from alternative work) to develop their talents to the full. Artists need money for the same reason. But professional hockey need not be commercial hockey. Because of the costs of staging competitions between professionals, it may be necessary to charge admission to the hockey game. But it is not necessary to vest unconditional property rights in the admissions. Only in North America has spectator sport been both professionalized and commercialized. In other countries, commercial profits from spectator sport are closely controlled by the state, sometimes limited and sometimes forbidden altogether. It has not been the salaries that have hurt hockey – in fact, they have contributed to the high level of skill developed by its players – but rather the exploitation of the game for private profit.

The most galling consequence of this commercialization for Canadians is that nearly all the best hockey games are played in the United States! Where hockey is played at its best in Canada – in Toronto's Maple Leaf Gardens and Montreal's Forum – it is impossible to buy a ticket. As Ralph Allen loved to write, hockey is Canada's religion.[3]

Weekends are centred around it, election campaigns and religious observances are altered to fit its scheduling, and during the annual Stanley Cup playoffs, the whole country stands still. Every family grows up listening to or watching "Hockey Night in Canada." Why we save all our enthusiasms for hockey is difficult to explain. Whatever the reason, hockey is the Canadian passion. Yet because spectator hockey is privately owned, most Canadians are prevented from seeing it at its best. What community would permit property rights in its national religion?

The Canadian community invests a great deal in the production, as it were, of good hockey players: it creates the social environment that encourages young players to aspire to greatness in the sport and to devote the necessary long hours of practice; it provides him with arenas in which to play and coaches to perfect his skills. The size of the investment is often considerable. Every hamlet boasts an arena, although its construction often requires years of saving and months of volunteer labour. Many a municipal budget is spent largely on minor hockey, to the deliberate neglect of alternative programmes. Because the development of good players is thus essentially a community enterprise, the choicest fruits of this enterprise – games between the most highly skilled of athletes – should be a community benefit. Yet they are not. If not exported directly for sale in the United States, the best games are sold here in Canada under monopoly conditions at outrageous prices.

Given the importance of hockey to Canadians, it seems incredible that major Canadian cities like Halifax, Quebec, Hamilton, Winnipeg, Regina, Calgary, Edmonton, and Vancouver do not have professional hockey teams of the highest rank. Yet they do not. But given commercial hockey's goal of profit maximization, the explanation is all too apparent. Bigger profits can be made in the United States. Take the case of Vancouver, for example. At long last a group of businessmen in that city have been offered (as of September 1969) first refusal on a newly created NHL franchise. If the Vancouver syndicate agrees to buy the $6 million franchise (no announcement has been made at the time of writing), it will bring a third NHL team (of fourteen teams) to Canada. At the most recent NHL expansion, that of 1966, Vancouver was refused a franchise and all six new franchises were awarded to US cities. The reason: television revenue. The expansion (to Philadelphia, Pittsburgh, St Louis, Minneapolis, Los Angeles, and Oakland) placed teams in the remaining northern US television markets and thus enabled the NHL to get a national TV contract from CBS. A Vancouver franchise would have brought little additional television revenue to the league, for NHL hockey (the games of the Montreal and Toronto teams) was already beamed at the Vancouver area. And the Vancouver market meant nothing to CBS.*

The commercialization of the game has affected the location of minor league teams too. Although it is difficult to trace a direct relationship between the growth of minor league hockey in American cities and the decline of similar operations in Canadian cities, I think the two developments are closely related. During the past decade senior semi-professional commercial teams in several Canadian cities have folded; and in 1969 the always strong junior clubs have been hit. This time, raiding has been direct: the semi-professional US college teams are luring Canadian boys away with "athletic scholarships."[4] Since the commercial game has socialized almost all Canadian athletes to the idea of playing in the United States, there is little reason to stay.

Commercialization has made hockey a high-priced, exclusive form of entertainment. In home games neither Montreal nor Toronto has played to less than full capacity for the last twenty years. Although

---

*   Jones, "Economics of the National Hockey League," 18-19. Also "By Dick Beddoes" *Globe and Mail,* Jan. 21, 1969. Clarence Campbell has said that Canadian public opinion forced the league to guarantee one of the new franchises to Vancouver. "NHL hand forced by voice of people," *Toronto Daily Star,* Sept. 12, 1969. But I suspect that television revenues played a significant role in this decision too. CBS has been losing money on its contract with the NHL and W. C. McPhail, its vice-president for sports, has said that unless the rating for hockey telecasts improve, the present one-year contract will not be renewed. "NHL Given One Year to Attract TV Fans," *Toronto Daily Star,* Aug. 5, 1969. With the immediate prospects for television revenue diminishing, the importance of a strong franchise, self-sufficient at the box office, becomes much greater. Although it cannot offer much television revenue, Vancouver is likely to sell all of its seats. When five of the six present expansion clubs are losing money, that old-fashioned box-office revenue Vancouver promises can be very appealing.

the seating capacity of both arenas has been increased, the demand
for tickets far exceeds the supply. Because of their private monopoly,
the owners have been able to determine prices as they please and to
restrict the sale of tickets to anyone they choose. In both cities, the
option on season's tickets has become a property right, too. It is not
unknown for people to bequeath them in their wills. In Toronto
more than 90 per cent of the tickets to Maple Leaf games are pre-sold
to season's subscribers. Despite this tremendous demand for hockey
seats, neither of the owners appears interested in distributing seats to
a wider segment of the public. It may be a national game, but it is
only a privileged – and well heeled – few that are able to watch professional games in person.

Commercialization of the game has even affected traditional Canadian television habits. The larger US market has given the American
network priority over the Canadian networks in the telecasting of
weekend games. They are now scheduled to suit CBS. When there is a
conflict, the Canadian network must be happy with second choice.
This is why "Hockey Night in Canada" is telecast in the afternoon
during the playoffs.[5]

Commercialization, moreover, has disrupted amateur hockey. The
profitability of commercial hockey depends primarily upon two factors: the availability of the best players and competition from alternative hockey attractions. Salaries and promotion costs – the main
costs of spectator hockey – are determined by the existence of other
potential employers, and ticket sales vary according to the ability of
the team to field "star" players and according to the performance of
other teams of equal calibre in the same area. If commercial teams
could completely control the player market and eliminate all professional hockey competitors – in short, if they could gain monopoly
control over the sport – then profits could be maximized. This is, in
fact, what the NHL has done. Until the late 1940s a number of semi-
professional ("amateur") leagues, some of which were operated on a
profit basis, competed with the NHL for hockey players and spectators. Although they enjoyed only a small percentage of the market,
the NHL considered them a threat to its financial security. The NHL
eventually won this competition – by completely outbidding its rivals
for players – and Canadian senior hockey has been a wasteland ever
since.[6] It is difficult to determine the extent to which the NHL's

monopoly has reduced the number of hockey teams operating in Canada, but I believe this number to be considerable. In other countries, where professional sport has not been commercialized and where no profit motive exists to encourage the elimination of rival teams, large professional leagues thrive.* In Canada, good senior hockey is but a memory.

Through its victory over senior "amateur" hockey, the NHL gained almost complete control over the association which governs all amateur hockey in Canada and directs its development, the Canadian Amateur Hockey Association. Virtually every youngster who plays organized hockey outside his school, for example, possesses a registration card from the CAHA or one of its affiliates. Although not all school boards are affiliated with the national organization, most of them use the CAHA rule-book and CAHA-approved referees. As the NHL controls the CAHA and closely supervises all its actions, it enjoys undisputed control over every aspect of the game.

By means of a series of legal agreements which it has persuaded the CAHA to sign, the NHL dictates the rules used in amateur hockey leagues and the conditions of amateur status. It dictates how the CAHA administers its programmes and spends its funds. And until three years ago, it controlled the hockey career of every boy over fourteen years of age, through an elaborate system of sponsorship of amateur teams. In 1967 a special committee of the National Advisory Committee for Fitness and Amateur Sport studying Canadian hockey, observed:

If any organization is to operate independently, it must enjoy control over its own procedures. For a sports governing body, this means it must be able to determine the eligibility of its own members, the playing rules of its competitions, and it must be free to determine how to spend its own funds. The Canadian Amateur Hockey Association enjoys fully none of these essential rights. Under the 1958 agreement (the agreement then in effect), it has abdicated certain of these responsibilities to the National Hockey League. In order to be able to function independently, we firmly believe amateur hockey must be free of control by the NHL.[7]

* For example, Australia, where in Melbourne alone thirty-six professional football clubs operate successfully.

The 1967 NHL-CAHA agreement replaced the "sponsorship" system with a universal draft of players twenty years of age, but the other forms of NHL control remained the same. In a subsequent report, the Hockey Study Committee concluded: "The CAHA failed to achieve the autonomy which the committee felt to be essential for the good of amateur hockey when it agreed to the 1967 NHL-CAHA agreement ... The committee is concerned because the *amateur* and the autonomous status of the CAHA is even more in question than it was under the 1958 agreement."[8]

The NHL-CAHA agreement has but a single purpose: to control the development of talent for the NHL's entertainment industry, now largely American-dominated. Few of the commercial hockey operators would dispute this conclusion. All hockey players and coaches seek to make their careers within the commercial leagues, they would argue. And the integration of amateur and commercial hockey supposedly ensures that players will receive a proper apprenticeship and thus make an easy transition to the professional, commercial leagues. But if one assumes, as the Fitness Council's study committee assumed, that amateur hockey is based upon an entirely different set of values and objectives, then he must conclude that NHL control is harmful.

At the community level, professional domination is harmful in many ways. The "win-at-all-costs," "beat-'em-in-the-alley" ethic of the professionals has so pervaded minor league hockey that it has soured the game for many youngsters, teachers, and parents.[9] The scramble to gain control of young players (the Fitness Council study discovered that the registration cards of boys as young as fourteen and fifteen were being bought and exchanged on the basis of their playing abilities,[10]) has disrupted many homes and the education of many young hockey players. As part of its study, the hockey committee compared the records of Ontario high school students who played hockey for teams *not affiliated* with the school with those of other students. The results bore out what has been widely believed:

From this research, we can now report there were significant differences in certain respects between the two groups, and that sound reasons exist to indicate these differences were related to the playing of Junior OHA hockey.

It is important to note that the hockey-playing and non-hockey-playing [students playing hockey for school teams are included in

the "non-hockey-playing" population] students in this study were
alike in their first year in secondary school ... After a similar start in
Grade 9, a divergent pattern of school behavior began to appear
which became most pronounced around the fourth and fifth years of
secondary schooling.

The hockey-playing students performed progressively more poorly
on Grade 11 and Grade 12 school examinations. On every one of six
standardized achievement tests given in Grades 10 and 11, they also
performed more poorly than their non-hockey-playing peers. In
terms of completion of Grade 13, only 5.9 per cent of the 511 hockey
players graduated compared with 10.7 per cent of the non-hockey-
playing group.[11]

As long as amateur hockey is considered by the NHL as a training
ground for its professional players, the disruption of education must
follow.

NHL control prevents thousands of Canadians who enjoy hockey at
the community level to conduct the game as they see fit. One recent
illustration should suffice. In the 1967 agreement, the amateur association agreed to lower the age of junior competition to enable the
NHL to turn young players into professionals a year earlier. At the
CAHA meeting a year later, the regional association representing
200,000 of 265,000 registered players voted to re-establish the higher
age limit. But the CAHA national executive, which bargains with the
NHL, refused to make the change.[12] Early in 1969 CAHA executive
secretary Gordon Juckes formally requested permission from the
NHL to raise the age limit, but the NHL has refused to reconsider.[13]
The reduced age limit is a serious blow to junior hockey, depriving
the clubs of their most experienced players and banishing the players
to the uncertainties of senior hockey. It is because they have lost a
full year of junior hockey that so many young players are accepting
US athletic scholarships. At a US college they are guaranteed a few
extra years of good competition.[14] The new age ruling has also led to
the establishment of two maverick junior leagues, one on the prairies
and one in western Ontario.[15] The breakdown of junior hockey is a
steep price to pay for the inability of the national association to
conduct its own affairs in the face of NHL domination.

The NHL-CAHA agreements have hampered our hockey teams in
international competition as well. The lengths to which the NHL may
go to eliminate senior competition and protect its monopoly profits

is readily demonstrated by its now successful attack on the Bauer experiment with the National Hockey Team. Prior to the 1964 Winter Olympic Games, the CAHA chose one of the top amateur teams in the country to represent Canada in international competition. Early in the 1960s, however, it became clear that a single amateur club, no matter how much it was supplemented by amateurs from other clubs, could no longer guarantee the success in international hockey that the Canadian public expected. The Russian, Czechoslovakian, German, and Swedish teams were steadily improving. Even the United States was entering teams equal to the best senior teams in Canada. At this time senior hockey in Canada was on the wane, particularly because of the opposition of the NHL.

In 1964, upon the initiative of the Reverend David Bauer, a truly national amateur team was selected and trained to represent Canada at the Olympics. An important component in the Bauer plan was that members of the National Team would be encouraged to combine university study with their hockey playing. In 1965 the team moved to Winnipeg, and two years later a second national team was formed and located in Ottawa. Although both these teams have proven far superior to any single senior team, they have been unable to regain Canada's supremacy in international hockey. In the 1969 World Tournament, Canada finished fifth. Largely as a result of these losses, a non-profit Hockey Canada Corporation has been established to finance and administer the National Team. Hockey Canada's first objective was to persuade the International Ice Hockey Federation to allow nine instantly reinstated professionals to play in international competition. The Montreal Canadiens and the Toronto Maple Leafs, both represented on Hockey Canada's Board of Directors, have promised to supply the players. Now that international hockey competition promises to be opened to professionals, the need for a specially trained national amateur team has disappeared. But all the same, it will be instructive to consider why that experiment failed.

It is popularly held that Canada could never have regained the world hockey championship with a team of amateurs, but was fated to the bottom of the world league until it could be represented by the NHL's professional players. Without question, the NHL exhibits the best players in the world, but that is not being contested. The real question is whether a team of specially prepared Canadian semi-professionals could beat the rest of the world. The NHL never gave Father Bauer a chance to prove his case.

If the National Team was to prosper, it had to include the top amateur players in the country. This the NHL never allowed it to do. In the 1967 NHL-CAHA agreement, the CAHA agreed that none of its teams (including the National Team) could "approach, negotiate or discuss employment with an unsigned drafted player before October 21 in any playing year without prior consent [of the NHL]." The NHL players' draft is simply a gentleman's agreement between member clubs not to negotiate with a player "drafted" by another club. But an "unsigned drafted player" is still an amateur player. By this clause, the National Team was prohibited from discussing hockey with the most talented young players until two months after it began its practices.[16] In another clause, the CAHA agreed not to use any of its player-development funds for the development of players for the National Team.[17] And finally to restrict the National Team, the CAHA national executive recently voted that "Canada's National Team not recruit junior-age hockey players," a ruling that eliminates 10,770 registered junior players as potential candidates for the team.[18] The Hockey Study Committee concluded, "It is rather tragic to note that professional hockey is obviously concerned about competition from one CAHA amateur team (the National Team) while it enters into agreement with the CAHA to develop to the highest possible level literally thousands of amateur teams from Senior to Bantam to serve its own purposes."[19] What is ahead for the National Team as selected and organized by Hockey Canada, is difficult to predict. Vis-à-vis the rest of the world, its performances can only improve. As professional players and unlimited body checking will now be permitted in international play, Canada should regain her world supremacy in the March 1970 tournament and should enjoy a playing edge for several years to come. The real problem will arise years later when the Europeans improve to the calibre of the Canadian-based NHL teams. Suppose Montreal, Toronto, and Vancouver all experience bad years. Can Hockey Canada get help from Chicago or Los Angeles? Not likely. At present only the Canadian-based teams contribute to the National Team, although Canadian citizens will continue to form most of the other eleven teams in the league. The NHL Players' Union has urged that all Canadian hockey players be allowed to play for Canada,[20] but the American-based teams are not expected to permit their players to participate. These US-based Canadians may even return to haunt us as members of the US National Team.

It has often been claimed that, without commercialization, Canadian hockey would never have become the national institution it now is, nor would Canadian hockey players be able to earn as much money from the game as they do today. But professional sport in other countries – British soccer, for example – has proven successful, without commercialization. Commercialization is not necessary for the success of professional sport. Yet it *is* necessarily responsible for the problems of Canadian hockey, the flight of the game to the United States, and the NHL's ruthless drive for monopoly. Once profit maximization became the goal of the NHL, it was inevitable that its leaders would transplant the game to the richer markets of the United States and seek monopoly control of the sport here in Canada. So that it could enjoy monopoly prices for its games, commercial hockey has driven good senior hockey out of business. So that it could dominate the supply of players, it has gained tight control over amateur hockey, with the result that hockey at the local level has been severely hampered and the Bauer experiment with the Canadian National Hockey Team has been sabotaged. It is perhaps difficult to believe that the same organization which brings us the Stanley Cup Playoffs each spring also works against what I have argued are the Canadian interests in hockey, but that conclusion is inescapable.

The true villains of the piece are not the owners of the NHL teams, but rather the institution of commercialized sport which they personify. Stafford Smythe and his colleagues on the NHL Board of Governors have not acted deliberately to depress Canadian hockey; they have merely tried to maximize profits for their hockey corporations. It is unfortunate that the by-products of these business decisions are so unpleasant. The profit motive simply should have no place in spectator sport. Since a sport like hockey is so much a part of the national culture and since the community contributes so much to the development of its athletes, the staging of hockey games should properly be a community enterprise.

To decommercialize Canadian hockey, each of the Canadian clubs should be compelled to become non-profit corporations. Several advantages would immediately ensue. A non-profit NHL team would plough back all its profits into community hockey. (Although the NHL now boasts about the sums of money it pays annually to the

CAHA for player development, these payments appear to be small in relation to profits.* Such a change should also bring about a more open ticket selling policy. More significant benefits would depend, of course, upon the extent to which the teams abandon their profit maximization objectives and seek to become a community service. If professional hockey could assist schools and amateur clubs in the development of sportsmanlike hockey in Canada – and not simply publicize itself or interfere, as it does at present† – then the benefits would be tremendous.

To repatriate Canadian hockey, however, a more radical step is necessary: the creation of a truly national non-commercial professional hockey league with teams in at least a dozen Canadian cities. To get started, the Canadian league would immediately have to buy players away from the existing NHL, as the fledgling American Football League bought players from the established National Football League to get started several years ago. Government backing might initially be necessary, but I am confident the new league could soon stand on its own feet. The existing NHL clubs only "own" players ultimately because each of them have agreed not to seek another team's players. In fact, most players are on one-year contracts. The existing NHL will not give up its present monopoly without a tremendous struggle; but with determined leadership, the new league could be formed.

If hockey stays commercialized, the Canadian community will continue to be exploited by it, while the best brand of the sport will be marketed elsewhere. Change will be difficult to effect, however, and not only because of the opposition of the commercial sports

---

* The CAHA receives about $800,000 annually from the NHL and its affiliates, or about $20,000 per commercial team. For the six months period ending February 28, 1969, Maple Leaf Gardens declared a profit of $810,090 or $1.10 per share. At the time, a single share was selling for about $28.

† One constructive – albeit commercial – contribution some professional players are making to Canadian hockey is the establishment of summer hockey schools. If these could be co-ordinated with community recreation programmes, even more boys could enjoy this specialized form of instruction.

operators and their apologists, the sports press.* Sport in Canada rarely generates its own change, but tends to be shaped by other forces in the society.† Until more Canadians become concerned about the effects of unregulated commercialism upon other aspects of Canadian society, it is unlikely they will ever be concerned about the effects of commercialism in sport.

* A few sports journalists have complained about the size of commercial sport's profits, however. See, for example, Melvin Durslag, "Owners Want Blood and the Law Helps," *Toronto Daily Star,* Sept. 20, 1969. For an illuminating account of the mechanics of sports promotion, see Bruce A. MacFarlane, "The Sociology of Sports Promotion," unpublished MA thesis, McGill University, Aug. 1955.

† It is questionable whether sport has been a force for change in any society. I know of only one case where sportsmen en masse have been in the vanguard of social change. In 1848, when Prussia invaded the German State of Baden to suppress Baden's newly promulgated liberal constitution, the Hanau Turnverein, a sport club, sent 300 armed gymnasts to repel the invaders. P. C. McIntosh, *Sport In Society* (London, 1963), p. 189.

POSTSCRIPT

In the few weeks since this article went to the editor, American interests have moved one step closer to total control of the NHL. Three days before Christmas the Medical Investment Corporation of Minneapolis acquired majority ownership of the Vancouver Canucks and the NHL's fourteenth franchise. John Munro, the federal minister of health and welfare, has begun to express concern about "the apparent transfer of power in the NHL to US owners although our country is still and is likely to continue to be the main source of talent for US teams," but he is quite unwilling to challenge the NHL's power over Canadian hockey. In particular, he has condemned the National Team to dependence upon handouts from the NHL for its players. In a recent reply to suggestions that Hockey Canada hire Bobby Hull for the National Team, Munro said: "Now remember that Hockey Canada is representative; it includes the NHL. Mr Hull has a contract with the NHL. Hockey Canada cannot encourage him to breach that contract unless it wants a war, financial and otherwise – and no co-operation from the NHL. *We know how a lack of co-operation in recent years hurt the National Team"* (italics mine).

At the moment the National Team's most serious antagonists are Canada's fellow members in the International Ice Hockey Federation who have just reversed their earlier decision to allow professional players in the 1970 World Championship. Canada has quite rightly refused to go along with this doubledealing and has withdrawn from the tournament. But we should not vent all our rage upon the opportunistic Europeans. After all, if the NHL had not already wrecked Canadian amateur and semi-professional hockey, the National Team would not be quite so dependent upon those professional players.

BK

January 5, 1970

NOTES

1 Nancy Howell and Maxwell L. Howell, *Sports and Games in Cana-dian Life* (Toronto, 1969), p. 60.

2 Frank J. Selke, *Behind the Cheering* (Toronto, 1962), p. 102.

3 Christina McCall Newman, ed., *The Man from Oxbow: The Best of Ralph Allen* (Toronto, 1967), p. 18. See also Frank Moritsugu, "Let the Probers Look at THIS Religion," *Toronto Daily Star,* April 17, 1965.

4 "Kids Turning to U.S. Colleges," *Telegram,* March 24, 1969; "Only Two Junior Hockey Clubs Escape U.S. Raiding Parties," *Globe and Mail,* Sept. 6, 1969.

5 "U.S. TV Networks Still Dictates NHL Playoff Times," *Toronto Daily Star,* Sept. 25, 1968.

6 *Report on Amateur Hockey in Canada by the Hockey Study Com-mittee of the National Advisory Council on Fitness and Amateur Sport* (Ottawa, 1967), p. 10. Referred to hereafter as *First Report.* A more popular explanation for the decline of senior hockey is tele-vision, but the Hockey Study Committee indicates that the decline was well advanced by 1954, before television was widespread in Canada.

7 *First Report,* p. 10.

8 *Report on Amateur Hockey in Canada by the Hockey Study Committee of the National Advisory Council on Fitness and Amateur Sport* (Ottawa, 1968), pp. 9-10. Referred to hereafter as *Final Report.*

9 "Fathers, Mothers, Punch Imlach, Are the Curse of Kids' Hockey," *Toronto Daily Star,* Jan. 21, 1965. Also Newman, ed., *The Man from Oxbow,* pp. 18-20.

10 *First Report,* pp. 15-16.

11 *Ibid.,* p. 27. The comparison was made with the assistance of the Carnegie Data Bank of Information about Ontario secondary school students.

12 *Final Report,* pp. 13-14.

13 "NHL in Control, CAHA Requests Age Limit Boost for Its Juniors," *Globe and Mail,* Jan. 29, 1969.

14 "Kids Turning to U.S. Colleges," *Telegram,* March 24, 1969.

15 "CHA rebel sees growth in Ontario," *Globe and Mail,* Jan. 29, 1969.

16 *Final Report,* p. 6.

17 *Ibid,*

18 *Ibid.,* p. 5.

19 *Ibid.,* p. 6.

20 "Players Association Wants 25 Best in NHL to Play Russians," *Globe and Mail,* May 30, 1969.

James Laxer

A doctoral student in history. He has contributed essays to *Canadian Dimension* and the *Canadian Forum*.

The Americanization of the Canadian student movement

During the past decade, left-wing thinkers in Canada increasingly have recognized that the goals of Canadian independence and socialism are interdependent. Continental integration has become so pervasive that those who value an independent Canada and those who reject the values of corporate capitalism are beginning to share a common agenda. Canadian nationalists are starting to realize that only large-scale government intervention in the economy can win back control of this country for Canadians; socialists are more and more aware that we cannot build a better society if Canada does not possess sovereign power. It is in the interest of North American capitalists to weaken the Canadian state and to limit it to the passive function of maintaining a peaceful and secure climate for investment. In contrast, it is in the interest of Canadian socialists to resist any decline in our national sovereignty and to demand that the state serve as an instrument for setting alternative social priorities, based on the satisfaction of human need rather than profit.

The necessary connection between the pursuit of Canadian independence and socialism has become an axiom of the Canadian left. But, for several reasons, the New Left student movement in Canada has had difficulty in grasping and acting upon this political axiom.

Youth and students form the New Left in Canada. The group originated with a peace movement that arose in the political doldrums of the late 1950s. Following the acquisition of nuclear weapons by Canada in 1963, certain elements of the Combined Universities Campaign for Nuclear Disarmament (CUCND) became convinced that "social change" was the only route to peace. This theme evolved at the same time as white students were involving themselves in the civil rights movement in the United States. From the early 1960s, the Canadian New Left derived much of its style and ideology from the United States, and American-centred issues filled its political agenda. A direct connection in terms of ideas and personnel can be traced from the Students for a Democratic Society (SDS) and the Student Non-Violent Coordinating Committee (SNCC) in the United States, through the Student Union for Peace Action (SUPA) to the Company of Young Canadians (CYC) and the Canadian Union of Students (CUS). Throughout these years there was little contact between the New Left and the traditional Canadian left (traditional Canadian left here referring to democratic socialists in the CCF-NDP, as well as to workers and farmers in the trade union and co-operative movements). Today's

Canadian student movement still bears the stamp of American influence. It has been unable to formulate a political strategy relevant
to Canadian society.

The American New Left has its roots in a cultural revolt of the
young against the dominant values of American society, a revolt
which has developed from the beatniks to the hippies. It began, not
with a concern over the fundamental conflicts in US society, but
with the rejection of the sterile cultural and personal outlook of the
majority of its people. Through the evolution of their own vocabulary, dress, and music, these youth movements developed great internal strength and deeply influenced their adherents. The life-style
which distinguished them from other sections of middle-class society
was intended to serve as the basis for a counter-community. The
identification of its participants with American black culture made
this youth revolution a potential base for a radical movement. As the
black revolutionary movement took shape, its style and orientation
were transmitted through the emerging New Left to masses of white
youth. It was this tie with the black movement that made it possible
for much of the American New Left eventually to transcend mere
cultural revolt.

The American youth movement has had a wide influence on the
life-style and culture of young people in many parts of the world –
especially in Canada. But the American youth revolt and the New
Left political movements have not been co-extensive. The New Left
groupings, whether their origins were anarchist, Christian pacifist, or
socialist, have evolved within the broader youth revolt. It is the
association of the American New Left with the youth revolt that has
given the movement its impact on young people outside the United
States, and particularly in Canada.

Unfortunately, the cultural rebellion of the young in Canada has
been far less suitable as the basis of a radical political movement
than it was in the United States. The identification of middle-class
Canadians with a second-hand culture based essentially on that of
American blacks has not put Canadian youth automatically in a
politically meaningful position. Rather, it has tended to cut them off
from traditionally radical sections of the Canadian population. In
Canada, a primary aim of the left should be the struggle against
domination by the American empire in order to achieve true independence. Obviously the goal is removed from the orientation of the
New Left.

In general, American radicalism tends to be an inappropriate guide for Canadian radicals because it is conceived out of the conditions of the heart of the empire rather than the conditions of a dependent country. American radicals to a large degree are concerned with preventing or checking the exploitation of much of the world by their own country. This leads such radicals to be quite unconcerned about the effectiveness of American national institutions. When Canadian radicals, influenced by the American New Left, adopt the same attitude to the effectiveness or survival of Canadian institutions, it has far different political implications. It benefits the world when American radicals challenge the right of US institutions to continue their economic and military domination of peoples abroad. This has reinforced the New Left's distrust of organizations and institutions in general. A similar attitude to Canadian institutions, however, results merely in a further softening-up of this country for American takeover.

In the immediate political situation, it is important for socialists to fight vigorously for Canadian control of Canadian institutions of all kinds. Such issues will unmask the continentalism of Canadian capitalists, and their dependence on the Americans. Significantly, the Canadian New Left has never waged a political campaign in which the American takeover of Canada (economically, politically, or culturally) was a central issue.

Socialists in a dependent country face a complex problem: they must seek power from domestic capitalists in such a way that they do not simply enhance the power of the foreign corporations at the expense of the local middlemen. In particular, Canadian socialists must chart a course that avoids two dangers: enhancing state capitalism through a too conservative fear for the fate of Canadian institutions; and facilitating American penetration by seeking power in a way that merely weakens Canadian institutions and undermines the beliefs of the Canadian people in their power to resist. Social democracy in Canada has failed because it has encouraged the growth of state capitalism (the welfare state) without having fought a determined battle for national independence. The Canadian New Left has failed because its American perspectives have made it insensitive to the demands of a socialist struggle in a dependent country. The New Left has been blind to the process needed to unite with potentially radical social forces in Canada. Instead it has placed its own unique life-style ahead of the general interests of the Canadian left. Some will object that New Leftists are now vitally concerned with achieving an alliance with the working class. The critical question is whether they are prepared to adapt their political methods and priorities enough to make such an alliance possible. To date they have not been, partly as a result of the powerful impact of American radicalism on the development of the Canadian movement.

As well as the perspective of American radicalism the Canadian New Left has adopted some specific American political issues. It has spent much effort on questions which are marginal to Canada – the race question or the draft – and when it has addressed itself to broader questions such as Vietnam, its demands for a Canadian response to the war generally have not been central to its campaign.

Three sets of notions have influenced the Canadian New Left as a result of its contact with American radicals: the idea of participatory democracy; suspicion of institutional structures and all complex forms of social organization; and belief in minority groups and the poor as central agents for social change.

The concept of participatory democracy originated in the United States as an attempt to revitalize and deepen the meaning of American pluralism. Pluralism is based on a view that society is an aggregate of individuals who come together in many different kinds of groupings to pursue their individual interests. Those who called for participatory democracy pointed out that the disadvantaged in society took no part in decision-making; their demand was for a voice for the poor – in other words, a call for an operative rather than a sham pluralism. Some Americans in the New Left felt that their society could not accommodate real pluralism, and that an attempt to make it operative would reveal fundamental antagonisms in America. This was an attempt to smuggle a concept of class struggle in the back door, an understandable tactic in a country whose ideology denies the reality of class. Intrinsically, however, participatory democracy does not transcend the liberal theory that there is a harmony of interests in society which will be realized if all groups of people are able to make their views known.

Along with the radical pluralism of the New Left came its suspicion of institutional structures and complex forms of social organization. American young people who were beginning to reject the society into which they were being socialized started to question the very right of society to socialize its youth. This was a necessary phase. Without a developed socialist tradition, young Americans naturally tended to reject all social organization, having as yet no idea of the concrete possibility of an alternative. The left-wing traditions indigenous to the United States tended to be individualist and anarchist and pushed them in the same direction.

The trouble with this rejection of the "system" was that often there was little discrimination between disavowal of capitalism and the rejection of complex, industrial society in general. The tendency to concentrate on the evils of bigness and complexity in institutions, rather than on the necessity for their social control, has compounded the problems of the New Left in two ways. It has made more difficult the quest for alliances with other groups seeking a humanist rather than a capitalist industrial society, and it has made almost impossible the building of a political organization capable of acting in a united way and on a national scale. The anti-organizational bias lingers on in the Canadian New Left; and although it is no longer explicitly espoused by radical student intellectuals, to a marked degree it still holds them back from involving themselves in organizations in Canada which may be important in the struggle for national independence.

Adopting the third notion and focusing attention on minority groups and the poor, the Canadian New Left came to see the urban and rural poor and disadvantaged minority groups such as the Indians and Métis as holding the greatest promise as agents of total social change. This assumption has been less useful in Canada than in the United States because no minority group here is analagous to the American blacks in terms of numbers, exploitation, and strategic location in the great urban centres. Moreover, the tendency to concentrate on minority groups has resulted in the failure of the New Left to appreciate the seminal importance of the exploitation of Canadian society in general by the American empire.

To those familiar with the experience of socialists during the last century, it is plain that only by being brought into contact with already organized groups in strategic areas of Canadian society will the urban and rural poor and disadvantaged minority groups be able to play a role in a movement for fundamental change. This change could result only from a revitalized movement of workers and farmers fighting for democratic control of the work situation and for the achievement of a socialist regime in Canada.

The American orientation of the Canadian New Left has been entirely understandable. It has stemmed from the general Americanization of this country and from the accompanying malaise of Canadian politics. The estrangement of the New Left from the traditional Canadian left has hardly been astonishing when one considers the timidity of Canadian social democracy as it emerged from McCarthyism and the Cold War of the 1950s. It would have been remarkable indeed if a youth movement born in such circumstances had possessed clarity of vision regarding the Canadian drift towards colonial status.

In the fall of 1964 SUPA, successor to the CUCND, was founded. Until its demise in the summer of 1967, it was *the* organization of the Canadian New Left. During its brief history it had a major impact on youth organizations in Canada – especially the CYC and CUS – and greatly influenced the Student Christian Movement and even the YMCA. Today, however, there is no such New Left organization in Canada. The term "Canadian New Left" now refers to people who are in the political and intellectual tradition of SUPA.

It is always difficult to measure the degree of continuity from one organization to another, particularly when one is dealing with a youth organization that has left few written records behind it and with individuals whose ideas have undergone a rapid evolution. But the continuity of personnel from SUPA to the staff and intellectual apparatus of the Canadian Union of Students in 1968-9 was striking. Ex-SUPA people, who were in many cases the most experienced politically, occupied positions ranging from field worker to president of CUS.

SUPA served as the major instrument for drawing American New Left ideas into Canada and for diffusing them among Canadian youth organizations. Its task was made easier by the general tendency of Canadians to accept innovations from the United States. Civil rights activities in the United States and the common currency of the American youth revolt made SUPA instantly recognizable to Canadians; its instant image greatly amplified its influence on Canadian young people. SUPA had many of the advantages of an American branch-plant corporation in merchandising its brand-name products.

The specific inspiration for SUPA projects came from the Economic Research Action Projects (ERAP), which were loosely affiliated with

SDS. Of greatest importance was the Newark Community Union Project (NCUP) which attempted to create "an inter-racial movement" among the poor in Newark, New Jersey, in the mid-1960s. One crucial aim of the organizers of NCUP was to find a non-black constituency of poor people for SDS. However, the project largely failed in its attempt to involve local whites and ended, in effect, as a black organizing venture.

NCUP served as the inspiration for a number of SUPA projects. Personal contacts played a large part in transmitting this kind of activity from Americans to the Canadian New Left. Some of this contact came from Canadian New Leftists who spent time working with radicals in the United States. Particularly important, however, was the influence of the American Tom Hayden of NCUP. Hayden's personal magnetism had a pronounced effect on the attitudes of SUPA leaders in Toronto and Montreal.

In Canada, ERAP and especially NCUP spawned the Kingston Community Project and the Toronto Community Union Project (TCUP). Both of these projects attempted to apply the ghetto organizing techniques used in American ERAP work. But, of course, the Canadian urban poor did not have the powerful common identity of American black ghetto dwellers, and it became clear that attempts to organize them on a residential basis would not result in the birth of a major social movement.

SUPA members undertook projects among the blacks in Halifax, the Indians and Métis in Saskatchewan, and the Doukhobors in British Columbia. There was never any serious effort in SUPA to work with organized labour. In part, this failure stemmed from the low opinion of the American New Left for the AFL-CIO, but it was an inappropriate prejudice when applied to Canadian labour with its significantly different political tradition.

SUPA's approach to community organizing revealed a basic failure to develop a working analysis of Canadian society.* This failure was

---

* Indeed, this was the reason offered for the demise of SUPA in the summer of 1967 by the organization's short-lived successor, the New Left Committee. A statement of the committee asserted: "Key to SUPA's failure was its inability to develop a coherent analysis of the structure of modern capitalism and of its specific characteristics in Canada. Instead SUPA remained ideologically confused, uncritically

a determining factor governing SUPA's relations with the rest of society. It meant that a developing left-right split within the organization often turned on sentiment rather than on clear-cut strategic disagreements. The militants tended to oppose activity in mainstream organizations, both because these were seen as the "enemy" and because such activities would enhance the position of the liberal wing within SUPA.

As the split in SUPA developed, the liberal wing of the organization increasingly was attracted to the Company of Young Canadians, where it saw an opportunity to continue its previous activities in a more affluent setting. After SUPA went defunct, the former left wing of the organization gravitated towards CUS, particularly after the election of Peter Warrian as CUS President at the 1967 Congress.*

While there was a marked split in the Canadian New Left between the liberals and the militants, both groups exhibited common characteristics in their behaviour in the CYC and CUS. Both the left and the right continued to reflect the rootlessness that has often been characteristic of middle-class radicalism. One of the problems of the rootless left is that much of its search for new meaning in life tends to go on at the level of style and form. The Canadian New Left has fallen victim to this kind of thinking more easily than has the American New Left. The clear and pressing character of the race question and the draft in the United States has provided a powerful corrective to a radicalism of form. In Canada, though, vital issues have been clouded by the enormous cultural impact of the United States.

Because of the tendency to form a counter-community (particularly in the early days of the New Left) and to adopt American issues and style, the Canadian New Left has remained, in effect, largely outside

---

eclectic. It drew on various elements of the pacifist – direct action approach and ill-defined SDS notions of "participatory democracy." But the war in Vietnam, the powerlessness of the poor, the authoritarian governing of the universities, were never traced to their structural roots in the political economy of modern capitalism, and the constituencies essential to revolutionary change were only vaguely defined and analysed."

* The majority of former SUPA members took neither of these routes, of course. Most of them simply dropped out of politics, although a few went into the NDP.

Canadian society. For the New Left, Canadian institutions and traditions have been without substance or value, the entire society has
appeared as a gray, uniform, and hostile force. Not understanding
Canadian history and particularly the history of peoples' movements
in Canada, New Leftists have been incapable of evolving a strategy
that rises above the level of sentimental militancy and expediency.

It is no accident that many SUPA members were attracted by the
alternative prospects of using or wrecking the CYC. One SUPA member writing in the organization's Centennial Newsletter advised fellow
radicals to "Use the CYC to destroy the CYC." But for many in SUPA,
activity in the CYC was not part of a strategy, but a comfortable substitute for one. Those driven there because of a lack of understanding
of Canadian society were not likely to find it in the CYC, where one
day inspiration was sought from VISTA and the next day from the
Red Guards.

Whatever its original intentions had been, New Left activity in the
CYC eventually appeared to the public as careerism and low-level
pocket lining. The radicals in the Company ended up as a standard
pressure group – they took what they could and left.*

The militant wing of the Canadian New Left began its career in CUS
with all the floundering that is characteristic of rootless radicalism.
The CUS Congress in the fall of 1968 resulted in a highly radical
stance for the organization but provided little in the way of radical
strategy. In the months following the Congress more than half the
schools pulled out of the union as CUS lost referendum after referendum. With no clear goals for the student movement or the university,
the CUS leadership slipped into the *de facto* building of a minority
radical union. While this was in itself unobjectionable, the mainstream national union was being crippled by the actions of a small
group at the centre, with little debate taking place within the student
movement at large on the possibility of alternative strategies.

Today radical student intellectuals in Canada have advanced beyond
the early New Left notions, and have to some extent transcended the
specifically American style that characterized the movement a few
years ago. This is due both to the recent impact of European student
radicalism and to an appreciation among some groups that have been

---

* It must be stressed to the credit of large numbers of SUPA people that
they never went along with the CYC game, and that those still active
in the student movement are mainly those who stayed outside.

associated with CUS of the need for radical research on the Canadian economy and society.

Another reason for the change in the political tone of the New Left is the regional shift in influence that has occurred within the movement. During SUPA's heyday, Toronto was the political and intellectual centre of gravity, with an English-speaking group in Montreal being next in importance. Saskatchewan, the other important centre of the New Left and the one having most contact with the democratic socialist tradition in Canada because of its strong CCF background, had relatively little influence on the dominant eastern groups. Since 1967, however, the balance has shifted decisively to the west, with a group at Simon Fraser achieving the kind of influence that the New Left around the University of Toronto once had. The shift in influence to Saskatchewan and British Columbia is one reason for the strong socialist emphasis within the movement today. Significantly, these are the provinces with the most powerful socialist traditions in Canada. The national importance of the New Left groupings there has marked the eclipse of Toronto libertarianism as the movement's dominant focus.

It may already be untrue to speak of the Canadian student movement as simply an offshoot of the American New Left. In spite of this, however, it remains substantially the case that the perspectives of the Canadian student movement are still affected materially by the horizons and world-view of the American movement. Those who cannot see beyond the American New Left can be expected to view Canada largely within this perspective. There is now a tendency among some student radicals to regard Canadian history as colonial history pure and simple, marked by a mere transition from the British to the American empire. Such a conclusion, denying as it does any important "national" experience on the part of English Canada, could make it simpler to reject the need for a specifically Canadian road to socialism. This would allow some New Leftists to return with a clear conscience to their original goal of creating the second American Revolution.

The perspective of such people overlooks the fact that even a colonial nation has a history which largely determines the kind of political movement that can arise within it. It is important to note that few in the New Left would deny the validity of French-Canadian "national" experience, in spite of the fact that French Canada has been even more colonial than English Canada. One can only conclude that the peculiar difficulty of the New Left in appreciating the unique experience of English Canada and its exploitation by the American empire results from a perspective similar to that of the American New Left, which makes it difficult to identify with an English-speaking, predominantly Anglo-Saxon, people. Since WASPS are seen as the "bad guys" in the United States, it is difficult to perceive that working-class WASPS in Canada form the core around which any successful radical movement will be established.

One reason for the tendency of the New Left to underestimate the importance of Canadian "national" experience is the obvious bias of historical hindsight: the Canadian bourgeoisie is now a willing dependent of the American capitalists – therefore, there is a tendency to underrate the extent to which it ever had distinctive interests and was able to shape Canada in its own image.

One might ask, what is the relevance of these disagreements about the past, as long as we all now agree on the need for an independent socialist Canada? The difficulty is this: the Canadian New Left perspective leads not to an independent Canadian struggle but to continental radicalism. In the long run, the present Canadian New Left perspective is not suited to a struggle for an independent socialist Canada. Either the perspective must change, or the New Left will be forced to go over to the continental strategy that was hinted at in several of the papers presented to the CUS Seminar in May 1969.

Central to the problem is the fact that New Leftists feel as alienated from Canadian society as their American counterparts do from American society. They do not experience a gut anger over the reduction of their country to a colony; they have no honest rage about the destruction of Canada as an historical entity. Unlike Quebec student radicals who experience imperialism as the degradation of their own society, the Canadian New Left does not prefer its own country over the United States. How, then, can New Leftists seriously consider themselves part of an anti-imperialist movement in this country? The problem is not one of political tactics or militancy, but the identification of those who take part in the struggle with the Canadian people as individuals and as members of a political community. If the New Left can make such an identification, its militancy and vitality will make it central to an anti-imperial coalition; if not, it will remain on the margin of things, merely distracting attention from the central facts of the Canadian situation.

George Martell

A member of Point Blank School and an editor of *This Magazine is about Schools*. He teaches sociology at Atkinson College, York University.

What can I do right now?
Notes from Point Blank School on the Canadian dilemma

[This is a slight revision of an article that originally appeared in *This Magazine is about Schools*.]

I started these notes six months ago when I wrote the introduction to Clay Borris' story of making his film, *Parliament Street*. Clay had been a client/a student/a friend of mine for almost four years. I hoped that in talking about my relationship with him I'd be able to be clearer about what Point Blank School* means to me and why I think it may be one of a number of institutions on which we can build an alternative system to the present governing structure in this country, or at least in English Canada. I didn't get very far in the writing, however, and I soon gave it up. Clay was too close to me and still too far away for me to discuss him without becoming either sentimental or clinical. The same was true of the school. I had no solid hold on it. In the past couple of years I've done so much insane wheeling and dealing – making it up and doing it too, being serious and bullshitting all the while, as everybody does in keeping these places alive – that I was not sure what my feelings were for the place, what it was I loved, and what I cared for elsewhere. I'm still not sure, even though the school continues to be more livable than any place I have been.

I started these notes again after listening to a taped interview Clay made with another eighteen-year-old kid from Parliament Street, Charlie Macdougal. From the age of nine Charlie had spent most of his life in jail or in training school, and on the tape he talked non-stop for almost two and a half hours about the quality of that life: its humiliations, its brutality, its bad sex. For hours afterwards I was angry, and the anger brought me back to realizing the extent to which I believed that the creation of schools like Point Blank was necessary for simple human dignity. They were a clear matter of justice. The school's reason for being then – in the first telling, anyway – did not require a detailed study of my own survival tactics (which are still unclear to me) or of the personal needs of a very small group of adults and kids I know and care for. This made it easier for me to write these notes: as a response to Charlie, not Clay.

Charlie is very much an abstraction for me. I've never met him. I haven't even seen him about the neighbourhood. The kids at Point

---

* Point Blank School is a small free school for neighbourhood kids in the Cabbagetown area of downtown Toronto. It has a membership of about forty people, and its administration and curriculum are developed entirely by its teachers and students through democratic processes.

Blank tell me, for his age, he's one of the toughest guys on Parliament
Street. "You otta see him when he gets drunk ... fuckit, is he ever
wild ... crazy bastard ... scares the shit right outta me." I don't know
how I'd react to his whole person. I've just heard his voice on the
tape talking to Clay, who interviewed him. However, while listening
to Charlie – intelligent, almost gracious, very cool and hoarse – I knew
I believed every word he was saying, even if, as a consummate con-
man, he made it up. I don't think he did – I think most of the events
he relates in fact happened – but whether he did or not finally doesn't
matter that much to me. Because the burden of what he says is what
every other kid says who's spent some time in our prisons for children. That's important not so much because a lot of other kids back
him up and so offer more proof that the objective conditions of
prison life are inhuman, but because a lot of kids say the same thing
period. That is *what* they say. That is *what* they have to tell us. They
don't tell us something else. When Charlie Macdougal talks as he did
to Clay those are the only words he uses; they are how he decides to
present the world of his prison to us and so also to himself at that
time. Whatever the personal and public con involved, the words at
that moment are his mind. He has no other.

For me his words are one final reality, one final part of his humanity, no matter how articulate his body may be in love and
violence. Without his words and his knowledge that they are in some
important sense true, he is a slave and has no chance of becoming a
man. If his words do not hold at least one important level of reality
for him and for us, the consequences of that fact lead me to greater
despair than I am capable of handling. I simply believe that they are
true, and hope at Point Blank we can effectively encourage more kids
to use words – films, paintings, etc., being words too – in the same
way.

Yet finally I don't think that's an adequate reason to be at Point
Blank. I don't think you can encourage people to describe the human
reality of a corrupt social system and leave it at that, hoping that
with some natural dialectic of consciousness they'll do something
about destroying that system on their own. It seems to me it's not
possible to let others suffer needlessly and do nothing except help
them write about it and do a little writing yourself. I don't like the
idea of "witness." It seems to me I'm less of a man if I don't put my
whole self on the line, and do it in a way that makes a difference to
the society as a whole.

To put this another way, I think the society is corrupt enough that I'd like to join the revolution, but I'm not certain what that means. Of course, I'm hoping that maybe one's begun – a revolution that's peculiarly modern – and that somehow I've joined it by being part of the free-school movement, but I'm not at all sure, especially in this country.

It may be – and I don't mean to brush this aside lightly – that I am too frightened to look closely at the militant argument that oppression must greatly increase in North America, and soon, and that we all must get ready for violent, confrontation politics: the friends of Ronald Reagan are going to have to be met head on and killed, or they'll kill us. I don't think that's the situation, mostly on hunch or intuition. I also don't think there are many people on the left in North America who think it's the situation either and actually believe we're going to fight a traditional revolution, with widespread bloodletting and the repression that goes with it. I don't think the left is prepared seriously to take on the police and the army, and I don't think they want to get prepared. The confrontation, particularly in the United States, on the campuses and in the ghettoes, still seems like theatre to me – violent theatre maybe in which brave individuals stand to lose a lot, including their lives, in making symbolic gestures of defiance.– but theatre nevertheless, without the potential to go further in the near future. Whatever the chance of a violent revolution in the United States, however, one thing I'm certain about is that a violent revolution will come much later in Canada. The explosive forces in America's cities and in her oppression of peoples of the third world are simply not ones we have to face right now.

But a non-violent revolution is something else. One idea that has been recurring to me lately is that we may actually have more potential for building a base for a non-violent revolution in Canada than in the United States simply because we have more time and space, fewer problems, less immediate government repression. Building a base for a non-violent revolution assumes, of course, that a violent revolution won't happen in the States. If it does, then fledgling institutions like Point Blank will be wiped out as we all pick sides. So I'm assuming America won't be faced with a violent revolution, at least not in the traditional mould. If I assumed otherwise, then I wouldn't be able to do very much, except sit around and wait for the action to start south of the border.

When I think about it, I'm not sure of this last point. Even if I did come up with a general analysis that said free schools would likely be historically irrelevant, I'd no doubt go ahead with my present work anyway, because I like what I'm doing, I don't know what else I could do, and my optimism is of a desperate kind. When it comes to large intellectual matters (leaving aside the rest of my life) I'm simply not to be trusted. I've got too much that's personal at stake. Nevertheless, I would like to put down a couple of general impressions I have about this country that correspond to what my "common sense" (as McLuhan uses that term) tells me are political realities for English Canadians like myself. I want to do so because the argument that emerges tends to support those people who are currently working in the cities, trying to build up, in a miniscule way and without much success, alternative institutions to the present system of government. We can use some support.

The argument is made at the expense of those who take a strong Canadian nationalist stand and are convinced that a humane socialism can emerge in conjunction with a new national spirit. I'm uneasy about this. For while I think that hope is illusionary, the benefits of the 49th parallel in relieving us of some of the burdens of empire, are undeniable. It's a matter of priorities. Maybe it comes down to this: support Mel Watkins in his bid to radicalize the NDP on a nationalist platform, but don't spend the majority of your time at it.

The first point I want to make, then, is that it no longer seems likely that the Canadian nation-state can serve as a framework in which something threatening to corporate capitalism can take place. As a country, I believe, we have had it. Our culture, our politics, our economy are almost entirely packaged in the US, whether by the radical left or the great corporations. It's not so much we're a colony, we're an integral part of the empire. We're Americans now, and I think we have to begin dealing with that fact; we must think in terms of this continent. The time for polite studies on the dangers of extra-territoriality is past. It's no longer helpful to try to find the touch of toryism in our bourgeois fragment which is going to lead us through liberalism to fabian socialism and freedom from Yankee imperialism. It's ceased to be pertinent to speculate on how to man the barricades against the infiltration of American behaviourist professors or how to tap French-Canadian nationalism for English-Canadian radicalism so we can all fight GM together. This kind of discussion has become painfully academic, quite removed from the day-to-day experience of most Canadians. For the game is up. We've been bought, and right now we don't mind very much. We just don't want to deal with it. "It's ok. alright." The PM has his finger on it: "These are the facts of life," he says openly, "and they don't bother me." Then Trade Minister Jean-Luc Pepin tells us: "We must remember that foreign direct investment involves interdependence more than dependence. While foreign participation in Canadian industry exposes us to external decision-making, we should remember that such exposure does not apply in one direction only. The country and company investing in a foreign land also expose themselves to the possibility of unfavourable foreign actions." The steely-eyed Canadian mouse, roaring in the board rooms of America. And Mr Trudeau continues: "This is where Canadians can prove whether they are entrepreneurs or not, and whether their assessment of the future is as good as the Americans ..." in the "industries of tomorrow."

It's embarrassing to have such patently dishonest leaders, I agree, but do you know anyone who is actually going to do something about preserving this country's independence? What kind of action are you going to get from the US residents who own 60 per cent of Canadian manufacturing, who own 74 per cent of Canadian petroleum and natural gas, who own 59 per cent of Canadian mining and smelting, to mention only three prominent areas of control? What about the foreign investors (mostly American) who financed 44 per cent of all net capital formation in Canada between 1954 and 1965? How do you think they'll advise their governments? Do you think there's going to be a strong nationalist stand taken by Canadians whose livelihood depends on this investment? Say by our big businessmen who now operate almost entirely within a continental or an international economy? Or the 80 per cent of Canadian trade unionists who belong to AFL-CIO unions? Or those for whom the increasingly complex apparatus of the welfare state, financed by this investment, provides a job or a handout? What about the political parties financed by the great corporations, the unions and the affluent middle classes? Or the people who run the media and the universities, who get their money from the government and the corporations. How will they act? Or the millions of immigrants who couldn't get into the States? Or the suburbs reading *Time* and *Readers' Digest* (supported by the federal government) and watching Doris Day on the CBC? We have to get serious. It's over. There is not one powerful group in this country, or outside it, prepared to lose anything important to them in order to protect Canada's sovereignty, because, frankly, they don't see that they have anything substantial to gain. Canadians knew what they were getting with Mr Trudeau, and they are not, as the left likes to make out, all that disillusioned with him. It would have been nice to have had a little more parliamentary glamour, a little more public humanity, but they'll vote for him again. Who else can make it as easy for them to lose the country they don't have? Who can do anything other than that?

We don't have a choice, as people like Walter Gordon hoped in 1967, "to do the things that are necessary to regain control of our economy, and thus, maintain our independence" or else "acquiesce in becoming a colonial dependency of the United States, with no future except the hope of eventual absorption." And because we don't have this choice it's hurtful to set up the problem in this way, for it always comes down to the question of the "will of English Canada" to survive and then a deluge of exhortations not to be apathetic. It leaves us nothing specific to do, except perhaps protect the 49th parallel (saving our sons from the draft, etc.) – a political border that probably doesn't need much protecting because the Americans will get what they want from us peacefully. For when we get past the question of keeping the Yanks at bay, we turn to mush. Take, for example, Kari Levitt in her otherwise very clear and useful article, "Canada: Economic Dependence and Political Disintegration in Canada" cited earlier in this book. The final paragraph:

In English Canada there exists the possibility that the cultural integration into continental American life has proceeded to the point where Canada no longer is a meaningful national community. Yet here there is the possibility that the current reaction among the younger generation against domination by the efficiency-mongers of big business, big government or big anything may revive the "conserving" nationalism which derives from the desire to shape the conditions of life within a community which individuals can control. Only the emergence of a new value system within English Canada can ensure the existence of a nation here. "Man and His World" indicates that the option is still open.

The fact is the "new value system" of youth that is to revive English Canada is at one with the value system of radical American youth, and the emergence of what can be called "youth culture" is a phenomenon that takes in all of North America. I can't imagine Mrs Levitt denying that; it seems so plain. Just take a look at the lineups outside *Alice's Restaurant.* And the reference to Expo I find as embarrassing as Mr Pepin's remarks about the possibility of Canadian economic retaliation. When you have to turn (as almost every journalist in the country has turned) to the efficient administration of a world's fair on an artificial island to find the emergence of some unique national soul, you're in considerable trouble.

It seems to me that there is no way out but to recognize that there is only one real question for us now: what kind of Americans are we going to be? Are we going to buy the life-style of the great corporations or are we going to reject it? There are only two choices, and the people who have chosen the second way of acting are that loose collection of groups in both Canada and the US called the New Left. In these terms Canada's democratic socialists (in the NDP) are buying the corporate life-style, although they would like it to be considerably more humane – a concern which involves more government control, nicer Canadian entrepreneurs, and better welfare benefits. In the short run, making capitalism run more decently is good because it lessens economic hardship and frees people up to act. But this is finally peripheral (though perhaps a necessary first stage) to the New Left push for a society that is fundamentally opposed to corporate capitalism, a society in which we are controlled by neither the government nor the corporations, and in which we do not have to prove whether we are "entrepreneurs or not," and yet a society which also does not deny our nature as North Americans.

What does it mean to be a North American? First of all, I think it means that we are unalterably bourgeois. In the past our society, like that of the United States, has generally believed that a man's essense is his freedom. We have had no other respectable tradition that has said otherwise. Our society was largely built at a time when the articulation of bourgeois ideals was at its height. Hobbes prettied by Locke was, in the end, the philosopher who counted, and the practical creed that emerged was ideally suited to mastering the frontier. As in America our conservatives are mainly old-fashioned liberals, who have a nineteenth century version of what it means to be autonomous: to will a destiny outside the destiny of others, and so deny the very notion of destiny. There is no acceptable Tory or old-line Socialist view that an imposed external order is necessary to put down human greed. What theory of a corporate society some of our ancestors might have brought from Britain had no roots to grow and in the end our loyalists wanted every bit of freedom their Yankee counterparts had to make a buck. When they wrote the BNA Act, with the help of the British government, they had at least the good taste not to deny that. The "Union," they declared, "would conduce to the welfare of the Provinces and promote the interests of the British Empire," and left it at that. "Peace, Order, and Good Government" was necessary to keep the money where it was, and let those people who had it make more of it. The Declaration of Independence still embodied what public ethics there were:

We hold these truths to be self-evident, that all men are created equal, that they are endowed by their creator with certain unalienable rights, that among these are Life, Liberty, and the pursuit of Happiness. That to secure these rights, Governments are instituted among Men, deriving their just powers from the consent of the government – That whenever any Form of Government becomes destructive of these ends, it is the Right of the People to alter or to abolish it, and to institute new Government, laying its foundation on such principles and organizing its powers in such form, as to them shall seem most likely to effect their safety and happiness.

This statement is still the basis from which we all begin, although many of us may have gone some distance from it. In spite of the enormous extent of their social and economic control, the managers of the corporations still come on with the message that North America is the land of the free enterpriser, that Horatio Alger is alive and well at Standard Oil. It's not that they don't know that everyone is aware that's nonsense, it's just that they can't say anything else. Any defence of a status-quo hierarchy is not considered to be right and defensible. It's not part of the American dream. It goes against the Canadian grain. Even the current bunch of law and order advocates must couch their language in terms of individual freedom; and because our university presidents and our businessmen and our politicians have to bullshit and act against their publicly expressed values, it makes them weak and loses them the loyalty of the young.

Freedom is still the operative value in North America, no matter how perverted, and any revolution that hopes to be successful has to take that into account. It's no longer helpful to think of a revolution, then, as the replacement of one class by another, the conquest of one group by another. From this perspective the confrontation politics in the American ghetto, on the campuses, in the theatre will succeed only as a prelude to another kind of revolution in which our experience of freedom is expanded. Americans finally don't like imposed laws, even if the laws result in a more just distribution of goods.

The practical wisdom of the New Left (if I can group everyone from the hippies to the militants under that title) has always appeared to me to lie in their understanding of the necessity of freedom. It seems natural for them to act in a way that assumes an expanded area of freedom is open to them, partly because of the increased democracy in their middle-class homes and warmer, less repressive, child-rearing habits. This is their great political strength: they haven't backed away from bourgeois freedom. In fact, they are pushing it much further than the bourgeois ever expected it to go, and in so doing – with all the pain and the chaos involved – are facing up to what it means for all men to be free, for them to have equal opportunities to fulfil their capacities as men. That means that the New Left has somehow had to deal with the fact of community: that our destinies *are* caught up with the destinies of other men, that all our freedoms are interlocked. A fact our grandfathers denied, and one which bewildered our fathers. The New Left has come at a time when no remnant of the frontier is left, when an urban civilization has to be built in North America or there will be no civilization at all. They are no longer prepared to accept the schizophrenia of the frontier and the new frontier, to live choosing between extreme polarities: moving on and staying put, being individualistic and standardized, competitive and co-operative, pious and free-thinking, responsible and cynical. They don't want children brought up any longer to face the situation in which, as Eric Erikson shows, they are asked at pretty much the same time, to "get the hell out of here" or "stay and keep the bastards out," two of our most sweeping slogans for action. For the first time a large group of people in North America know clearly that things have stopped being that simple.

What the New Left (including the free schools) has been pushing for, more than anything, is some kind of humane social order. They know in their bones that the world has been a madhouse too long.

It's no life just to leave your choices open; that finally just burns you out, dries you up. What they are after – as most people have always been after in one way or another – is some new union of freedom and necessity, some order in which they can be complete, in which they can work at what they love. The only way you can get history off your back is to take it all into account. Psychotherapy isn't enough. You have to deal with everybody, a whole society, its present and its past.

Why Herbert Marcuse has been the most influential philosopher of the New Left, in spite of his incredibly heavy language, is that he makes the above point very strongly, and puts the current movements for freedom in the context of the past oppression of European thought and institutions. For many, he provides the strongest theoretical basis for what they know everyone around them is feeling, making the present manifestation of the general human desire for unity more intelligible. He is also an old man who has remained a revolutionary and knows that the young are right in demanding an order, now, in which an individual's life instincts are not denied. Any individual. All must be assumed to have equal claim on freedom. You can trust human love to be socially creative. Eros is culture building. Sex sublimates itself. His central argument (found in *Eros and Civilization*) is this:

In the light of the idea of a non-repressive sublimation, Freud's definition of Eros as striving "to form living substance into ever greater unities, so that life may be prolonged and brought to higher development" takes on added significance. The biological drive becomes a cultural drive. The pleasure principle reveals its own dialectic. The erotic aim of sustaining the entire body as subject-object of pleasure calls for continual refinement of the organism, the intensification of its receptivity, the growth of its sensuousness. The aim generates its own projects of realization: the abolition of toil, the amelioration of the environment, the conquest of disease and decay, the creation of luxury. All these activities flow directly from the pleasure principle, and at the same time, they constitute *work* which associates individuals to "greater unities"; no longer confined within the mutilating dominion of the performance principle, they modify the impulse without deflecting it from its aim. There is sublimation and, consequently, culture; but this sublimation proceeds in a system of expanding and enduring libidinal relations, which are in themselves work relations.

This non-repressive sublimation, as a reflection of the life instinct, swallows up Freud's death instinct, as that instinct's basic objective is the termination not of life but of pain, the absence of tension. So paradoxically, Marcuse argues, the conflict between life and death is more reduced the closer life comes to being pleasurable:

Pleasure principle and Nirvana principle then converge. At the same time, Eros, freed from surplus repression, would be strengthened, and the strengthened Eros would, as it were, absorb the objective of the death instinct. The instinctual value of death would have changed; if the instincts pursued and attained their fulfilment in a non-repressive order, the regression compulsion would lose much of its biological rationale. As suffering and want recede, the Nirvana principle may become reconciled with the reality principle. The unconscious attraction that draws the instincts back to an "earlier state" would be effectively counteracted by the desirability of the attained state of life. The "conservative nature" of the instincts would come to rest in a fulfilled present.

Death would cease to be an instinctual goal. It remains a fact, perhaps even an ultimate necessity – but a necessity against which the unrepressed energy of mankind will protest, against which it will wage its greatest struggle.

In this struggle, reason and instinct could unite. Under conditions of a truly human existence, the difference between succumbing to disease at the age of ten, thirty, fifty, or seventy, and dying a "natural" death after a fulfilled life, may well be a difference worth fighting for with all instinctual energy. Not those who die, but those who die before they must and want to die, those who die in agony and pain, are the great indictment against civilization.

Having said this, however, what do you do if you see, as Marcuse does, that "unfreedom has become part and parcel of the mental apparatus"? How do you react to your knowledge that the majority of citizens are under the illusion that they are free, that their government is democratic, that their culture is honest, that the life style of the great corporations is the way to happiness, or at least that they have nothing else to say. In the past, from Plato to Rousseau, the answer to this problem (never carried out in a just fashion) has been the Tory-old-line-Socialist answer: an order has to be imposed to ensure the good life, to ensure that men don't act greedily. What Marcuse says (very much of the New Left) is that "the idea of an educational dictatorship exercised by those who have acquired knowledge of the real Good" is "obsolete." All men can be trusted to be reasonable:

Knowledge of the available means of creating a humane existence for all is no longer confined to a privileged élite. The facts are all too open, and the individual consciousness would safely arrive at them if it were not methodically arrested and diverted. The distinction between rational and irrational authority, between repression and surplus-repression can be made and verified by the individuals themselves. That they cannot make this distinction now does not mean that they cannot learn to make it once they are given the opportunity to do so. Then the course of trial and error becomes a natural course in freedom. Utopias are susceptible to unrealistic blueprints, the conditions of a free society are not. They are a matter of reason.

While individuals may be capable of handling much greater freedom than they now have, the majority of them don't feel the immediate need of it.

The situation we face is this: "Radical change without a mass base seems to be unimaginable. But the obtaining of a mass base – at least in this country – and in the foreseeable future – seems to be equally unimaginable." The way out, of course, is to go and get a mass base. From there, however, things get difficult because corporate capitalism, temporarily at least, is pretty stable, particularly with its increasingly close rapport with the Soviet Union and its tight control over access to the mass media. The result is that you can't meet the establishment head on, except through the theatre of confrontation, in which you hope for a widespread expansion of consciousness. Now, useful as that is, it's not enough. What concrete change can be accomplished, particularly when a centralized and co-ordinated movement is neither possible nor desirable? What Marcuse envisages (in a recent speech) is "local and regional political action against specific grievances – riots, ghetto rebellions and so on, that is to say, certainly mass movements, but mass movements which in large part are lacking political consciousness and which will depend more than before on political guidance and direction by militant leading minorities."

What Marcuse goes on to suggest is that "the strength of the New Left may well reside in precisely these small contesting and competing groups, active at many points at the same time, a kind of guerrila force in peace and in so-called peace, but, and this is, I think, the most important point, small groups concentrated on the level of local activities, thereby foreshadowing what may in all likelihood be the basic organization of libertarian socialism, namely small councils of manual and intellectual workers, soviets, if one can still use the term and not think of what actually happened to the soviets, some kind of what I would like to call, and I mean it seriously, organized spontaneity."

I find myself very sympathetic to Marcuse's whole position, but the kind of solution he suggests, a solution many other people suggest also, has to be adapted somewhat to the English-Canadian scene, because our "specific grievances" aren't half as big as America's. We don't have a war on our hands. We don't have a great racial problem. French Canada we can forget in our day-to-day living and for centuries we have so crushed our Indian peoples that they can rely now on little more than our charity. Our cities are still livable, at least for the next ten years or so.

That means that we don't have problems that will rally masses of people immediately to the left, but it also means that we don't have to waste a lot of very good energy fighting for things to stop so life can begin again. I think it means that we can build in our cities – and some people have tried and are trying to build – "small groups, concentrated at the level of local activities," groups that are living institutions, that can provide the basis for an alternative system of government, commerce, and education. We can do it, I think, with a much broader range of citizens than is open to the American radical because the society is not as repressive here. In a very small way we've begun, particularly with residents' associations, the co-op movement, and the free schools, in which the push for a much more workable democracy is fundamental. As they presently stand, these institutions are ludicrously underdeveloped; but in this country they have enormous potential and they can be organized now, within the existing framework of law. They have potential not only as a basis for an alternative system for society, but also as a power bloc within the established system. (If strong residents' associations covered Toronto, say, and controlled the vote at all levels of government, that would mean a great deal.) If institutions like these were organized on a large scale there would likely be considerable pressure from both inside and outside the country to stop their growth. But it might come late, and we might be far enough along the road to have gathered a substantial group of people in Canada committed to this kind of action. This will be strong commitment. You can rely on it because it is built (by people, necessarily, of many classes) on the experience of trying to create a livable world together, and on the knowledge and love of life that comes from that, even if it is mostly the knowledge and love of a life that could have been. As a basis for a movement I think that's good, whatever Canada's fate.

Thinking this, I think also that the energies of the militant students on our campuses are not directed at that sector of Canadian society where they'll do the most good. It's not that I don't buy the radical critique of the universities. It seems to me that universities are a good deal more corrupt than most radicals suspect, and I believe too that the current mode of confrontation with the academic establishment is useful, because the language is not yet hackneyed and so is communicable. However, it seems to me that in its present form, protest in Canada (as opposed to the US where you have to fight against the war) shouldn't take up that much time. Demanding justice from the administration in various ways has many good results, but I don't think anyone should get caught in the bag of trying to take over the administration of the universities. First, because administrators finally do what they're told to do by the people who pay them, and so if you take over their jobs you're then going to have to deal seriously with the corporations and the government; when you do this you'll be doing it without a mass base. Second, and more important really, I haven't found the multiversity to be a place to learn very much, except perhaps some old technology that is useful. I don't believe it's a place where you can learn much that's serious – in the humanities, the sciences, or the arts – no matter how humane the administration becomes or how open the procedure is for choosing and running courses. The form as well as the content is corrupting.

It seems to me, then, that the major thrust of Canadian student radicals should be to encourage students to prepare themselves to leave the universities to go into the cities and work to build the institutions of a livable society. Right now that probably means residents' associations, producer-consumer co-ops, and free schools, although it can mean many other institutions as well. And just as it appears possible to organize a wider range of citizens here than in America under the banner of local democracy, I suspect it may be possible also to organize a wider range of students than on American campuses not when you ask them to occupy Simcoe Hall (which still perhaps should be occupied sometime) but rather when you ask them to go downtown or into the suburbs to build societies that are run by the people who live in them.

In North America powerlessness is felt over a very wide range of classes. What the majority of us want back – and it is a *majority* – is our dignity as citizens. The students who come will not be particularly responsive to a radical ideology. What they will have is a deep but inarticulate sense that something is badly wrong, both in the university and in the society at large. Coming into the cities to work at something they know is good, they will become radicals in their own way, not through well-meaning manipulation, but by living day to day in situations where repression is seen and felt, and where they are fighting it for solid long-term ends. The commitment that arises from this experience can be trusted to last considerably longer than the commitment that comes from understanding your university president is a fink and does not care about your personal well-being. Most people knew that before they came.

The position I'm putting forward here – and one I hope circumstances will allow me to hold onto – is in all ways a non-violent one, in which the emphasis is placed on building up a new society peacefully. I have an ambivalent feeling about this position. The gestures of those people in the United States (and to a much lesser extent in this country) who break the law and go to jail or get their heads kicked in by the local cops, move me a great deal; and I know these actions are appropriate to the violence and horror of the American empire, of which we are a supporting part. I am frightened of that kind of action, and I have not done it. Partly because of the fear. Partly because I can't convince myself that these actions are worth the risk, in terms of results, in Canada. And partly because I have no real sense of outrage for the issues at stake. If I had I would not be in this country. I would be in Hanoi. Further, while I'm a little sad about Canada's demise, I don't care that much about it. For whatever reasons of personal history and social context, the anger needed to sustain my action on either an international or a national front is not there. I'd like it to be, but it's not.

What it comes down to is that right now, as a Canadian living in downtown Toronto, I do not feel seriously threatened. My imagination isn't very active. I don't sense that I may soon lose something I love, particularly something I love well enough to die for or suffer imprisonment for. If I thought someone was going after my family or my friends or the school, then I'd be prepared to do something pretty serious. But that's as far as I go. Point Blank is the largest social unit I can get solidly angry about. It is the largest abstraction I can imagine fighting for ... fighting for the whole of it, not just parts of it. It is here – if I can use these terms – that I am just beginning to feel like a citizen who knows he must take into account the larger realities of the polis. We're very new at the school and I may be badly disillusioned, but here I have the feeling that I can consider the general good and not sense that I am betraying what is best in myself in doing so, that I can fuse my destiny with those of others and know, whatever their political opinions and they are many, that I am tied to them. It is my first society, and for all the hassels I am more content than I have ever been in my life.

I have also the sense at Point Blank that by living here (or in whatever arrangements emerge from this group of people or others we join or who join us) I'll be able to develop, as others will, a livable political theory for this continent, assuming we are all pushing in a general way for local control. Right now I don't know what I want specifically from a society, and I don't know what I am capable of giving. Before this time I had had no experience with a fairly large group of people from whom I was not severely alienated, although, like many others again, I kept that alienation to myself out of fear and ambition. The result was I made no commitments, and I ran no risks. I must now make those commitments and run those risks, because unless I do I will not have felt through my capacities as a citizen. Without having done this I will not be capable of responding humanly to the building of the society that must emerge out of the ashes of this one, and I will be capable of acting abstractly and tyrannically. Thus, while schools like Point Blank are a matter of justice for Charlie Macdougal, the communities that emerge from them and other institutions like them are also a human necessity, both for Charlie and for people like myself.

My hope is that in Canada, if we can hold the border long enough and keep the corporations back a little, we may have the chance of building these societies in our cities, both as a political base (which is useful no matter what happens at the top) and a humanizing environment. It's a very long shot, but I think it's the only realistic chance we've got, here in northern America. I believe we should put most of our energies towards it.

Gerald L. Caplan and James Laxer

Gerald Caplan is a regular contributor to *Canadian Dimension*, the *Canadian Forum*, and other journals. He teaches history at the Ontario Institute of Studies in Education.

Perspectives on un-American traditions in Canada

Canadian socialism lacks a self-contained theoretical framework.* It has never come to grips with Canada's uniqueness: its British heritage, its propinquity to the United States, its dual nationalism. Instead, it has merely modified the British Fabianism which was the birthright of its earliest Canadian supporters; in Canadian terms, this meant opposing Lockean liberalism with welfare liberalism, or creating the CCF against the Liberal and Conservative parties. Thus imprisoned by its derivativeness, it failed to perceive the major theme in Canadian history since as early as 1918. Rejoicing in Canada's escape from the empire, socialists ignored the more insidious process whereby we were becoming perhaps the first neo-colony.

The purpose of this essay is, first, tentatively to indicate why Canadian socialists have only just begun to perceive the reality of the American role in Canada, and, secondly, to begin the enquiry as to whether there exists a tradition of Canadian radicalism which contains a serious component of opposition to American imperialism. We will argue that both the CCF/NDP and the Canadian trade union movement reflect a moderate left tradition, upon which a more radical ideology and strategy can, in theory, be built. Whether, as a result of transforming these two institutions into meaningful instruments of an anti-imperialist struggle, Canadian socialists can succeed in winning power in Canada, is a question we shall examine in conclusion.

In this essay we take as a given the proposition that American imperialism threatens the very existence of the Canadian nation, and that it is the chief enemy of the world social revolution which we believe essential to the creation of a more just and humane international order. Because assumptions such as these are uncommon in an intellectual community dominated by liberals, socialist scholars often do little more than challenge conventional beliefs, and as a result they rarely get beyond first principles. In our case, we take it that this book in itself provides the documentation for our view of the contemporary American state. While recognizing that our position

---

*   In this paper we refer only to English Canada when we talk of "Canada." When we speak of "socialism," we mean such institutionalized structures of workers, farmers, and middle-class progressives as the CCF/NDP, organized labour, and the co-operative movement.

is far from unchallengeable, we nevertheless have chosen here merely to assert it explicitly as the basis for the substantive argument which follows.

Socialists in Canada have not always been concerned to protect Canadian independence from the threat of American domination. In fact, their strong concern with the national question is a relatively recent phenomenon. The primary reason for this is that socialists in Canada have tended to borrow their ideas on national sovereignty from either liberals or conservatives, depending on the period in question, while they themselves have viewed the evolution of Canadian nationhood from differing perspectives.

Liberals generally have considered the most important events in the evolution of the Canadian nation to be those associated with gaining constitutional autonomy from Great Britain: the struggle for responsible government, and the acquisition of the right to set our own foreign policy. This liberal school of thought, which is associated politically with the Laurier-Mackenzie King tradition, has considered the establishment of close economic ties with the United States to be the most sensible development strategy for Canada.

Opposing this perspective has been the tradition of tory-nationalism. Tory-nationalists consider the great events in our history to be those concerned with the maintenance in Canada of a society distinct and separate from that of the United States. Since the era of John A. Macdonald, these men have been associated historically with the protection of Canadian industry, the British connection, and positive state intervention in the economy in the interest of national development.

Where does the left fit into this picture? Before the 1960s Canadian socialists tended to echo the liberals on the national question. The western progressives, who became one element of the CCF, were passionate free-traders who had turned away from Laurier only after the defeat of his reciprocity policy in 1911. The intellectuals who joined the CCF and drafted the Regina Manifesto were in many respects left-Laurier liberals. Thus Frank Underhill would find it easy to agree with Mackenzie King that Canadian independence would be achieved if Canada loosened her ties with Britain and affirmed her North Americanism. Thus the Regina Manifesto blamed the depression of the 1930s on economic nationalism and pledged the CCF to oppose the development of a new economic British empire. No mention was made of the danger of an American takeover of the Canadian economy, even though direct American investment already existed on a large scale in Canada by 1933.

The attitude of Canadians (including Canadian socialists) to the United States has shifted markedly from one period to another, tending to favour either the traditional liberal or the traditional tory view. Sometimes Canada's differences from America, and sometimes her similarities to America, have been emphasized depending on the context of the period and on the perspective of the observer. During the Civil War, the strains of violence in American society appeared more salient than the common commitment of the two countries to the ideal of nineteenth-century liberalism. When Canadian and American forces were landing together in Normandy, it seemed more pertinent that two democracies were fighting Nazism than that Canada had agreed to a permanent alliance with the United States in the establishment of the Joint Defence Board in 1940. Today, the issues of the war in Vietnam and internal racial violence combine with the American takeover of the Canadian economy to modify a traditional Canadian view of the United States as both a society to be emulated, and a powerful ally and protector against chimerical threats from abroad. At certain points the landscape of history casts into relief the features Canadians fear in the United States, while at others it projects largely what they admire. Clearly the main determinant in the attitude of Canadians to the United States has been changes in it rather than in ourselves.

The vacillating love-hate sentiments of Canadians toward Americans derives from the fact that English Canadians enjoy their own exclusive collectivity and yet also are a part of the larger American collectivity. This aspect of the English-Canadian consciousness has been reaffirmed periodically by such events as the War of 1812, Confederation, and the rejection of reciprocity in 1911. The idea of Canada as counter-America is based on a set of notions that recur continually in the English-Canadian attitude to the United States: that the United States is too big, too unmanageable, and too violent; that Canadians can be grateful for the border, and for all the empty space that exists between them and the North Pole; that as a marginal power we enjoy the luxury of being a more relaxed and humane people. In peaceful times Canadians have been conditioned to think that it is better to let the Americans take the lead; we will follow at a safe distance, enjoying the material benefits of America but eschewing the social pitfalls. However, in periods when the situation in the United States is most menacing, Canadians tend to focus on the features in their own society which distinguish them most from their neighbour and from their neighbour's view of man.

America now shoulders the burdens of world empire and will continue to do so for the foreseeable future. The end of American isolation has meant that America's inherent imperialist tendencies are now on permanent display. As a result of this change in America's world position, a permanent polarization has occurred in Canadian thinking regarding the United States, replacing the previous tendency of Canadians to vacillate from the tory to the liberal pole.

Canadian liberals (including in this sense many Conservatives and NDPers), who by and large share the world-view of the American empire, seek continental integration socially and economically, even if they have minor policy differences with the Americans from time to time. Those who are not in sympathy with America's world aims and with her social system are taking up the struggle for Canadian independence. Increasingly, this means Canadian socialists. Ironically, at the same time as conservatism is disappearing as a viable force in Canadian society, socialists are taking up the conservative view of the national question. With the disappearance of Britain as an important factor in Canadian affairs and with the reduction of the national bourgeoisie to a junior partnership in American enterprise, Canadian conservatism has become mere sentimentality.

As socialists take up the burden of being the prime defenders of Canadian independence, they are attracted to conservative intellectuals such as Donald Creighton and Harold Innis who have paved the way for them. The transition of Canadian socialists from the liberal to the tory view of Canadian nationhood is most conspicuous if one compares *Canadian Dimension* in the 1960s to *Canadian Forum* from the twenties to the fifties.

The Innis-Creighton metropolitan school stressed the evolution of Canadian society as the product of a commercial-communications system centred on Montreal, but having its ultimate point of origin

in Britain. Thus they rejected a claim of the frontier thesis that
Canadian social practice was "forest-born," a thesis which Frank
Underhill applied to Upper Canadian radicalism. Logically, of course,
the frontier influence transcended such irrelevancies as nation boundaries. It therefore naturally identified Canadian progressivism with
its American counterpart, leading ultimately to a theory of a continental identity of interest on the left. For the metropolitan school
the important features of our society had their ultimate origins on
the other side of the Atlantic and not in North America. Kenneth
McNaught's study of Woodsworth, which stressed the British origins
of his social philosophy, was important in extending the metropolitan
thesis to Canadian socialism. Gad Horowitz and Cy Gonick, writing
in *Canadian Dimension,* refined the shift in the Canadian socialist
perspective by developing the thesis that socialism and national independence are necessarily reciprocal demands in Canada. Only with
their work in the 1960s did Canadian socialist thought advance beyond the anachronistic continentalism of the *Canadian Forum* in
the fifties. It is above all the national question which has led to a
revitalized Canadian socialism, and which is now the leading item on
its agenda.

We repeat: for Canadians who wish to pursue the elusive goal of an
egalitarian socialist society, American imperialism is the major enemy.
The struggle against this enemy, however, must not be waged by the
mindless imposition of strategies which have evolved in wholly un-
parallel situations. The social movement which alone can mobilize
the resources for this struggle must be true to its discrete traditions
and environment. For Canadian socialists, this means that while we
need to draw upon the experiences of homologous movements elsewhere in the world, a successful anti-imperialist strategy must be
rooted in Canada's unique geo-political position and in the organic
traditions and culture of popular movements in this country.
    What we are referring to is much more substantial than the con-
ventional conceits of editorial writers when comparing Canada and
the United States. While it is empirically valid, for example, to point
to Canada's greater tolerance and the comparative lack of violence in
its history, it is not clear whether the characteristic in question is one
of reasonableness or of colonial passivity. What we are calling for is
a serious investigation of the historical evolution of popular culture

in Canada. Of special importance to the left, of course, is the history
of working-class consciousness as it developed in its unique Canadian
setting.

It is the Marxist historian, E. P. Thompson, who has most persuasively undermined the simplistic fundamentalism of too many of his
fellow Marxists. As he made clear in his monumental work, *The
Making of the English Working Class,* "The changing productive relations and working conditions of the Industrial Revolution were
imposed, not upon raw material, but upon the free-born Englishman
– and the free-born Englishman as Paine had left him or as the
Methodists had moulded him."[1] The implications of regarding the
emergence of the British working class as a unique socio-cultural
phenomenon are obvious and should guide us in studying the Canadian working class: classes vary in their political and cultural tradition
from one nation to another as a function of their differential historical experiences.

We take a truism. Canada was an integral part of the British empire
at the time of the evolution of the British working class, while the
United States was not. Our organic relation to the empire, compounded first by the conscious rejection of the United States by the
Loyalists and then by immigration from the British Isles, has stamped
a British mark on the English-Canadian character which sharply
distinguishes it from the American. Because of this relationship, we
shared directly in the social experience of Britishers which Americans
missed after their revolution. A dialectic was at play: as Americans
deliberately severed their original European roots, Canadians, equally
deliberately, reaffirmed theirs. Of course, Canadians could hardly escape the influences, both intangible and material, which increasingly
permeated from the south; but they wholly consciously remained
un-American.

The large-scale British immigration to Canada during these and
later years inevitably resulted in the transplanting of important
elements of that working-class culture and consciousness in Canada.*

* It is true that many working-class immigrants to Canada became farmers, and indeed contributed weightily to our radical agrarian tradition. But many remained urban workers; for the industrial boom
beginning by the 1850s greatly increased the size of the existing
labouring class.

Because they were entering a British country, these immigrants were able to retain their traditions, their social and political attitudes – in short, their culture. Prominent in that culture was Protestant evangelicalism, a fact which reflects the central role which religion played in popular culture in the nineteenth century.

Divergent religious traditions have been an important factor in creating significant differences between Canadian and American political and social experiences. To be sure, similar kinds of evangelicalism were to be found in both countries. Yet there were also significant distinctions: Americans were not touched as Canadians were by certain British experiences, while unique and critical aspects of American social evolution did not influence Canadian developments. When the Protestant evangelical creed in America severed its European ties, it cut off its adherents from the old world in terms of both historical tradition and present reality. American Protestantism thereby became a potent element of American nationalism and served to sanction its notable messianism. America, and its Protestant faith, were seen as a new force for the salvation of man. No comparable force helped mould the tradition of the Canadian working class. Nor was the latter affected by the slave-owning south, whose cultural impact was transmitted through migration to a substantial section of the white working class in the great cities of the American midwest and west.

In Canada, evangelicalism, principally Methodism, retained its British orientation. Methodism was the dominant creed among the working people of English Canada, as it was among their counterparts in England. Common religious institutions served as vehicles to spread throughout Canadian society the culture of tens of thousands of British immigrants. It was in this way that Canadians shared in the cultural evolution of the English working class. This relationship significantly influenced the types of social movements which later arose in English Canada, and it made a socialist perspective considerably more palatable to English-Canadian than to American workingmen.

The variety of evangelicalism which transformed itself into social gospel was much more common in Canada than in the United States, a function largely of the retention by Canadians of religious ties with Britain. By the end of the nineteenth century, a significant number of Canadians had come to see trade unionism and socialism as practical manifestations of Christianity.[2] By 1918 the declarations of both the Methodist and Presbyterian churches on social reconstruction were further to the left than those of the major Canadian political parties, and they had an honourable place in the forefront of the reform forces in this country.[3] Yet once again the ambiguity of the Canadian position must be noted. It is true that the route from British Methodism, to Canadian Methodism, to social gospel, to social democracy in J. S. Woodsworth is only the most spectacular example of a well-travelled path, which led finally to the victory of the CCF in Saskatchewan. But it is equally true that the road from reactionary, fundamentalist, American protestantism led north to Social Credit in Alberta. At the same time, Saskatchewan also was influenced by labour-farmer, populist, and co-operative movements which sprang up in Montana and North Dakota. But perhaps more significant than the very real distinctions between the red-necks and the social gospellers is that they all worked within the flexible ideological framework of nineteenth-century liberalism.

Similarly, the socialism which British working-class immigrants were transporting to Canada, and which so influenced our own socialist tradition, was one of welfare-statism. Indeed, while the battle for labour emancipation, as Keir Hardie called it, was everywhere a difficult one, upward social mobility in North America seemed so much more common than in Britain that a strategy of piece-meal, ameliorative reforms seemed the most reasonable strategy to pursue. Ideologically more rigorous immigrants from Europe could serve to keep the labour tradition honest in the corrupting atmosphere of go-getting Americanization, but they were unable to re-orient the overriding reformist approach.

We no more intend to suggest that the Canadian working class is simply the transplanted British working class than we would argue that Canada is nothing more than Britain in the new world. But if Canadian workers were the basis for whatever radicalism exists in the Canadian tradition, it is the British connection which legitimates the existence of that tradition. It is, therefore, hardly necessary to agree with the main thrust of Gad Horowitz's argument that British toryism in Canada gave rise to its dialectical opposite of socialism.[4] What in fact happened was that a socialist tradition was brought here, and was moulded and modified in its new environment.

As in its attitude towards politics, so in its view on labour emancipation, the new movement was torn schizophrenically between its internationalist and its more nationalistic tendencies. Thus, though both intellectually and pragmatically there were good reasons for associating with American unionism, as early as 1873 Canadian working men established the first national central labour organization, the Canadian Labour Union,[5] and the first Canadian Labour MLA was elected in Ottawa in the following year.[6] Even in those years, as Logan tells us, British immigrants and British ideas were vying with American influences in unions which were already part of North American internationals.[7] In fact ever since there has been a vigorous movement for autonomous or independent Canadian unions, which has resulted in the establishment of Canadian executive structures and newspapers in most unions with international affiliation. At times, this drive has been associated with a move by labour to the left, as in the case of the One Big Union, or to political activism, as in the creation of the NDP.

The culture and traditions of the Canadian working class are the lifeline of the Canadian left. The great achievements of the Canadian left – the political affiliation of many of the trade unions and the strength of social democracy – grow out of that culture and tradition. As with all traditions, this one "has independent life and force, and must affect the behaviour of political movements."[8] Such a situation is unusually significant in the Canadian context, where the immediate task of the left is to prevent the complete assimilation of the country by the American empire. For we cannot honestly ignore the twin ambiguities which run through the Canadian tradition: the one, that classic love-hate relationship with our great neighbour to the south; the other, the dilution of the British socialist tradition with British liberalism and the ethos of Horatio Alger.

Canadian radicals must come to grips with this contradictory position. We must show that in the present situation, the only tenable solution for maintaining Canada as an independent sovereign power is by extending and developing that tradition which has its roots in the social gospel, in welfare-state social democracy, in the preservation of Canadian institutions from domination by stronger foreign powers. Whether our cultural traditions provide an adequate foundation for such a task is a question we must face squarely.

The NDP is the most important institutional expression of the Canadian left. More than any other organization, it embodies the cultural and political traditions of the Anglo-Canadian working class. The

NDP was created in 1961 through the collaboration of the CCF and the Canadian Labour Congress. The new party retained the reformist approach of the CCF, while evolving an organic relationship with the labour movement of a kind never had by the CCF.[9] The NDP brings together the essential constituencies – workers, farmers, students, intellectuals – that are necessary in building a mass socialist movement.

However, the NDP also exhibits the timidity that is characteristic of social democracy in Western Europe. The Cold War days of the 1950s have left their mark on the NDP, which was born at the end of a long ideological retreat on the part of its predecessor, the CCF. Retreating further and further from any fundamental criticisms of capitalism, Canadian social democrats began to lose even the memory of the days when they had considered themselves a real alternative. Instead they became little more than a pressure group for a number of welfare measures. In effect, they promised a government that would make capitalism more humane in the interests of the little man. Most serious has been the failure of the NDP to deal with the problem of Canadian independence and to appreciate the global threat of US imperialism to the establishment of socialism anywhere in the world.

It is not surprising that when a fresh sense of radicalism was experienced in the 1960s, its young proponents tended to ignore the NDP. Quite naturally, young people, who were willing to struggle for a society in which the large majority of people actively determine the shape of the social order, found NDP welfarism less than inspiring.

In spite of the alienation of the young left from the NDP, certain compelling and unique features in the Canadian political situation make it vital for the new radicals to attempt to radicalize the tens of thousands of New Democrats who make up the only mass left political grouping in Canada. Our location next to the heart of the American empire imperils not only the socialist cause in Canada, but also the very survival of the nation itself. The Canadian left is faced with the imperative of building an anti-imperialist movement in the very near future: a fact which necessitates the creation of the broadest possible left grouping. Efforts to radicalize the NDP are the logical point of departure in building an anti-imperialist movement.

If a mass anti-imperialist movement in Canada can win power at all, it can do so only by co-ordinating the struggle for democracy at the local level with that of winning elections at provincial and federal

levels. Community democracy is essential, both because it is the
most meaningful form of democracy and because only through the
experience it provides can power be gained at the national level. And
it is only in a strategy to achieve state power that the central struggle
to liberate Canada from the American empire can be waged. This in
turn will facilitate the democratic control of Canada, and it is also
the means by which we can contribute to the international struggle
for a socialist world. Towards this end, both the NDP and the trade
union movement must be radically restructured and reoriented to be
equipped to play their proper roles in the struggle.

The NDP's predecessor, the CCF, was largely a transplant of British
Methodism, British Fabianism, and British Labourism. Not surprisingly, therefore, it was from the first characterized by two serious
deficiencies. In the first place, it had an inadequate theory of social
change, and no concept of how society is transformed from a capitalist to a socialist one. There was instead the naïve conviction that
the cumulative effect of selective nationalization plus social welfare
measures would automatically produce a qualitatively new society;
the whole would be greater than the sum of its parts. Secure in its
chiliastic faith, the central role of property and the realities of power
relations could blithely be ignored at worst, vastly oversimplified at
best.

From this sprang the second weakness which reduced the effectiveness of the CCF, as it had the British Labour party and other European social democratic parties. Strategy for these parties consisted
exclusively of attempts to gain control of legislatures through electoral means. This had two significant effects. First, it reinforced the
illusion that all power resided in governments, and obscured the
reality that power is distributed, however unequally, among a number
of societal institutions – governments, churches, schools, the mass
media, and above all the corporations. Second, the CCF inevitably
ended up directing all its energies towards winning elections. The
party consequently became susceptible to offering policies that were
immediately attractive, rather than those that were honestly complex
and demanding.

The result finally was intrinsically alienating, for it implied individual powerlessness to influence one's immediate environment. Only
parliaments could effect significant changes; the mass of Canadians
could do nothing but vote for "the party of their choice"; socialists

could do nothing more than try to convince neighbours to vote for the CCF. It was the New Left which had to remind us that it is an abdication of responsibility to concentrate on electoral power at the expense of one's immediate community. The socialist must fight for democracy and equality where it most immediately and directly touches people: in factories, in apartment buildings, in shopping centres, trade unions, neighbourhood associations, schools, and universities. Like its predecessor the NDP, while legitimately interested in (but improperly understanding the nature of) central power, irresponsibly ignored local power. A priority for radicals, therefore, is to work within the NDP in order to transform its strategic thrust. We must help to make it understand its position as the parliamentary wing of the larger Canadian socialist movement, and the central national instrument in the struggle against American imperialism. For, as European experience has shown, a social democratic party that comes to power without a mass socialist movement can continue to function only at the pleasure of the most potent organized force in society, the capitalist class.

Similarly, any strategy for building a broad social movement in Canada necessarily involves the problem of revitalizing and extending the labour movement. We hasten to say at the outset that this is no simple-minded call for the repudiation of international unionism. Only labour's enemies could seriously demand that Canadian unions voluntarily surrender their resources while powerful American-dominated multinational corporations proliferate in Canada. But it is surely not unreasonable to demand that Canadian unions maintain power in their own hands adequate to transform their organizations into vehicles for radical social change, with no restrictions on such activities from external forces.

We are, moreover, convinced that socialists must become involved in efforts in their trade unions to raise questions of worker participation and control at every level of industrial decision-making, and in organizing new sections of the labour force. A bureaucratized union, remote from its membership, is as unsatisfactory as a nationalized industry in which workers remain powerless and alienated. The support of progressive legislation is not enough; the point to be stressed again is that democracy is most vital where it most directly affects everyday life. Socialists must encourage a major takeover by unions of management's present prerogatives; but equally they must insist upon a major takeover by rank-and-file workers of the labour bureaucracy's present prerogatives.

A third potential community of allies in the struggle to create an independent socialist Canada is the student movement, which has developed during this decade into a serious force in its own right. One of us has dealt elsewhere in this book with the limitations of the Canadian student movement, and we would here only restate one central argument: as long as it is motivated by American issues such as the draft and race, and as long as it fails to come to terms with such radical traditions as Canada offers, it will remain an ineffectual force in Canadian society.

It is our conviction that, as necessary conditions for building an anti-imperialist social movement in Canada, the NDP must be weaned from its obsession with electoral politics; the trade union movement must democratize itself while winning increased control in industrial decision-making; and the student movement must be de-Americanized. Two questions logically follow: Can these institutions be transformed in the manner we advocate? And if they can, will we then have the sufficient conditions for a successful socialist strategy? Clearly no facile answers will suffice for such vexing questions; but we can at least indicate the role of radical scholars in helping to come to grips with them.

We have already referred to the derivative nature of the ideas of Canadian socialists on the evolution of Canadian nationhood. Without a full tradition of socialist scholarship in Canada, socialist scholars, working in isolation, have been obliged to rely almost totally on liberal and conservative historians for their perceptions of the Canadian past. Thus their own views on the national question are predominantly traditional.

This raises the same kinds of problems for socialist scholars in studying Canadian history as are experienced by all modern students of the medieval period. How can one avoid the biases of those whose writings alone can admit one to the period in question? We must face a further and related problem. Canadian historical writing has tended to be narrowly political in its orientation, dealing largely with the evolution of the thinking of political leaders in Canada. A small group of historians have studied a small group of political leaders with whom they have had much in common in terms of social position and orientation. Almost no work has been done on the evolution of popular culture in Canada. This leads one to conclude that much of what has been said about the ideas of ordinary Canadians on the national question is little more than the wishful thinking of historians, or reflections of what political leaders think their constituents think.

Another problem arises. The traditional tools of historical scholarship make it difficult for us to deal with certain problems of the greatest importance. Without a new social science that marries the approaches of historians and sociologists, how can one deal with the fundamental problem of the effect of technological change on social relations and popular culture? It is this very problem that faces anyone concerned with the evolution of popular culture in Canada.

The problem confronts the Canadian historian in this way. Mackenzie King before 1939, as seen through the eyes of historians, was the last traditional political leader in Canadian history. The 1940s appear as a gray transitional period – neither in the realm of history nor in the contemporary world. Then one comes to the 1950s – and here the tools of the historian become obviously inadequate. Even though St Laurent and Pearson are the natural successors of King, they inhabit a wholly different kind of society from his (or at least different from the society historians claim King inhabited). Technological change and continental integration – the two great facts of contemporary Canada – do not lend themselves to the examination of traditional historians.

One overriding difficulty emerges from this. We have built our case on the evolution of a reformist tradition in Canada that goes back over a century; and yet, we have few guidelines by which to judge how much cultural and social continuity has survived the vast technological changes which have occurred in contemporary Canada. Therefore, it is not possible for us to weigh with precision the importance of the factors of cultural continuity which we have stressed.

In conclusion, we cannot say with certainty that the Canadian left can be transformed in the way we have suggested; nor can we predict whether such a transformation would make it a wholly effective force against American imperialism. Everything we know suggests that such a transformation will be necessary; whether it will be sufficient is another question. The crisis that faces this country is such that one can only propose that we begin to move in the direction proposed in an active political way, at the same time developing new tools of analysis that can bring greater precision to our understanding of the course of Canadian evolution.

NOTES

1 (London, 1968), p. 213.
2 Richard Allen, "The Social Gospel and the Reform Tradition in
   Canada, 1890-1928," *Canadian Historical Review,* XLIX, no. 4
   (Dec. 1968), p. 385.
3 *Ibid.,* p. 392.
4 Horowitz did recognize, however, certain difficulties in applying the
   Hartzian approach to English Canada: see *Canadian Labour in Politics*
   (Toronto, 1968), p. 15.
5 Eugene Forsey, "Unions and Cooperatives," J. M. S. Careless and R. C.
   Brown, eds., *The Canadians, 1867-1967* (Toronto, 1967), p. 492.
6 *Ibid.,* p. 498.
7 H. A. Logan, *Trade Unions in Canada* (Toronto, 1948), p. 46.
8 Eric Hobsbawm, *Labouring Men* (London, 1968), p. 377.
9 See *inter alia,* Gerald L. Caplan, "The Failure of Canadian Socialism:
   The Ontario Experience, 1932-1945," *Canadian Historical Review,*
   XLIV, no. 2 (June 1963).

Ian Lumsden

A frequent contributor to *Canadian Dimension* and other periodicals. He teaches political science at Atkinson College, York University, and his main interest is in the political economy of underdeveloped areas.

American imperialism and Canadian intellectuals

The Americanization of Canada is first and foremost a function of
the penetration of the Canadian economy by American monopoly
capitalism.[1] Americanization is not merely a synonym for industrialization or modernization, as some would contend. Nevertheless, the
effects of American economic imperialism[2] cannot be fully understood unless they are related to the character of the technology and
ideology which evolved first in the United States, and which now
facilitates its increasing control over Canada.

The continued technological supremacy of the United States, and
the increasing technological backwardness of other countries relative
to it, are the products of the global capitalist system which the
United States dominates. While the process of technological development may reach varying stages in different countries, it does not
ensure that they will all ultimately follow in the footsteps of the
most advanced industrial country. In fact, what happens is that the
hinterlands of the capitalist system contribute in diverse ways – capital, natural resources, and skilled manpower – to the further advance
of technology in its metropolises.[3] Admittedly, some part of the
new technology is subsequently extended to the hinterlands, but
its impact and catalytic powers are restricted by the boundaries
of branch-plant enclaves. Conversely, the technological progress of
the hinterland or satellite economies depends largely upon the extent
and manner of their integration with the metropolitan economies,
particularly with the economy of the United States which increasingly
dominates the global capitalist system. The industrialization of Sweden, for example, clearly a more developed country than Canada,
does not reflect as strong a degree of Americanization as Canada
owing to its more independent economic development in the past.
On the other hand, the industrialization, such as it is, of the underdeveloped Latin American countries ensures their partial Americanization long before they reach European levels of development.
The fact that the phenomenon we know as Americanization exists
throughout the capitalist world despite enormous economic dispari-
ties within it, demonstrates that it is more a function of American
economic penetration than of industrialization or modernization.

Americanization, then, is the process by which the nature of a
country's development, particularly its economic development, becomes increasingly determined by that which has taken place in the
United States. The fundamental characteristic of the United States is

that it has become an *overdeveloped*[4] industrial society, committed to producing goods as an end in itself, and divorced from the satisfaction of genuine social needs – be these of the nation as a whole, or of large numbers of its citizens who live at its margins. The deprivation of the poor accompanies the satiation of middle and upper middle class wants.

The recent development of the advanced countries, and in particular that of the United States, has been distinguished by the emergence of a new phenomenon, to which Jacques Ellul has given the name "technique." The technique of post-industrial society, based in part upon technology and in part upon a distinctive methodology, creates the impression of having *"absolute efficiency ... in every* field of human activity."[5] So rational do these new procedures appear to be that they distract attention from the ends they purport to serve. Moreover, they are particularly well suited to the American economy, geared as it is to omnivorous civilian and military consumption. Such is the basis of the bureaucratic rationalism that now pervades US institutions. These institutions are largely in the hands of "experts," who alone can lay claim to a mastery of various specialized techniques. The experts administer a society which has created "a proficiency of technical means that now oscillate absurdly between the production of frivolous abundance and the production of genocidal munitions."[6] In the face of the "expertise" of these men and the economic power of those who employ them, even the most educated laymen must share the sense of powerlessness of the masses.

America is the home of corporate liberalism and bureaucratic rationalism in more than one sense. The tendency to rationalize the status quo and to downplay the extent to which the real commitment is to profit maximization is peculiarly American. American political thought has always been characterized by what Daniel Boorstin has called the notion of "givenness." By this he means that America's political values are considered inherent to its way of life. Americans have "an unprecedented belief in the normality of [their] kind of life to [their] place on earth."[7] Increasingly, however, they have also come to assume that the United States must be the pacesetter for the rest of the world in things cultural, economic, and technological. It is no accident that this belief coincides with the need of the multinational corporation to destroy resistance to its products, and thus to homogenize the world in America's image. As John F. Kennedy himself reminded us, not enough attention has been paid "to the part which an early exposure to American goods, skills and American ways of doing things can play in forming the tastes and desires of newly emerging countries."[8]

Ideology plays a key function in legitimizing the process of Americanization by masking the reality of American economic imperialism in the name of the technological imperative. The basic assumption of US corporate liberalism is that fundamental structural changes are to be conceived as offering solutions neither to the domestic problems within the heart of the empire nor to those within its hinterlands. The role of the liberal ideologist, both within and without the United States, has been reduced to that of diverting attention from the root causes of the problems facing American imperialism and of opposing those ideologies that could crystallize opposition to it – principally, socialism and nationalism. Increasingly, he has become no more than an advocate of social engineering and crisis-managing in his attempts to cope with the contradictions that are emerging with increasing strength and frequency in the United States and in the remainder of the global capitalist system which it dominates.*

The inability of American imperialism to manage its contradictions by liberal means, whether they be located in Harlem or in Vietnam, is more and more apparent. Neither spectacular technological advances nor vast increases in its economic productivity can disguise the fact that America more and more often has had to resort to outright repression as the only way out. Despite its superficial rationality, America's post-industrial system, in fact, grows more and more irrational. For its basic mode of operation is still that of the market: the parts are rational, the whole irrational. "The giant corporation withdraws from the sphere of the market large segments of economic activity and subjects them to scientifically designed administration. This change represents a continuous increase in the rationality of the parts of the system, but it is not accompanied by any rationalization of the whole."[9]

---

* The careers of McGeorge Bundy, former Kennedy aide and now president of the Ford Foundation; of Robert McNamara, former secretary of defence and now president of the World Bank; and of Lester Pearson, former prime minister of Canada and later head of a World Bank task force, illustrate the point.

Who can doubt, then, that the possibility of developing a saner and more humane world hinges upon the dismantling of the American economic empire, together with its perverted educational and scientific estates? We must accept the fact that the transformation of Canada, Americanized as it is, is now linked to the overthrow of the whole imperial system. The counterpart of un-American activities within the United States is the activities of anti-imperialist socialists abroad. There is nothing xenophobic or chauvinistic about this. To be anti-American is to recognize that it is American monopoly capitalism that buttresses the process of Americanization in Canada, and to oppose all those domestic forces that have become apologists for, and hence accomplices to, the extension of American influence both within Canada and throughout the remainder of the global capitalist system.

A call for rejection of American domination need not be based on fantasies about the past. With George Grant we can accept the death of the old Canadian nation. What we call for now is a search for a new one – one based upon the recognition of the fact that Canada is physically part of North America, and that this country has come to share many of America's political and cultural values, along with the economic integration that has been impelled forward by its corporate élites. Its special status within the empire, as it were, nevertheless demands a distinct political programme that is appropriate to Canadian conditions. What is primarily at stake is not political status, but its content and perspectives.

A growing number of Canadians agree with some or all of the foregoing analysis. But the left in Canada must accept the fact that it has so far failed to channel its energies and emotions. At no time has it developed the requisite political analysis and programme that would lead to a broad movement for socialism and independence. However, the increasingly explicit repressive and racist basis of American society, coupled with the inability of the Canadian federal and provincial governments to cope with Canada's own domestic economic problems – such as inflation, regional depression, pollution, housing, and labour unrest – suggests that a constituency for such a movement may yet emerge. Much depends upon the formulation of a political programme and the emergence of socialist leaders capable of radicalizing the political consciousness of the Canadian people.

The New Democratic party has, so far at least, failed to provide either. Neither has the New Left been particularly successful in its attempts to radicalize Canadian students. The explanation for their respective failures is by no means peculiar to the Canadian left. It also explains the present impasse of the British Labour movement.[10] Too much attention has been paid to what Gramsci termed "political society" and too little to "civil society" as the main source of a state's strength.[11] The NDP has been obsessed with parliamentary politics and has allowed quasi-constitutional issues – such as that of bilingualism and Quebec – to distract its attention from the question of extra-parliamentary power, which is much more pertinent to the issue of the Americanization of Canada. The New Left, on the other hand, may have become so mesmerized by the dynamic revival of American radicalism that it, too, has been distracted from the need to devise strategies that are appropriate to Canadian institutions and their cultural peculiarities.[12]

The NDP is not a radical organization. It has acquired a commitment to social democracy rather than to democratic socialism. But that does not mean that socialists should be indifferent to its fortunes, for it may well attain federal power in the future, in addition to gaining control of an increasing number of provincial governments. If it does so, it will undoubtedly accelerate the evolution of a more complete domestic welfare state. This is, of course, desirable in itself, and no socialist worthy of the name would attempt to deny it. We must be clear, however, that the expansion of the welfare state is likely to occur regardless of which party is in office. Post-industrial capitalism has the means to pursue such a programme without undergoing fundamental structural changes. On the other hand, nothing short of such changes is likely to offer an acceptable solution to problems of structural unemployment, of despoliation of the domestic environment, or of Canada's continued participation in the exploitation of the underdeveloped countries by developed nations.

The NDP, judging by its present leadership and programmatic statements, does not appear to be an organization that will be able to reverse the process of Americanization. To be sure, it promises a more rational administration of resources, and it reveals a greater awareness of the need to protect Canada's interests. But it does not offer to dismantle the framework of Canada's corporate capitalism, or to transform Canada's relationship to other countries. How could it, when this is basically determined by non-governmental institutions, by multinational corporations in particular, which do not identify with the interests of Canada and which frequently are not even accountable to the Canadian government? Although the 1969 Winnipeg policy convention of the NDP demonstrated the desire of many of its members for a genuine socialist programme, the leadership of the party remains, *en principe*, as committed to the existing corporate technocratic structures as are the leaders of the other national parties. The explanation for this, and for many other factors which determine the NDP's non-radical character, lies in its concern for electoral gains rather than for the transformation of popular consciousness.

Nevertheless, the NDP remains the only organization of the left that has succeeded in reaching a broad spectrum of the working class, upon which ultimately any socialist counter-hegemony must largely be based. Accordingly, participation in the NDP may provide radicals with an opportunity to inject a genuinely socialist content – one that revolves around questions of property and class – into its present liberal framework; and in the process to help legitimize the idea of class politics among the electorate as a whole. A precondition to the establishment of a socialist hegemony, it need hardly be stressed, is the demystification of the "pseudo-politics"[13] – such as Trudeau-mania – which continue to hypnotize the majority of Canadian voters.

The reversal of the Americanization of Canada can come about only through the substitution of a new world-view among its people in place of their addiction to the "American way of life" and their adherence to the values perpetuated by the North American bourgeoisie. These values are diffused through a wide variety of cultural, educational, and social institutions. They will not easily be dislodged. In spite of this, socialists must always keep this axiom of radical analysis in mind: when a hegemony of socialist values has been established, the election of a socialist government will follow sooner or later. Where it is absent, the chance election of a purportedly left-wing government is quickly revealed to be inconsequential to the implementation of socialist goals. The recent history of the Labour party in Britain offers an object lesson to all who place electoral considerations above the struggle, long and disheartening though it may be, to establish a new political and social consciousness amongst the masses of the population.

The struggle to forge a counter-hegemony of socialist values in

Canada will take many forms and experience many unforeseen turns of events. Clearly, one variant or another of confrontation tactics, and the fight to democratize institutions, non-governmental as well as the purely political, will be decisive issues; for changes in consciousness are not merely the response to reason and rationality, but are based upon personal experience of struggle, and change of life style. This is the all-important insight of the New Left. Since consciousness is also moulded by political ideas, however, the role of intellectuals becomes crucial to the prospects of developing both a radical movement and a socialist hegemony within Canada.

The task of socialist intellectuals consists of unmasking the real function of all those social and cultural institutions that inculcate bourgeois values into the masses, and hence legitimate and perpetuate their political domination. They must propagate an alternative worldview to which the masses can relate in terms of their own experience, and devise political programmes which facilitate its extension. Given the extent to which the mass media and institutions of education have become integrated with the corporate world, the prospects of developing a socialist intelligentsia in Canada, and the tasks that lie ahead of them, are not particularly propitious. Nevertheless, this must be among the first priorities of a Canadian radical movement; for there is scant evidence that an insoluble economic crisis lies ahead of Canada in the foreseeable future, and it seems that nothing short of this would lead to the spontaneous development of a socialist consciousness among the majority of the Canadian people.

Universities should, but do not in practice, offer conditions in which socialist intellectuals may emerge. The organization and nature of Canadian universities in part explain why this is so, and in part suggest why the present situation may soon be changed.

Canadian universities are not yet as large, impersonal, or corrupt as the larger colleges in the United States. There is so far only one counterpart at most – the University of Toronto – to the giant US multiversity, which is an institution defined not only in terms of its numerical size, but also in terms of its diverse economic functions and sources of income. Multiversities in the United States provide key research services to the public and private sector of the economy – most conspicuously to the military and the giant corporations that are at the forefront of technological innovation. Canadian universities do not, as yet, have quite the same character. In the first place, the branch-plant nature of the economy detracts from the need for research in Canada, and second, the Canadian attitude to education, being more élitist than that of the United States, has tended to put a brake upon the mindless expansion of post-secondary "schooling."

The contradiction between what the liberals claim the university is or should be, and what the modern university has actually become is not nearly as marked in Canada as it is in the United States. The empire builders within the administration and faculty have not yet made it in the continental "big league." With very few exceptions, possibly only the University of Toronto, they never will. Their income and research funding is paltry in comparison to that of leading US universities. For example, in 1968, MIT received $108 million from the Pentagon alone.[14] Social scientists have, perhaps, become the most corrupt branch of the academic establishment. But to my knowledge no Canadian social scientist has received grants for counter-revolutionary research that are remotely comparable to the hundred thousand dollars that David Apter was offered by the US Airforce to study the military implications of his work on the politics of modernization.[15]

For these and other reasons – such as the questions of enrolment of minorities, the state of ethnic studies, and so forth – Canadian universities do not contain the explosive elements that are to be found in the United States. Nevertheless, in practice, they are equally opposed to the humanistic tradition which universities supposedly uphold in liberal societies. They are institutions dedicated to schooling rather than to education. The alienation of many students and, indeed, of some of the faculty, accrues from this central fact. Canadian universities are by implication dedicated not to corporate research, but to training the future technostructure that will operate corporate business.

The most characteristic feature of Canadian universities in recent years has been their Americanization. Among its most pernicious effects has been the "professionalization" of formerly humanistic disciplines.[16] Canadian students are now increasingly taught by faculty whose academic standing is measured by their "professional reputation" rather than by their intellectual abilities. Accordingly, faculty members have become intellectually conservative and loath to engage in controversy that has not been sanctioned by their professional norms. They have ceased to involve themselves in public issues other than in their capacity as paid "consultants." Thus Canadian universities are by and large devoid of intellectual vitality. They have abdicated a crucial function of the university – that is, the promotion of "*rational* and *effective* social criticism."* Instead they have become universities and faculties "on the make," obsessed by social and professional status.

The tragedy is that the academic staff, far from stimulating the critical faculties of their students, have reinforced, *by their own example,* the tendency to regard the university as an institution whose main function is to provide one with a "meal-ticket." The majority of students, particularly of graduate students, soon become indifferent "towards anything not bearing directly on one's own academic grades, one's paycheck and one's future career prospects."[17]

Nevertheless, the universities retain as much potential for radicalism (and hence for the development of socialist intellectuals) as any other institution in Canada. Nowhere is the contradiction between the promise of corporate liberalism, and what it actually offers, so glaring. The university concentrates large numbers of middle-class youth at a time when they are ripe for political reflection, and yet not irrevocably integrated within the American way of life. On the other hand, as Eugene Genovese has reminded us, universities remain institutions which, despite their ties to the corporate world, are the most

* Christian Bay, "Academic Government and Academic Citizenship in a Time of Revolt," cus mimeo., p. 2. The flood of American faculty members that now threatens to submerge Canadian universities will not improve matters either. They are the model upon which the younger Canadian faculty have based themselves. Moreover, it is perhaps pertinent to note that these American visitors, or immigrants, as the case may be, are overwhelmingly liberal in their ideology. They consist in large part of individuals who either want to take a sabbatical from the United States, or who want to attempt to recreate their American dream in Canada. The fact that they pay no taxes for the first two years would obviously be particularly attractive to them. Conversely, Canadian university communities have to my mind been greatly enriched by the presence of the handful of us radicals who have come to Canada, but few of them remain here (e.g., Andre Gunder Frank, Mickey and John Rowntree, and Eugene Genovese).

tolerant of dissenting values.[18] By their very nature and functions
they are likely to remain so. Accordingly, the contradiction between
the original aspirations of the hoards of students and the faculty bent
on pursuing their private interest will surely become more acute. The
clash between the minority of student radicals and the insecure
liberal establishment will in all probability lead both to more authori-
tarianism and to a superficial liberalization of the curriculum. But
this will not remove the discrepancy between student expectations
and faculty response. The "silent majority" of students may join
the faculty and the public at large in calling for more order on the
campus; but this will only increase dissent among the radical minority
against the established order, and their numbers will increase. Ultimately though, it must be recognized that Canada is neither the
Bay Area nor Manhattan. The larger social issues which lead to the
military occupation of a campus are absent. We may conclude that
although universities will become more overtly conservative as a
whole, they do not promise in the foreseeable future to be like
Ronald Reagan's reactionary offspring in California.

As a result of these new conditions, the universities may yet be able
to make a vital cóntribution to the future of socialism in Canada.
Paradoxically, this hope is related to the destruction of the illusions
of some radical students that they can somehow convert the campuses into springboards for nation-wide revolution. This is an impossible goal. The working class, their principal would-be allies, are
becoming increasingly intolerant of the doctrinaire attitudes and even
political ignorance of many radical students. The radical task in Canada will be long and laborious. The sooner students take cognizance
of this fact, in addition to the fact that they have even fewer allies
than students in the United States, the sooner they will develop the
political maturity that will allow them to play the role that they are
uniquely fitted to play in Canada – that is, as an intellectual vanguard
that challenges and rejects the hegemony of bourgeois values over
the rest of the nation. In the absence of intellectuals among the
faculty, and in the absence of a radical intelligentsia outside the
university, students are most able to fulfil the function that has been
abdicated by the NDP – that of political agitation and of encouraging
"the masses to be discontented with their lot."[19]

Moreover, by forsaking their present adventurism, radical students are likely to focus upon issues that are directly relevant to their most immediate constituency – the rest of the student body. Vietnam, classified war research, and racial discrimination against black students may be directly relevant to US students, but they do not affect Canadians to the same extent. By comparison, the task of radicalizing the Canadian student with respect to domestic issues seems unglamorous, but it is strongly pertinent to the long-term needs of a Canadian radical movement. Such a commitment will make a real contribution to the development of socialist analysis and political leadership which is so evidently lacking on the Canadian left.

In addition to developing their own separate analysis and organization, radical students can play a crucial role in exploiting the present conditions within the university to the long-term benefit of socialism in Canada. That is to say, whereas at present there is virtually no radical scholarship taking place within Canadian universities (or many radical faculty being employed for that matter) – a situation that is masked by the liberal's claim that scholarship is non-ideological – the polarization of the universities can be invoked to demand radical course offerings, appointments, and so forth. This is something that the liberal establishment may be prepared to tolerate in order to demonstrate the sincerity of its pluralist pretensions and to accommodate, in part, the radical minority. It will do so, provided that faculty and students engage in radical activity that is appropriate to the university – that is, provided that their dissent on the campus is limited to non-violent demonstrations, research, and political exposés, and other forms of essentially intellectual radicalism. At the present time tactics involving one or another form of physical obstruction seem counter-productive in Canadian universities. This seems a modest goal, but since even this has been ignored in recent times, it makes all the more absurd the mechanical imitation of tactics devised by European and US students under quite different conditions. It is perhaps appropriate to note that the radical resurgence in Europe and the United States has been preceded and accompanied by the emergence of a socialist intelligentsia.

The role of radical students is potentially vital. It may help to create the conditions from which radical intellectuals will emerge. For embarrassing though it may be, the paltry output of socialist intellectuals in Canada must be underlined. There is no radical scholarship that bears comparison to that of the United States and most European countries, or of many Latin American countries for that matter.* There are neither first-class socialist journals nor a radical press, notwithstanding the valiant efforts of *Our Generation* and *Canadian Dimension.* I do not, of course, mean to imply that liberal scholarship is much better, but evidently it has so far (unfortunately) been able to withstand the socialist challenge fairly effectively.† The absence of a socialist intelligentsia is critical, for it ensures that radical critiques will be characterized by their negative, destructive character, rather than by a plausible and attractive alternative vision of the society we wish to transform. And in the absence of such vision, who can blame the masses for continuing to succumb to the bourgeois gospel?

Radical students are thus the main hope at present for the injection of some intellectual vitality into the university. The effectiveness of their contribution is conditional, however, upon the use of means that are appropriate to a Canadian university – which by and large does not yet engage in overt counter-revolutionary research, which does not yet engage in much classified military research, which does not yet discriminate overtly against racial minorities, and which does not yet play a role that is as critical to the industrial system as its major US counterparts. The revitalization of the university's critical function in response to the students' introduction of ideological critiques of liberal "scholarship," is a precondition to the subsequent emergence of radical intellectuals among the faculty, and a socialist intelligentsia among the community at large.

By stressing the importance of students and intellectuals I do not mean to downplay the relevance of other social groups. Indeed,

---

* The *New Left Review* in England, and *Monthly Review* and the defunct *Studies on the Left* in the United States are examples of what I have in mind.

† In this respect, it is perhaps worth stressing that merely branding liberal intellectuals as bourgeois ideologists is unlikely to achieve very much with respect to their demystification. Only superior scholarship by socialist intellectuals is likely to do that. For example, there is clearly a great need for a systematic critique of the ideological assumptions underlying the principal textbooks and monographs dealing with Canadian history and politics, and an examination of their treatment (non-treatment, really) of the American influence upon Canada.

radical analysis does not emerge abstracted from its social setting. Socialist scholarship, radical politics, and mass discontent interact and reinforce one another. In this respect, the main factor that has contributed to the revival of radicalism in the United States, and which has, conversely, been absent in Canada, has been the Vietnam war. It is the ever-present factor of being conscripted for service in Vietnam that has politicized students with respect to all the other repressive features of North America. Although Canada has been only indirectly involved in the Vietnam war, its political climate has nevertheless been affected by it, as is true of all the other western allies of the United States. Accordingly the growing economic, political, and military contradictions within the American empire as a whole will determine, as much as any other single factor, the prospect for a radical movement within its junior partner to the north.

Ultimately, the Canadian response to events occurring largely outside its boundaries will be determined in large part by the quality of available radical analysis, leadership, and organization. The slim prospect of avoiding the militarism and repression that are increasingly engulfing the United States depends upon the success of Canadian radicals in forging a new political and social consciousness for Canada. Much remains to be done.

NOTES

1 For the best analysis of the American political economy see Paul A. Baran and Paul M. Sweezy, *Monopoly Capital* (New York, 1966).

2 See Harry Magdoff, *The Age of Imperialism* (New York, 1969), for an analysis of US economic imperialism. See also James Petras, "Notes on Imperialism and Revolution," *Canadian Dimension,* Feb. 1969.

3 See, for example, Andre Gunder Frank, *Capitalism and Underdevelopment in Latin America* (New York, 1969), and Rodolfo Stavenhagen, "Seven Fallacies about Latin America," in James Petras and Maurice Zeitlin, eds., *Latin America: Reform or Revolution?* (New York, 1968).

4 See Irving Louis Horowitz, *Three Worlds of Development: The Theory and Practice of International Stratification* (New York, 1966), pp. 70-1.

5 Jacques Ellul, *The Technological Society* (New York, 1964), p. xxv.

6 Theodore Roszak, *The Making of a Counter Culture* (New York, 1969), p. 13.

7 *The Genius of American Politics* (Chicago, 1953), p. 33.

8 Quoted by Harry Magdoff, "The Age of Imperialism," *Monthly Review,* vol. 20, no. 6, p. 36.

9 Baran and Sweezy, *Monopoly Capitalism,* p. 337.

10 See Perry Anderson *et al., Towards Socialism* (London, 1965), in particular Anderson's essays on the "Origins of the Present Crisis" and the "Problems of Socialist Strategy."

11 For appraisals of Gramsci's contribution to modern socialism, see John M. Cammett, *Antonio Gramsci and the Origins of Italian Communism* (Stanford, 1967); Eugene D. Genovese, "On Antonio Gramsci," *Studies on the Left,* vol. 7, no. 2 (March-April 1967); and Alastair Davidson, *Antonio Gramsci: the Man, his Ideas,* Australian Left Review Publications, 1968.

12 This phase of the Canadian New Left has come, or is coming to an end. See, for example, Steven Langdon, "Pat-a-Cake Politics," *The Varsity* (University of Toronto) Oct. 31, 1969, and Alan Morinis, "Towards a New Radicalism," *The Seer* (Winters College, York University), Oct. 31, 1969.

13 For the distinction between politics and "pseudo-politics" see Christian Bay, "Politics and Pseudopolitics," *American Political Science Review,* LIX, 1 (March 1965).

14 *Time Magazine,* Nov. 7, 1969. For information on the Pentagon contracts of other leading US universities see the North American Congress on Latin America, *Research Methodology Guide,* mimeo Compare, for example, the $50 million received by Johns Hopkins University in 1966 with the grants for *all* Canadian universities from the same source. These appear to total under $3 million in 1969. *Canadian Dimension,* Oct.-Nov. 1969.

15 *N.A.C.L.A. Newsletter,* vol. 11, no. 5 (Sept. 1968), p. 11. Another American who should be well known to Canadian students, Seymour Martin Lipset, is listed as having received (in spite of his claim to be a "man of the Left") $95,000 from the Airforce to study the "Implication of Comparative National Development for Military Planning." *Ibid.*

16 See Edmund Wilson, *The Fruits of the M.L.A.* (New York Review of Books Pamphlet) for a devastating analysis of the academic discipline of English literature.

17   Bay, CUS mimeo., p. 11.

18   See Eugene Genovese, "War on Two Fronts," *Canadian Dimension,* April-May 1969, and Eugene Genovese and Christopher Lasch, "The Education and the University We Need Now," *New York Review of Books,* Oct. 9, 1969.

19   Gad Horowitz, "Toward the Democratic Class Struggle," in Trevor Lloyd and Jack McLeod, eds., *Agenda 1970: Proposals for a Creative Politics* (Toronto, 1968), p. 244.

PREVIOUS ULSR PUBLICATIONS

The Prospect of Change edited by Abraham Rotstein

Nationalism in Canada edited by Peter Russell

An Independent Foreign Policy for Canada? edited by Stephen Clarkson

Agenda 1970 edited by Trevor Lloyd & Jack McLeod